Communications in Computer and Information Science 2400

Series Editors

Rationale

The CCIS series is devoted to the publication of proceedings of computer science conferences. Its aim is to efficiently disseminate original research results in informatics in printed and electronic form. While the focus is on publication of peer-reviewed full papers presenting mature work, inclusion of reviewed short papers reporting on work in progress is welcome, too. Besides globally relevant meetings with internationally representative program committees guaranteeing a strict peer-reviewing and paper selection process, conferences run by societies or of high regional or national relevance are also considered for publication.

Topics

The topical scope of CCIS spans the entire spectrum of informatics ranging from foundational topics in the theory of computing to information and communications science and technology and a broad variety of interdisciplinary application fields.

Information for Volume Editors and Authors

Publication in CCIS is free of charge. No royalties are paid, however, we offer registered conference participants temporary free access to the online version of the conference proceedings on SpringerLink (http://link.springer.com) by means of an http referrer from the conference website and/or a number of complimentary printed copies, as specified in the official acceptance email of the event.

CCIS proceedings can be published in time for distribution at conferences or as post-proceedings, and delivered in the form of printed books and/or electronically as USBs and/or e-content licenses for accessing proceedings at SpringerLink. Furthermore, CCIS proceedings are included in the CCIS electronic book series hosted in the SpringerLink digital library at http://link.springer.com/bookseries/7899. Conferences publishing in CCIS are allowed to use Online Conference Service (OCS) for managing the whole proceedings lifecycle (from submission and reviewing to preparing for publication) free of charge.

Publication process

The language of publication is exclusively English. Authors publishing in CCIS have to sign the Springer CCIS copyright transfer form, however, they are free to use their material published in CCIS for substantially changed, more elaborate subsequent publications elsewhere. For the preparation of the camera-ready papers/files, authors have to strictly adhere to the Springer CCIS Authors' Instructions and are strongly encouraged to use the CCIS LaTeX style files or templates.

Abstracting/Indexing

CCIS is abstracted/indexed in DBLP, Google Scholar, EI-Compendex, Mathematical Reviews, SCImago, Scopus. CCIS volumes are also submitted for the inclusion in ISI Proceedings.

How to start

To start the evaluation of your proposal for inclusion in the CCIS series, please send an e-mail to ccis@springer.com.

Amey Karkare · Prajish Prasad · Arun Raman
Editors

Computing Education Research

17th Annual ACM India Compute Conference, COMPUTE 2024
Gandhinagar, India, December 5–7, 2024
Proceedings

Springer

Editors
Amey Karkare
Indian Institute of Technology Kanpur
Kanpur, Uttar Pradesh, India

Prajish Prasad
FLAME University
Pune, Maharashtra, India

Arun Raman
BITS Pilani K K Birla Goa Campus
Sancoale, Goa, India

ISSN 1865-0929 ISSN 1865-0937 (electronic)
Communications in Computer and Information Science
ISBN 978-3-031-84390-7 ISBN 978-3-031-84391-4 (eBook)
https://doi.org/10.1007/978-3-031-84391-4

This Springer imprint is published by the registered company Springer Nature Switzerland AG
The registered company address is: Gewerbestrasse 11, 6330 Cham, Switzerland

Preface

COMPUTE is an annual Indian conference supported by ACM India and iSIGCSE (India Chapter of Special Interest Group on CS Education). The focus of COMPUTE is to improve the quality of computing education in the country by providing a platform for academicians and researchers to interact and share best practices in teaching, learning, and education in general. This version of the conference was the seventh edition in the series and was held during Dec 5–7, 2024 at IIT Gandhinagar, Gujarat, India as an in-person event co-located with The International Conference on Technology 4 Education (T4E 2024) organized by the EdTech Society, India. The conference had five major themes as listed below:

1. **Computing Education Research:** Evaluation of Pedagogical Approaches and Interventions in CS Education, Evaluation of Technology-Based Learning Environments for CS Topics, Assessment and Evaluation in Computing Education, Student Engagement and Motivation in Computing Courses.
2. **Educational Data Mining and Learning Analytics:** Learning Analytics, AI in Education (AIED), Multimodal Learning Analytics (MMLA), and Educational Data Mining (EDM) applied in computing education contexts.
3. **Curricula Design and Experience:** Innovative Pedagogies in Computer Science, Synergistic Learning of CS Topics with Other Disciplines, Inclusivity in Computer Science Education, Industry-Relevant Computing Skills and Competencies, Digital Literacy and Everyday Computing.
4. **India-Specific Computing Education Research Issues:** Inclusive Education in Indian Diverse Socioeconomic and Language Contexts, CS Education and Challenges from the Digital Divide, CS Teacher Training and Professional Development in India, Gender Disparities in CS Education, Gaps and Challenges in Indian CS Education and CS Education Research.
5. **Responsible Computing:** Ethics in Computer Science, Digital Citizenship and Online Safety, Cybersecurity in Education, Digital Wellbeing.

COMPUTE 2024 received a total of 49 paper submissions from industry and academia in India. During the review process, 14 papers were desk rejected as they were incomplete or they did not match the theme of COMPUTE. For the remaining 35 papers, each was reviewed by at least three members of the program committee and subsequently discussed by the program committee chairs. The committee members were not involved in the review process of any papers that they co-authored. Only the final decision was conveyed to them. The platform (Microsoft CMT3) took care of any conflicts. After due deliberation, 12 papers were accepted as full papers, and 3 papers were accepted as short papers. Thus, 15 papers out of 49 were accepted for publication and were presented at the conference. Among the accepted papers, 1 paper has a mix of authors from not-for-profit organizations and academia, 1 paper has a mix of authors from industry and academia, and 13 papers are from academia. The committee also invited 12 other submissions to be presented as posters during the conference. The posters are not part of the proceedings, but it gave the authors a chance to interact with COMPUTE 2024 attendees and improve their work for submission elsewhere. The conference had five keynote speakers. Meenakshi D'souza, the 2024 winner of the ACM India Outstanding Contribution to Computing Education Award presented a talk on "*Computing Education in the Universities of India: The Trichotomy of Scale, Diversity and Quality*". Sudarshan Iyengar addressed the issue of AI education with his talk titled "*AI for India: Setting the Stage for Scalable and Inclusive Education in Artificial Intelligence*". Three keynote talks by Ayush Gupta, Norman Bier, and Shuchi Grover on "*Queering Technology Education, or, Why Research and Development in Technology Education Needs Gender Studies*", "*Learning Engineering: Improving Student Outcomes with Carnegie Mellon University and NAMTECH*", and "*Teaching with and about AI in K-12 Education: A Clear-Eyed Approach to Navigating the Road Ahead*" respectively were jointly held with the T4E conference.

December 2024

Amey Karkare
Prajish Prasad
Arun Raman

Organization

General Chair

Chitra Babu	SSN College of Engineering, India

Program Committee Chairs

Amey Karkare	Indian Institute of Technology Kanpur, India
Prajish Prasad	FLAME University, India

Publication Chair

Arun Raman	BITS Pilani Goa, India

Steering Committee

Chitra Babu	SSN College of Engineering, India
Neeraj Goel	IIT Ropar, India
Amey Karkare	IIT Kanpur, India
Mrityunjay Kumar	IIIT Hyderabad, India
Viraj Kumar	IISc Bengaluru, India
Needhara Misra	IIT Gandhinagar, India
Shitanshu Mishra	UNESCO, India
Prajish Prasad	FLAME University, India

Program Committee

Umair Z. Ahmad	NUS, Singapore
Chitra Babu	SSN College of Engineering, India
Satya Jaswanth Badri	IIT Ropar, India
Arnab Bhattacharya	IIT Kanpur, India
Neeraj Goel	IIT Ropar, India
Neelima Gupta	Delhi University, India
Ruchika Gupta	IIT Guwahati, India

Swaroop Joshi	BITS Pilani Goa, India
Ramamohan Babu K. N.	Dayananda Sagar College of Engineering, India
Amey Karkare	IIT Kanpur, India
Shitanshu Mishra	UNESCO, India
Neeldhara Misra	IIT Gandhinagar, India
Madhavan Mukund	Chennai Mathematical Institute, India
Vandana Naik	Goa State Higher Education Council, India
Nitin P. Patil	SP Pune University, India
Awanish Pandey	AMD India Private Limited, India
Prajish Prasad	FLAME University, India
Arun Raman	BITS Pilani Goa, India
Vishwas Rathi	NIT Kurukshetra, India
Deepti Reddy	SIES Graduate School of Technology, India
Ramprakash Rustagi	University of Maryland Baltimore, USA
Veena S.	PES University, Bengaluru, India
Vivek Sabanwar	IIT Bombay, India
Shubham Sahai	NUS, Singapore
Bhumika G. Shah	Gujarat University, India
Renuka Sindhgatta	IBM Research, India
Lakshmi T. G.	Shikha Institute of Education, Mumbai, India
Sujith Thomas	BITS Pilani Goa, India
Abhijat Vichare	ACM India, India

Sponsors and Supporters:

Contents

India-specific Computing Education Research Issues

Explain in Plain Language Questions with Indic Languages: Drawbacks, Affordances, and Opportunities

David H. Smith IV[1(✉)], Viraj Kumar[2], and Paul Denny[3]

[1] University of Illinois, Urbana, IL, USA
dhsmith2@illinois.edu
[2] Indian Institute of Science, Bengaluru, Karnataka, India
viraj@iisc.ac.in
[3] University of Auckland, Auckland, New Zealand
p.denny@auckland.ac.nz

Abstract.
Background: Introductory computer science courses use "Explain in Plain English" (EiPE) activities to develop and assess students' code comprehension skills, but creating effective autograders for these questions is challenging and limited to English. This is a particular challenge in linguistically diverse countries like India where students may have limited proficiency in English.

Objective: We evaluate the efficacy of a recently introduced approach called Code Generation Based Grading (CGBG) in enabling language agnostic "Explain in Plain Language" (EiPL) activities. Here students' EiPL responses generate code that is tested for functional equivalence to the original which was being described.

Method: We initially evaluate the correctness of code generated from correct EiPL responses provided in 10 of India's most commonly spoken languages. To evaluate the effectiveness of the approach in practice, we assess student success and perceptions of EiPL questions in a NPTEL (National Programme on Technology Enhanced Learning) course.

Results: We find promising results for the correctness of code generated from translations of correct EiPL responses, with most languages achieving a correctness rate of 75% or higher. However, in practice, many students preferred to respond in English due to greater familiarity with English as a technical language, difficulties writing in their native language, and perceptions of the grader being less capable of generating code from prompts in their mother tongue.

Keywords: Explain in Plain English · Explain in Plain Language · GPT-4o · Code Comprehension · Auto-grading

1 Introduction

Among the many skills introductory computer science students are expected to acquire are the abilities to read code and comprehend its purpose [11,15,31]. To

A. Karkare et al. (Eds.): COMPUTE 2024, CCIS 2400, pp. 3–17, 2025.
https://doi.org/10.1007/978-3-031-84391-4_1

develop and evaluate these skills, "Explain in Plain English" questions, where students are shown a segment of code and asked to explain it, are often used [21,22]. Informed by the Structure of the Observed Learning Outcome (SOLO) taxonomy [4], responses are not only graded on their correctness but also whether they describe the code's purpose (a *relational* response) or simply it's implementation (a *multistructural* response) [19].

To enable the use of these questions at scale, autograders have been developed and achieved remarkable success [2,11]. However, one shortcoming of the existing approaches is that they rely on a large quantity of human labeled data. Extending these approaches to a variety of languages would require a corpus of labeled data to be created for each language. A more recent autograding approach referred to as "Code Generation Based Grading" (CGBG) uses a Large Language Model (LLM) to generate code from a student's EiPE response and grades the generated code to check if it matches the functionality of the code the student was attempting to describe [10,27,28]. Though this approach currently has the shortcoming of not being able to distinguish between *multistructural* and *relational* responses, it comes with the benefits of being able to provide students more objective and specific feedback (e.g., generated code, test case results). In addition, it enables students to respond to questions in languages other than English, transforming what was formerly an "Explain in Plain English" question into an "Explain in Plain Language" (EiPL) question [10,27].

To explore the degree to which a state-of-the-art LLM (OpenAI's GPT-4o) is language agnostic, and by extension, the degree to which CGBG enables EiPL questions, in this paper we address the following research questions.

RQ1: How effective is the CGBG process for EiPL questions in the context of India's linguistically diverse landscape?

RQ2: How do students interact with EiPL questions and what are their perceptions of responding in their mother tongue?

As noted by other authors [17], limited English language proficiency among Indian students presents a notable barrier to the adoption of code comprehension activities such as EiPE questions. CGBG presents a unique possibility to address existing inequities in the assessment of code comprehension by potentially allowing students to respond in their mother tongue as well as other languages in which they have fluency.

2 Background

2.1 Code Reading and Comprehension Activities

Learning to program is often discussed as mastering a variety of skills, namely, learning to read, write, and trace the execution of code [13,31]. As is the case with mastering any skill, frequent practice along with timely and actionable feedback are essential [3,14]. Questions which address code writing and tracing are relatively easy to develop and deploy, even at scale [30]. However, code reading questions, which often involve students providing a natural language description of code, are more difficult to grade automatically [2]. This in turn limits their scalability, the variety of questions students have the opportunity to practice with, and the timeliness of the feedback students receive. This is particularly concerning in the age of AI code generation, where courses using generative AI tools must emphasize these skills to ensure students can validate the code they generate [8,24,29].

Perhaps the most common code reading activity is the "Explain in Plain English" (EiPE) question [21,22]. In these questions students are shown a segment of code and asked to provide an English description of the code's purpose rather than it's implementation. Fowler et al. found that instructors who include such questions in their courses particularly value them for developing and evaluating their students' ability to reason about the purpose of code [12]. Autograders, which rely on a large corpus of human labeled training data, have been developed and perform similarly to that of a trained teaching assistant [2,11]. Though these results are promising, they are limited to dichotomous feedback which can limit the ability of students to learn from that feedback [3] and can lead to distrust of the autograder [18].

Beyond the limitations relating to scale and the difficulties relating to autograders, EiPE questions suffer from a singular limitation: only accepting responses in English. All prior work, both in developing rubrics and creating autograders, has been done exclusively in the context of English language responses. To address this issue, Kumar [17] introduced *Refute* questions, where students are shown a segment of code and a stated task that it fails to achieve. To answer the question correctly the student must select an input which demonstrates that failure. The broader goal of these questions is to address the skills of task comprehension and code comprehension in a single activity that is not dependent on a student's ability to articulate the purpose of a given segment of code or the nature of an error in natural language [1].

2.2 Explain in Plain Language Questions

As previously noted, the scalability of EiPE questions is limited by the complexity of designing an autograder and the fact that autograders must be created on a per question basis. In theory, if multiple languages were to be supported, that would require the training of additional models for each language making the method largely intractable using previous approaches. A more recent approach to grading EiPE questions was developed by Smith IV et al. [28], referred to as "Code Generation Based Grading" (CGBG). This approach involves the use of LLMs to generate code from a student's EiPE response and then tests that code's functionality using unit tests as a proxy for grading the correctness of a student's response. When Denny et al. [10] and Smith IV et al. [27] incorporated the grading approach into a variety of CS1 lab activities they found that several students successfully responded to these questions in Chinese. This suggests the CGBG approach can transform the "Explain in Plain English" activity into an "Explain in Plain Language" (EiPL) activity. It must be noted that the approach is only as language agnostic at the LLM that supports it and model performance will inevitably differ amongst languages [32–34]. Nonetheless, this finding represents both a promising step forward and an area ripe for investigation, especially as the computing education community grapples for productive ways to incorporate LLMs into the curriculum and classroom practice [8,9].

2.3 Language Diversity in India and Computer Science Education

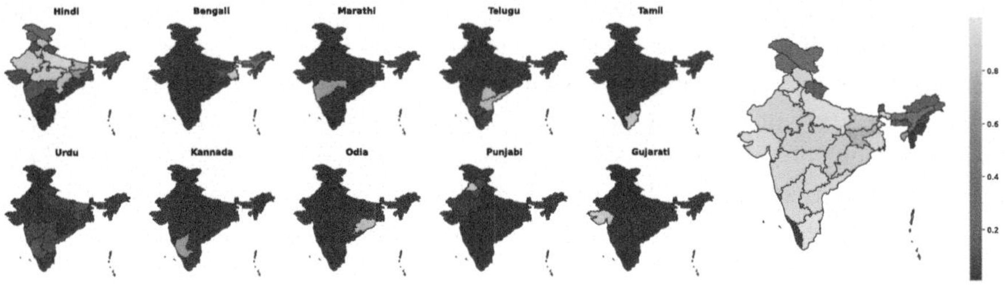

Fig. 1. The percentage of each state's population which speaks the given language as their mother tongue as reported by the 2011 census for the top 10 most spoken languages of India's 22 scheduled languages. It is important to note that this census predates the separation of the states of Ladakh and Telangana from the states of Jammu-Kashmir and Andhra Pradesh, respectively. As such, it may not be fully representative of the languages spoken in those states today.

As India's National Education Policy (NEP 2020) [20] notes,

> "*The aim must be for India to have an education system by 2040 that is second to none, with equitable access to the highest-quality education for all learners regardless of social or economic background.*" (p. 3)

Underlying this goal, the policy states *promoting multilingualism and the power of language*, *respect for local context*, and *respect for diversity* as being among its key principles. Though each of these are certainly laudable goals, multilingualism in particular serves as a barrier to the creation, adoption, and evaluation of curriculum given India's linguistic diversity (Fig. 1).

In the context of computer science, and perhaps Science, Technology, Engineering and Mathematics (STEM) courses more generally, we are fortunate than many of our core instructional materials are language agnostic. Though instructional materials, documentation, and question prompts must of course be translated, the underlying autograders themselves exist independently of natural language [30]. Code writing and debugging questions can be autograded using unit tests. Tracing questions are graded simply by checking if students entered the correct output. This leaves code comprehension activities, which require responses to be entered in natural language, as perhaps the only question in the context of introductory computer science which has historically required autograders to be built on both a per questions *and* a per language basis.

3 Methods

Our analysis of both the effectiveness of the approach and students' perceptions and interactions with these problems is divided into two parts. First, in Sect. 3.1, we present an evaluation of CGBG across a variety of Indic languages using expert translations of "gold standard" English responses to EiPE questions. The second evaluates students' interactions with and perceptions of EiPL questions in a online National Programme on Technology Enhanced Learning (NPTEL) course.

3.1 Evaluation of Expert Translations

As a first step towards evaluating the degree to which the Code Generation Based Grading (CGBG) process enables Explain in Plain Language (EiPL) questions in the context of Indic languages, we evaluate the model's performance on ten of the most commonly spoken languages from India's 22 scheduled languages. As shown in Fig. 1, by using this subset of languages, we cover a significant proportion of individuals for whom one of these languages is their mother tongue, according to the 2011 census [6]. As such, this represents the most conservative estimation of the proportion of speakers for each state who are proficient in one of these languages as we do not consider individuals who are proficient in multiple languages.

To perform this evaluation we begin with a set of CS1 level code segments in both C ($n = 5$) and Python ($n = 6$). Associated with each of these is an example of an English prompt that successfully generates functionally equivalent code and thus would be graded as 'correct' according to CGBG (Table 1). We invited participants with expertise in a range of Indic languages, recruited through convenience sampling, to translate these English descriptions of the code into the language(s) in which they self identified as being fluent. To obtain good-quality translations of these English descriptions in each of our target Indian languages, we distributed a survey to Computer Science faculty participants in Faculty Development Programmes (FDPs) for CS1 courses. Four such FDPs were led by one of the authors, and were conducted at institutions in Tamil Nadu, Karnataka, Maharashtra, and Uttarakhand. Prior to distributing the survey, we introduced faculty to EiPE questions as a way to assess code comprehension, and we described our study of EiPL questions for linguistically diverse student populations. Faculty translated English descriptions of the code into the language(s) in which they self identified as being fluent.[1] We then applied CGBG, using GPT-4o as our LLM of choice, to responses in each of the languages *post hoc* to determine how well the grading approach performs with respect to each language. Code was generated using the following prompt:

[1] Faculty were encouraged to preserve technical terms in English if they felt this was more natural, and were asked to transliterate non-English words in Latin script.

Generate a Python function called 'foo' that accomplishes the given task using the following instructions written in [SPECIFIED LANGUAGE]: [EXPERT RESPONSE]. The code should be returned in the following format:

```
def foo(<parameters here>):
    <code>
```

Note: The function should always return a value rather than print the result. Additionally, generate only the code and no additional test cases or explanatory text.

Here [SPECIFIED LANGUAGE] was replaced with the language the expert was translating the prompt into and [EXPERT RESPONSE] was replaced with the translation of the prompt.

3.2 Evaluating EiPL in an Online Course

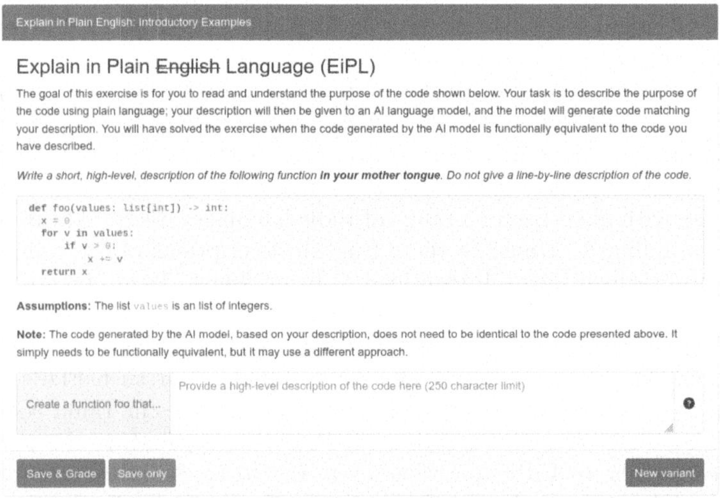

Fig. 2. An example of an EiPL question hosted on PrairieLearn.

Eight EiPL questions (Fig. 2) were then deployed in a Python programming course hosted by the NPTEL platform[2]. This was an accelerated course that aimed to teach students the fundamentals of programming with Generative AI in four weeks of instruction. The instructions of the EIPL questions alternated

[2] https://elearn.nptel.ac.in/shop/iit-workshops/completed/programming-with-ai-for-problem-solving/.

between directing students to respond in English and in their mother tongue. These questions were administered on the PrairieLearn platform [30] and students were provided with 20 attempts to answer each question.

Table 1. Success of expert translations for each language. The table highlights the ratio of successful to total responses in each language for each question.

	QID	Gujarati	Hindi	Punjabi	Marathi	Bengali	Telugu	Urdu	Kannada	Odia	Tamil
C	Reverse a String	2/2 (100%)	56/58 (96.6%)	4/4 (100%)	6/6 (100%)	8/9 (88.9%)	68/74 (91.9%)	4/4 (100%)	13/15 (86.7%)	4/4 (100%)	36/54 (66.7%)
	Check for Vowel Presence	1/1 (100%)	39/53 (73.6%)	3/3 (100%)	4/5 (80.0%)	6/7 (85.7%)	41/71 (57.8%)	5/5 (100%)	9/13 (69.2%)	3/4 (75.0%)	43/53 (81.1%)
	Count Even Nums	0/0 (N/A)	39/52 (75.0%)	1/1 (100%)	3/5 (60.0%)	5/8 (62.5%)	43/71 (60.6%)	4/4 (100%)	10/14 (71.4%)	2/2 (100%)	27/52 (51.9%)
	Find Last Zero Index	0/0 (N/A)	40/45 (88.9%)	1/1 (100%)	4/5 (80.0%)	7/7 (100%)	41/68 (60.3%)	3/4 (75.0%)	13/16 (81.3%)	2/2 (100%)	31/51 (60.8%)
	Sum of Positive Numbers	0/0 (N/A)	44/47 (93.6%)	1/1 (100%)	3/4 (75.0%)	7/7 (100%)	36/66 (54.6%)	2/4 (50.0%)	10/13 (76.9%)	1/1 (100%)	26/52 (50.0%)
Py	Prime Num Check	0/0 (N/A)	41/42 (97.6%)	1/1 (100%)	3/4 (75.0%)	7/7 (100%)	60/65 (92.31%)	4/4 (100%)	14/14 (100%)	1/1 (100%)	28/50 (56%)
	Generate Fibonacci List	0/0 (N/A)	35/40 (87.5%)	1/1 (100%)	2/3 (66.7%)	6/6 (100%)	59/64 (92.2%)	2/3 (66.7%)	9/11 (81.8%)	2/2 (100%)	41/48 (85.4%)
	Get All Even Nums	0/0 (N/A)	24/37 (64.9%)	1/1 (100%)	2/3 (66.7%)	6/7 (85.7%)	46/62 (74.2%)	3/3 (100%)	5/13 (38.5%)	1/1 (100%)	27/48 (56.3%)
	Get Largest Positive Num	0/0 (N/A)	34/39 (87.2%)	1/1 (100%)	3/3 (100%)	7/7 (100%)	54/61 (88.5%)	3/3 (100%)	12/13 (92.3%)	1/1 (100%)	43/47 (91.5%)
	Sum Even Nums in 2D Array	0/0 (N/A)	26/36 (72.22%)	1/1 (100%)	3/3 (100%)	4/6 (66.7%)	25/60 (41.7%)	2/3 (66.7%)	5/12 (41.7%)	0/1 (0.0%)	13/45 (28.9%)
	Check if Substring Exists	0/0 (N/A)	25/33 (75.8%)	1/1 (100%)	1/3 (33.3%)	3/7 (42.9%)	32/58 (55.2%)	3/3 (100%)	8/12 (66.7%)	0/1 (0.0%)	14/45 (31.1%)
	Totals:	3/3 (100%)	403/482 (83.6%)	16/16 (100%)	34/44 (77.3%)	66/78 (84.6%)	505/720 (70.1%)	35/40 (87.5%)	108/146 (74.0%)	17/20 (85.0%)	329/545 (60.4%)

4 RQ1: Success of Expert Translations

In total, we collected translations from 180 participants. Though the majority of the responses were in Hindi, Telugu, and Tamil, all languages except for Gujarati received responses for all 11 questions (Table 1). Overall, the model performed well with the majority of languages achieving above an 80% correctness rate overall. The one notable exception to this was Tamil which not only achieved the lowest correctness rate overall but also had a wide variance in correctness rates across the questions. This is particularly surprising given the large quantity of responses acquired for Tamil, but it aligns with prior work by Jordan et al. [16] which found GPT-3.5 to be poor at generating questions in Tamil.

Though less dramatic, there was also a reasonable amount of variance in the correctness rates for Hindi and Telugu for which we also had a large number of responses. These results call for further investigation to understand the nature of these "false negatives", particularly when considering the sensitivity of LLMs to the specific wording of the input prompts [7]. Future work should aim to distinguish between those that are due to the model's limitations and those that are due to ambiguities introduced through the translation process. The latter of these is particularly important as it may be used to inform instruction for students who are responding to EiPL questions in each of the respective languages.

5 RQ2: Students' Interactions with and Perceptions of EiPL Questions

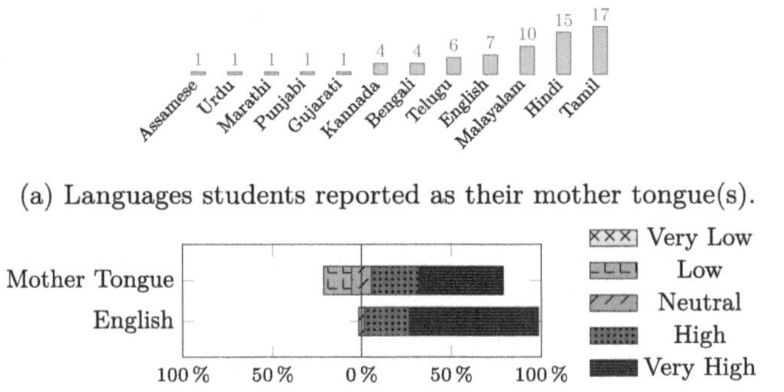

(a) Languages students reported as their mother tongue(s).

(b) "How do you rate your proficiency in *reading and writing*"

Fig. 3. Languages spoken by students who participated in the activities (Fig. (a)) and their proficiency in reading and writing in both their mother-tongue as well as English (Fig. (b)).

A total of 72 students participated in the study, with 64 providing responses to the survey. Students were asked to self-report their mother tongue(s) in a post-activity survey. As shown in Fig. 3a, participants spoke a wide variety of languages, notably, with several reporting English as one of their mother tongues. Students were also asked to report their proficiency in English and their mother tongue, with the majority reporting high proficiency in both, although proficiency in their mother tongue was slightly lower (Fig. 3b). Regarding the completion rate of the assignments, 90% of the students attempted some of the questions, and 65% completed all of them.

We report the results of: 1) how students chose to respond to the EiPL questions and the success of those responses in Sect. 5.1 and 2) their perceptions of responding in their mother tongue in Sect. 5.2.

5.1 Student Prompts for EiPL Activities

Though students were requested to respond in their mother tongue for four of the eight EiPL activities (due to the request they alternate between languages when answering) we observed that the vast majority of students' final responses on those questions were in English (78.8%). While some English responses were expected given that a number of students reported English as being among their mother tongues, the proportion of responses in English far exceeds the proportion of participants which fall under this category. This suggests many of the participants either had an aversion to, or difficulty with, responding in their mother tongue. As for the non-English responses, these often contained a mix of English and the student's mother tongue. For example,

- **Kannada + English:** "*s1 mathu s2 anagrams antha check maduvantha function*"
- **Hindi + English:** "*Ek list me kitni bar 0 ata hai wo count krne wala function*"

The success rate for students who opted to respond purely in English was 95.9% while responses in mixed or pure mother tongue had a success rate of 80%. Although we must be cautious about making inferences regarding this relationship, we make two observations. First, students in both categories enjoyed reasonable success suggesting the approach can be effective in practice. Second, our findings highlight the need for future work to better understand this disparity, which may be due to deficiencies in the LLM or other confounding factors e.g., the relationship between English proficiency and technical competence.

5.2 Perceptions of Prompting in English vs Mother Tongue

The results of the Likert questions from the survey indicated students were more inclined to perceive responding in English to be a more accurate assessment of their code comprehension skills (Fig. 4a). Similarly, and in keeping with the results of the previous section, the vast majority of students reported that they preferred to respond in English when given the option to respond in either English or their mother tongue (Fig. 4b).

One researcher performed reflexive thematic analysis on the complete set of responses to the open-ended questions using the guidelines detailed by Braun and Clarke [5]. This resulted in three primary themes: 1) students' greater familiarity with English as a technical language, 2) difficulties writing in their mother tongue, and 3) perceptions of the model as less capable in their mother tongue. We discuss each of these themes in detail below and provide examples of student responses to each.

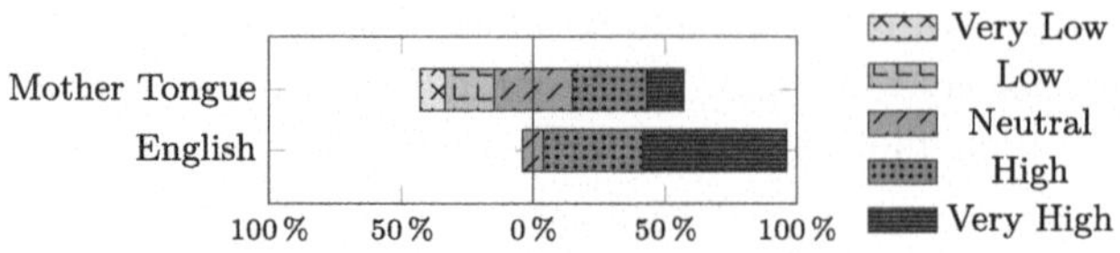

(a) To what extent do you disagree or agree with the statement "When responding in [given language], this task is an accurate way to evaluate my code comprehension skills?"

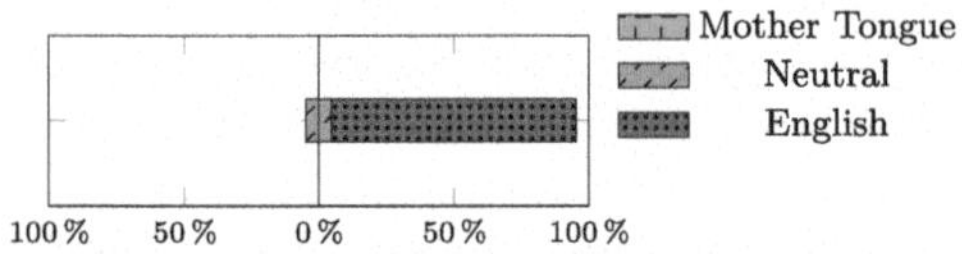

(b) Language preference when responding to EiPL questions

Fig. 4. Students' perceptions of the accuracy of the EiPL questions when responding in their mother tongue versus English (Fig. (a)) and their preference for responding in English or their mother tongue (Fig. (b)).

Students' Greater Familiarity with English as a Technical Language. Many students ($n = 10$) reported that they preferred to respond in English as it was the language they used most frequently when learning or discussing technical subjects.

- *"I rarely use my mother tongue with computers. So it has been difficult to explain specific technical ideas effectively in mother tongue. But the same is very easy with English."*

Several expanded further stating that they used their mother tongue and English in different contexts, with English being the language they used for technical subjects and their mother tongue being the language they used in more social settings.

- *"I am much more fluent in reading and writing in English compared to my mother tongue (Kannada). As I go to an English medium school, I speak, read and write English on a daily basis. However, I speak Kannada only with my family members and have never learnt how to read or write Kannada."*

Difficulties Writing in Mother Tongue. Related to the previous section, where students reported that they were more familiar with English as a technical language and their mother tongue as a language for general communication, a small number of students ($n = 3$) reported difficulties writing in their mother tongue.

- *"Not able to write in mother tongue but able to only comprehend whereas I have a strong control over English."*
- *"I am only able to speak in my mother tongue and not able to read or write. I am very proficient in English. Hence, I wouldn't be able to do the task in my mother tongue."*

These results reflect the results of the Likert question on language proficiency discussed in the previous section (Fig. 3b).

Perceptions of the Model as Less Capable in Mother Tongue. A number of students ($n = 7$) reported that they perceived the model to be less capable of producing accurate responses when prompted in their mother tongue.

- *"I was able to explain my requests well in English and the GPT code functioned well and gave expected results but I wrote the same in plain Hindi, and was struggling to get answers."*
- *"Sometimes the explanation given in mother tongue is not understood properly by the AI."*

One reported a specific instance where the model struggled to understand the prompt when it was in their mother tongue.

- *"In English I did not see any issue in comprehending the task by AI, but when I used my mother tongue from one particular question I found that AI unable to convert the 'sahi'* (**गलत**) *'galat'* (**सही**) *to true and false."*

This may highlight the need for mixing languages (e.g., Tamil + English = "Tanglish", Hindi + English = "Hinglish") when responding to EiPL questions where students use English keywords when referring to technical concepts and their mother tongue for other words. It may also be the case that, given many students reported using English when communicating in a technical context, they were less familiar with describing technical concepts in their mother tongue. This may have decreased the quality of their responses and led to the subsequent lower performance of the approach.

6 Discussion

Though the results relating to perceptions of the EiPL questions highlighted several challenges of deploying these questions in courses, the results of the expert evaluation are still promising. Additionally, it is important to note that these results will only improve as both the quality of the LLMs available and the size of the datasets continue to improve and increase, respectively. As such, the question of integrating EiPL questions into instruction is less a matter of "when" and more a matter of "how".

The results of the classroom study highlight the sensitivity to the local context when answering the question of "how" EiPL questions using CGBG are deployed. In particular, the qualitative analysis of the survey responses highlighted the students' greater familiarity with English for describing programs given its status as a technical *lingua franca*, and issues with the LLM misinterpreting certain terms from their mother tongue. Though the former may simply be a byproduct of the population taking the course in which the study was conducted, the latter is likely to persist across populations. This may suggest that, when introducing these questions to novices in the context of Indian education, using a mixed language approach (e.g., "Hinglish" [23]) could be beneficial. The primary goal is to reduce the overhead of the extraneous task of learning English, and to shift the focus towards learning to comprehend and describe code for populations where English proficiency is less common.

Previous work conducted in the context of undergraduate education in Tamil Nadu [25,26] found that students expressed positive sentiments toward bilingual instruction in Tamil and English. Looking ahead to the future of EiPL questions, as LLMs improve, they will increasingly enable multilingual code comprehension questions. As one student noted in the open-ended survey responses,

> "*Everyone is free to choose their language and it is wonderful if that option is available.*"

Though our results showed that performance varied between languages, the fundamental proposition of empowering students to demonstrate code comprehension in the language of their choosing, thus enabling these questions to be used more easily in a broader, global context is powerful.

7 Limitations

First, there is an inherent difficulty in curating a dataset of expert responses across multiple languages. Validating the 'correctness' of each response requires significant overhead, as experts in computing education, programming, and the specific language are needed for each evaluation. The lack of this kind of validation combined with the use of convenience sampling means that the quality of responses in the dataset we evaluated may vary across each of the languages. As such, the results we present should not be interpreted as the LLM's agreement with ground truth for each of the languages under consideration, but rather, its agreement with what we can assume are reasonably high quality translations.

The limitations of the evaluation of the EiPL questions in the NPTEL course are twofold. First, the accelerated pace of the course (4-weeks) means it likely attracted individuals already familiar with programming rather than novices. This may have contributed to an aversion for students to respond in their mother tongue due to their greater familiarity with using English in a technical context. Similarly, this was an online course rather than a traditional in person university course. Future evaluations should consider the use of these questions in a more traditional university CS1 context.

8 Conclusions

Explain in Plain English questions have been a traditional method for developing and assessing code comprehension skill in introductory computer science courses. However, challenges with grading these questions have limited their uptake, and present particular challenges in linguistically diverse regions like India. In our study, we evaluated the efficacy of the Code Generation Based Grading (CGBG) approach applied to ten of India's most commonly spoken languages. We demonstrated that CGBG can effectively generate and grade code from responses in multiple languages, achieving high correctness rates in most cases. While many students preferred responding in English due to familiarity and perceived precision, the approach shows promise for enabling responses in their mother tongue. Challenges such as difficulties with technical terminology in native languages and varying model performance were identified, highlighting areas for future research. This work underscores the potential of Explain in Plain Language (EiPL) questions to make computer science education more inclusive and accessible, paving the way for more equitable learning experiences globally.

References

1. Agarwal, N., Kumar, V., Raman, A., Karkare, A.: A bug's new life: creating refute questions from filtered CS1 student code snapshots. In: Proceedings of the ACM Conference on Global Computing Education, vol. 1, pp. 7–14 (2023)
2. Azad, S., Chen, B., Fowler, M., West, M., Zilles, C.: Strategies for deploying unreliable AI graders in high-transparency high-stakes exams. In: Bittencourt, I.I., Cukurova, M., Muldner, K., Luckin, R., Millán, E. (eds.) AIED 2020. LNCS (LNAI), vol. 12163, pp. 16–28. Springer, Cham (2020). https://doi.org/10.1007/978-3-030-52237-7_2
3. Bangert-Drowns, R.L., Kulik, C.L.C., Kulik, J.A., Morgan, M.: The instructional effect of feedback in test-like events. Rev. Educ. Res. **61**(2), 213–238 (1991)
4. Biggs, J.B., Collis, K.F.: Evaluating the Quality of Learning: The SOLO Taxonomy (Structure of the Observed Learning Outcome). Academic Press (2014)
5. Braun, V., Clarke, V.: Using thematic analysis in psychology. Qual. Res. Psychol. **3**(2), 77–101 (2006)
6. Chandramouli, C., General, R.: Census of India 2011. Provisional Population Totals, pp. 409–413. Government of India, New Delhi (2011)
7. Denny, P., Kumar, V., Giacaman, N.: Conversing with copilot: exploring prompt engineering for solving CS1 problems using natural language. In: Proceedings of the 54th ACM Technical Symposium on Computer Science Education, SIGCSE 2023, vol. 1, pp. 1136–1142. Association for Computing Machinery, New York (2023). https://doi.org/10.1145/3545945.3569823
8. Denny, P., et al.: Prompt problems: a new programming exercise for the generative AI era. In: Proceedings of the 55th ACM Technical Symposium on Computer Science Education, SIGCSE 2024, vol. 1, pp. 296–302. Association for Computing Machinery, New York (2024). https://doi.org/10.1145/3626252.3630909
9. Denny, P., et al.: Computing education in the era of generative AI. Commun. ACM **67**(2), 56–67 (2024). https://doi.org/10.1145/3624720
10. Denny, P., Smith, D.H., Fowler, M., Prather, J., Becker, B.A., Leinonen, J.: Explaining code with a purpose: an integrated approach for developing code comprehension and prompting skills. In: Proceedings of the 2024 on Innovation and Technology in Computer Science Education, ITiCSE 2024, vol. 1, pp. 283–289. ACM, New York (2024). https://doi.org/10.1145/3649217.3653587
11. Fowler, M., Chen, B., Azad, S., West, M., Zilles, C.: Autograding "explain in plain English" questions using NLP. In: Proceedings of the 52nd ACM Technical Symposium on Computer Science Education, SIGCSE 2021, pp. 1163-1169.

Association for Computing Machinery, New York (2021). https://doi.org/10.1145/3408877.3432539
12. Fowler, M., Chen, B., Zilles, C.: How should we 'explain in plain English'? Voices from the community. In: Proceedings of the 17th ACM Conference on International Computing Education Research, ICER 2021, pp. 69–80. Association for Computing Machinery, New York (2021). https://doi.org/10.1145/3446871.3469738
13. Fowler, M., Smith IV, D.H., Hassan, M., Poulsen, S., West, M., Zilles, C.: Reevaluating the relationship between explaining, tracing, and writing skills in cs1 in a replication study. Comput. Sci. Educ. **32**(3), 355–383 (2022)
14. Hao, Q., et al.: Towards understanding the effective design of automated formative feedback for programming assignments. Comput. Sci. Educ. **32**(1), 105–127 (2022)
15. Izu, C., et al.: Fostering program comprehension in novice programmers - learning activities and learning trajectories. In: Proceedings of the Working Group Reports on Innovation and Technology in Computer Science Education, ITiCSE-WGR 2019, pp. 27–52. Association for Computing Machinery, New York (2019). https://doi.org/10.1145/3344429.3372501
16. Jordan, M., Ly, K., Soosai Raj, A.G.: Need a programming exercise generated in your native language? ChatGPT's got your back: Automatic generation of non-English programming exercises using openAI GPT-3.5. In: Proceedings of the 55th ACM Technical Symposium on Computer Science Education, vol. 1, pp. 618–624 (2024)
17. Kumar, V.: Refute: an alternative to 'explain in plain English' questions. In: Proceedings of the 17th ACM Conference on International Computing Education Research, pp. 438–440 (2021)
18. Li, T.W., Hsu, S., Fowler, M., Zhang, Z., Zilles, C., Karahalios, K.: Am i wrong, or is the autograder wrong? Effects of AI grading mistakes on learning. In: Proc. of the 2023 ACM Conference on International Computing Education Research, ICER 2023, vol. 1, pp. 159–176. ACM, New York (2023). https://doi.org/10.1145/3568813.3600124
19. Lister, R., Simon, B., Thompson, E., Whalley, J.L., Prasad, C.: Not seeing the forest for the trees: novice programmers and the solo taxonomy. ACM SIGCSE Bull. **38**(3), 118–122 (2006)
20. Ministry of Education (Govt. of India): National Education Policy 2020 (2020). https://www.education.gov.in/sites/upload_files/mhrd/files/NEP_Final_English_0.pdf
21. Murphy, L., Fitzgerald, S., Lister, R., McCauley, R.: Ability to 'explain in plain English' linked to proficiency in computer-based programming. In: Proceedings of the 9th Annual International Conference on International Computing Education Research, ICER 2012, pp. 111–118. ACM, New York (2012). https://doi.org/10.1145/2361276.2361299
22. Murphy, L., McCauley, R., Fitzgerald, S.: 'Explain in plain English' questions: implications for teaching. In: Proceedings of the 43rd ACM Technical Symposium on Computer Science Education, SIGCSE 2012, pp. 385–390. Association for Computing Machinery, New York (2012). https://doi.org/10.1145/2157136.2157249
23. Parshad, R.D., Bhowmick, S., Chand, V., Kumari, N., Sinha, N.: What is India speaking? Exploring the "Hinglish" invasion. Phys. A **449**, 375–389 (2016)
24. Prather, J., et al.: The robots are here: navigating the generative AI revolution in computing education. In: Proceedings of the 2023 Working Group Reports on Innovation and Technology in Computer Science Education, pp. 108–159 (2023)

25. Raj, A.G.S., Ketsuriyonk, K., Patel, J.M., Halverson, R.: What do students feel about learning programming using both English and their native language? In: 2017 International Conference on Learning and Teaching in Computing and Engineering (LaTICE), pp. 1–8. IEEE (2017)
26. Raj, A.G.S., Ketsuriyonk, K., Patel, J.M., Halverson, R.: Does native language play a role in learning a programming language? In: Proceedings of the 49th ACM Technical Symposium on Computer Science Education, pp. 417–422 (2018)
27. Smith, D.H., Denny, P., Fowler, M.: Prompting for comprehension: exploring the intersection of explain in plain English questions and prompt writing. In: Proceedings of the Eleventh ACM Conference on Learning @ Scale, L@S 2024, pp. 39–50. Association for Computing Machinery, New York (2024). https://doi.org/10.1145/3657604.3662039
28. Smith, D.H., Zilles, C.: Code generation based grading: evaluating an auto-grading mechanism for "explain-in-plain-English" questions. In: Proceedings of the 2024 on Innovation and Technology in Computer Science Education, ITiCSE 2024, vol. 1, pp. 171–177. Association for Computing Machinery, New York (2024). https://doi.org/10.1145/3649217.3653582
29. Vadaparty, A., et al.: CS1-LLM: integrating LLMs into CS1 instruction. In: Proceedings of the 2024 on Innovation and Technology in Computer Science Education, vol. 1, pp. 297–303 (2024)
30. West, M., Walters, N., Silva, M., Bretl, T., Zilles, C.: Integrating diverse learning tools using the prairielearn platform. In: Seventh SPLICE Workshop at SIGCSE (2021)
31. Xie, B., et al.: A theory of instruction for introductory programming skills. Comput. Sci. Educ. **29**(2–3), 205–253 (2019)
32. Zhang, W., Aljunied, M., Gao, C., Chia, Y.K., Bing, L.: M3Exam: a multilingual, multimodal, multilevel benchmark for examining large language models. In: Advances in Neural Information Processing Systems, vol. 36 (2024)
33. Zhang, X., Li, S., Hauer, B., Shi, N., Kondrak, G.: Don't trust ChatGPT when your question is not in English: a study of multilingual abilities and types of LLMs. In: Proceedings of the 2023 Conference on Empirical Methods in Natural Language Processing, pp. 7915–7927 (2023)
34. Zhao, Y., Zhang, W., Chen, G., Kawaguchi, K., Bing, L.: How do large language models handle multilingualism? arXiv preprint arXiv:2402.18815 (2024)

HinglishEval: Evaluating the Effectiveness of Code-Generation Models on Hinglish Prompts

Mrigank Pawagi(✉), Anirudh Gupta, Siddharth Reddy Rolla, and Kintan Saha

Indian Institute of Science, Bengaluru, Karnataka, India
{mrigankp,anirudhgupta,siddharthrr,kintansaha}@iisc.ac.in

Abstract. Code-generation Models are Large Language Models (LLMs) that are fine-tuned to generate code from natural-language prompts. Prior work shows that such models can democratize programming by translating clear English-language prompts into code for simple programming tasks. In this paper, we explore whether this democratization can extend to novice programmers who lack proficiency in English but are able to craft clear prompts in another language. Specifically, we consider prompts in *Hinglish*, a mixture of Hindi and English that many students in India are comfortable with. We make two contributions. First, we propose a semi-automated technique to translate English prompts into Hinglish, and we use this technique to create HinglishEval: a Hinglish translation of the widely-used code-generation benchmark HumanEval. Second, we compare the performance of several popular open- and closed-source code-generation models on Hinglish and English prompts. Our findings suggest that although code-generation models are generally more effective at generating accurate code from English prompts, their efficacy with Hinglish prompts is promising.

Keywords: Large Language Models · Native Language Speakers · Novice Programmers

1 Introduction

In the evolving landscape of Generative AI, software development has been significantly influenced by the usage of Large Language Models (LLMs) such as GPT [1], Gemini [4], Llama [33], MistralAI [15], and Codegen [28]. Software developers are rapidly adopting AI coding assistants and have seen improved programming efficiency with such tools [29,32]. The structure of the prompt provided to these models plays a crucial role in the quality of the generated code [30]. Most models exhibit a high proficiency in understanding English prompts, as their training datasets predominantly consist of English text [24]. However, there is a significant gap in the performance of LLMs when prompted in English versus other languages [8].

A. Karkare et al. (Eds.): COMPUTE 2024, CCIS 2400, pp. 18–29, 2025.
https://doi.org/10.1007/978-3-031-84391-4_2

For non-native English-speaking (NNES) users, particularly in India, there is a demand to prompt these models in a more familiar language, such as Hinglish [27]. Hinglish is a blend of Hindi and English that is often used in technical contexts where important terminology may not have natural Hindi translations. It is marked by the frequent use of English words in sentences with usual Hindi grammar. This linguistic mix is not unique to Hindi. Similar blends exist for other languages like Spanish (Spanglish) and Chinese (Chinglish) as well. The prevalence of English in technical literature and discourse leads to a natural integration of English terms in conversations across various languages, resulting in these hybrid language forms. Since technical documentation is primarily available in English, NNES novice programmers find it challenging to adequately explain their queries while prompting LLMs for programming tasks like code generation, debugging, or code explanation [3]. Moreover, these programmers are also prone to misinterpreting LLM responses in a non-native language such as English. Addressing this language barrier by allowing novice programmers to prompt in their native languages can enhance both their learning experience as well the quality of their work on programming tasks.

To evaluate the performance of LLMs for code generation tasks, Chen et al. [9] proposed the pass@k metric to estimate whether at least one of the k LLM-generated solutions for a given prompt is "correct". In this context, a "correct" solution is one that *passes all the test cases.* We will utilize this metric[1] to evaluate LLMs on code generation from prompts in Hinglish. We will focus on prompts written in the Latin script since this is a natural way of typing Hinglish.

2 Background

Compatibility with native languages is important for increasing access to Computer Science education. Several recent studies have demonstrated that LLMs can help close this gap [2,11,18,25]. These models have become ubiquitous in recent times for their natural language and technical capabilities including code generation [16,22,31,35].

2.1 Native Languages in the Classroom

Previous studies have shown that the use of native languages in educational settings is crucial for effective learning [3,12,13]. For example, 122 Indian languages were recognized by the national census in 2011 [20]. Yet, technical communication often takes place in English or its blends with regional languages. Writing prompts in English can be challenging for NNES novice programmers who are more comfortable with Hinglish or other such blends with English. By supporting diverse languages, LLMs can eliminate the need for extensive translation of educational material and technical literature, by acting as an interface between such content and NNES students or their instructors [17].

[1] In this paper, we will consider $k = 1$.

2.2 Large Language Models on Native Language Prompts

Recent work suggests that LLMs have the ability to understand and respond to queries in different languages [19,26,37,39,40]. However, these capabilities are limited to only a few languages. More linguistically diverse datasets are therefore required to train LLMs in adequately comprehending queries in other languages. Our work focuses on the code-generation abilities of LLMs and indicates that the performance of LLMs when prompted in Hinglish is lower than when prompted in English. While this suggests that it is still challenging for LLMs to understand problems specified in regional languages, we observe that this gap is narrow and the abilities of these models are promising.

2.3 Related Work

The rise of LLMs has revolutionized the field of natural language processing. Their code generation and code explanation abilities [16,31] have impacted several aspects of CS education, especially introductory programming courses [2,25]. The multilingual abilities of these models [19,40] have shown promise in helping narrow the gap in access to technology for NNES users. In particular, they have been shown to help NNES programming students [12,13].

Previous work on evaluating LLMs for CS education has shown the utility of LLMs for both students as well as instructors [2,7,25]. In general, several benchmarks have been proposed to evaluate the programming capabilities of LLMs in various aspects of software engineering [5,6,9,14,21,23,38]. Our work builds upon previous work by developing a benchmark for evaluating code-generation by LLMs from prompts in a regional language like Hinglish.

3 Approach

3.1 Creating a Benchmark

Our study builds upon the widely-used HumanEval dataset [9] which contains basic programming exercises for evaluating the code generation capabilities of LLMs. Each exercise in HumanEval consists of a prompt, a set of test cases, and a ground truth solution. The prompt is an incomplete Python function definition consisting of a function header along with a *docstring*. The docstring is a comment that contains a purpose statement for the function, and optionally some test cases called *doctests*. We translate these purpose statements to Hinglish to create our benchmarking dataset. This translation is performed semi-automatically as described in the following sections.

Generating Base Translation. We extract the docstring from each prompt and provide one-shot prompts to GPT-4 to translate them to Hinglish, as illustrated in Fig. 1. This provides us with *base* translations which can then be manually verified and corrected. We adopt this approach based on previous work demonstrating that human-AI collaboration increases the efficiency and quality of translation [36].

System: You are a translator fluent in both Hindi and English. Today, you will convert docstrings of Python functions from English to Hinglish, which is a conversational form of Hindi in which we use English for technical words related to syntax or code, programming concepts, and mathematics. Note that all text must be in the Roman script, like in the example.

User:

```
Given a positive integer n, return the product of the odd digits.
Return 0 if all digits are even. For example:
digits(1) == 1
digits(4) == 0
digits(235) == 15
```

Assistant:

```
Diye gaye positive integer n ke odd digits ka product return karo.
Agar saare digits even ho to 0 return karo. Jaise ki:
digits(1) == 1
digits(4) == 0
digits(235) == 15
```

User: `<docstring>`

Fig. 1. Our prompt to GPT-4 for translating docstrings. We provide a persona through our system prompt, and then provide an example for the translation. We replace `<docstring>` with the docstring to be translated.

Manual Verification and Correction of Translations. A group of seven undergraduate students who can natively converse in Hinglish manually verified the base translations. Each *base* translation was verified by one student. In case of an incorrect translation, the student opened a pull request with the proposed correction. Pull requests were reviewed by one or two other students and merged only once a consensus was reached. We will refer to the final dataset of Hinglish prompts thus created, together with the test cases and ground truth solutions from HumanEval, as HinglishEval.

Besides grammatical correctness, these corrections usually focused on making the translations idiomatic to native speakers. In total, 74 base translations were manually corrected with an average edit distance of 24.76 characters per modified docstring. Listings 1, 2, and 3 respectively illustrate an original docstring in HumanEval, its base translation, and its manually corrected and verified translation.

3.2 Evaluation

Experimental Setup. We prompted each model under evaluation with both the English prompts in HumanEval as well as the Hinglish prompts in HinglishEval. We evaluated the generated code for each prompt by testing its equiva-

```
Write a function that accepts a list of strings.
The list contains different words. Return the word with maximum
number of unique characters. If multiple strings have maximum number
of unique characters, return the one which comes first in
lexicographical order.
...
```

Listing 1: Docstring in problem 158 of HumanEval.

```
Ek function likho jo strings ki list ko accept karta hai.
List mein alag alag shabd hote hain. Unique characters ki maximum
number wala shabd return karo. Agar multiple strings mein maximum
number of unique characters ho, toh lexicographical order mein
sabse pehle aane wala shabd return karo.
...
```

Listing 2: Base translation for docstring in problem 158 of HumanEval. The highlighted text was removed during manual correction.

```
Ek function likho jo strings ki ek list accept karta hai.
List mein alag alag words hain. Sabse zyada unique characters wala
word return karo. Agar multiple strings mein maximum number of
unique characters ho, toh lexicographical order mein sabse pehle aane
wala word return karo.
...
```

Listing 3: Manually corrected translation of docstring in problem 158 of HumanEval. The highlighted text was added during manual correction.

lence with the corresponding ground truth solution over the provided test cases. We configured the models to greedy decoding (0 temperature) and set the maximum number of output tokens to 512. We found this limit to safely accommodate all ground truth solutions. At 0 temperature, models behave deterministically and so we only generate one output for every prompt.

System Prompt. We provided a system prompt to each model under evaluation to provide a persona to the model along with relevant instructions. This system prompt is shown in Listing 4. The system prompt was not provided to models that did not offer such a facility, like models in the Gemma, CodeGen and Polycoder families. The main prompt (as described in Sect. 3.1) to the models was prefixed by the following: "Can you complete the following Python function?

Retain the function header and docstring". These prompts were provided in the appropriate format depending on the model under evaluation.

```
You are an experienced Python programmer. Complete the Python
functions from the given docstrings. Do NOT write anything except
the function definition. Avoid print and input statements.
```

Listing 4: System prompt for code generation.

4 Results

4.1 Performance Metrics

Pass@1. For each model, M under evaluation, we calculate the pass@1 values on HUMANEVAL (denoted by E) and HINGLISHEVAL (denoted by H), denoted respectively by $P_1(M,E)$ and $P_1(M,H)$. Note that $P_1(M,D)$ is the fraction of problems in dataset $D \in \{E,H\}$ for which M generated *correct* code. Under our evaluation, the generated code for a given problem is *correct* if it is equivalent to the corresponding ground truth solution over all the provided test cases. Further, we define Δ_M to be the difference in the pass@1 values of M between HUMANEVAL and HINGLISHEVAL, i.e., $\Delta_M = P_1(M,E) - P_1(M,H)$. Table 1 lists the values of $P_1(M,E)$, $P_1(M,H)$ and Δ_M for various models. Figure 2 shows the ratio of $P_1(M,E)$ and $P_1(M,H)$ values for each model. The figure excludes models with $P_1(M,E) = 0$ or $P_1(M,H) = 0$.

Item Response Theory. Item Response Theory (IRT) [10] is a psychometric model that utilizes statistical data to explain the relationship between intrinsic

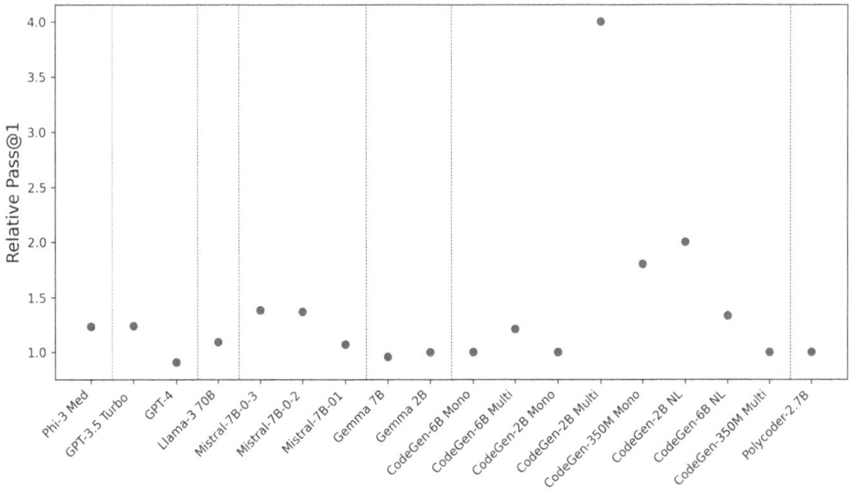

Fig. 2. Relative pass@1 scores, i.e., $P_1(M,E)/P_1(M,H)$ values.

Table 1. Pass@1 scores of different models on the HumanEval and the HinglishEval datasets.

Model Family	Model (M)	$P_1(M, E)$	$P_1(M, H)$	Δ_M
Phi-3	Medium-4k Instruct	73.78	59.76	14.02
GPT	4	71.95	79.27	−7.32
	3.5-Turbo	72.56	58.54	14.02
Llama 3	70B	71.95	65.85	6.10
Mistral	7B-Instruct-v0.3	39.63	28.66	10.98
	7B-Instruct-v0.2	31.71	23.17	8.54
	7B-Instruct-v0.1	27.44	25.61	1.83
Gemma	7B	13.41	14.02	−0.61
	2B	10.98	10.98	0.00
CodeGen	6B-Mono	15.24	15.24	0.00
	6B-Multi	10.37	8.54	1.83
	6B-NL	4.88	3.66	1.22
	2B-Mono	9.76	9.76	0.00
	2B-Multi	7.32	1.83	5.49
	2B-NL	4.88	2.44	2.44
	350M-Mono	5.49	3.05	2.44
	350M-Multi	3.05	3.05	0.00
	350M-NL	0.00	0.00	0.00
PolyCoder	2.7B	1.83	1.83	0.00
	0.4B	0.00	0.00	0.00
	160M	0.00	0.00	0.00

traits and observed outcomes. IRT has been employed to examine the usefulness of individual questions in standardized tests for human participants [34]. We utilize IRT to compare the relative performance of different models while accounting for each problem's difficulty and ability to discriminate models. This relative performance is called *latency*[2].

We assume that the difficulty of a problem specified in English (in HumanEval) is preserved during translation to Hinglish (in HinglishEval) and consider both versions to be the same problem. Therefore for every model M, we consider two *subjects* $E(M)$ and $H(M)$ which take the same problems in English and Hinglish respectively. We independently compare these two subjects from every model in the same IRT evaluation. We will denote the latency of a subject, X by L_X. Note that a higher L_X indicates better performance of X relative to other subjects in the evaluation.

[2] Note that throughout our text, we will exclusively use this term in the context of IRT, and it should not be confused with the same term for the delay between prompting LLMs and receiving their output.

We implement IRT using the 2-Parameter Logistic (2PL) model, which computes the latencies of the subjects being evaluated using the difficulty and discrimination values of each problem. We did not use the three-parameter model which also accounts for a guessing parameter for each subject while computing latencies. This parameter captures the ability of the subjects to correctly guess answers to problems. Since we executed models with greedy decoding, the responses of the subjects were deterministic. Therefore, we did not include this parameter. Table 2 lists the latencies of all the subjects in our evaluation. Broadly, it can be observed that most models understand English prompts better than Hinglish prompts, even for the same problems.

Table 2. IRT latencies of different subjects.

Model Family	Model (M)	$L_{E(M)}$	$L_{H(M)}$
Phi-3	Medium-4k Instruct	0.800	0.751
GPT	4	0.800	1.600
	3.5-Turbo	0.800	0.708
Llama 3	70B	0.801	0.800
Mistral	7B-Instruct-v0.3	−0.785	−0.800
	7B-Instruct-v0.2	−0.800	−0.821
	7B-Instruct-v0.1	−0.800	−0.800
Gemma	7B	−1.664	-1.612
	2B	−2.357	−2.394
CodeGen	6B-Mono	−1.600	−1.601
	6B-Multi	−2.383	−2.426
	6B-NL	−3.161	−3.587
	2B-Mono	−2.396	−2.392
	2B-Multi	−2.590	−3.956
	2B-NL	−3.401	−3.914
	350M-Mono	−3.832	−3.247
	350M-Multi	−3.869	−3.832
	350M-NL	−3.985	−3.985
PolyCoder	2.7B	−3.893	−3.958
	0.4B	−3.985	−3.985
	160M	−3.985	−3.985

4.2 Analysis

The positive Δ_M values for all LLMs except GPT-4 and Gemma-7B indicate that these models perform relatively poorly when prompted in Hinglish. A similar trend is seen when comparing the IRT latencies of the English and Hinglish subjects derived from each model. However, this gap is small and our evaluation demonstrates that both open- and closed-source models are promising in their utility for NNES novice programmers.

On inspecting bugs in the LLM-generated code, we found that many models produced code with logical errors when prompted in Hinglish even though they generated correct code from English prompts. This suggests a lack of comprehension of problem statements by these models when problems are specified in Hinglish. Listings 5, 6 and 7 illustrate some selected examples of such problems with high difficulty values.

```
def match_parens(lst):
    """
    Aapko do strings ki ek list di gayi hai, dono strings me sirf open parentheses '(' ya close parentheses ')' hain. Aapka kaam ye check karna hai ki kya in dono strings ko kisi order me concatenate karne se resulting string acchi banegi. Ek string S sirf aur sirf tabhi acchi maani jayegi agar usme saare parentheses balanced ho...
    """
    def is_balanced(s):
        ...
    return 'Yes' if is_balanced(lst[0] + lst[1]) else 'No'
```

Listing 5: Mistral-7B-v0.3's response for the Hinglish version of HumanEval problem 119. The bug in this response can be fixed by changing the highlighted text to `is_balanced(lst[0] + lst[1]) or is_balanced(lst[1] + lst[0])`.

```
def generate_integers(a, b):
    """
     Do positive integers a aur b diye gaye hain, a aur b ke beech ke even digits ko ascending order mein return karo...
    """
    return [i for i in range(min(a, b), max(a, b) + 1) if i % 2 == 0 ]
```

Listing 6: GPT-4's response for the Hinglish version of HumanEval problem 163. The bug in this response can be fixed by changing the highlighted text to `i % 2 == 0 and 0 <= i <= 9`.

```python
def words_string(s):
    """
    Aapko ek string di jayegi jisme words commas ya spaces se separated honge. Aapka task hai string ko words mein split karna aur words ki array return karna...
    """
    words = s.split(', ')
    words = [word.strip() for word in words]
    return words
```

Listing 7: GPT-3.5-Turbo's response for the Hinglish version of HumanEval problem 101. The bug in this response can be fixed by changing the highlighted text to `s.replace(',', ' ').split()`.

5 Conclusion

This study evaluates the code-generation abilities of LLMs from prompts in regional languages. This provides a perspective on their usefulness for NNES users, particularly novice programmers who may use these models for assistance in programming tasks. We present a benchmark to track the performance of newer and upcoming language models on such tasks. In particular, we note that while code-generation models are more effective at generating code from problems specified in English, their abilities with Hinglish are promising.

One immediate direction for future work is to expand this benchmark to other regional languages and their blends with English. Our benchmark evaluates models on a relatively small number of Python code-generation tasks, and future work can extend our approach to benchmarks involving other programming languages, other aspects of software engineering like code comprehension or debugging, and harder programming problems. User studies involving students and instructors should be conducted to better understand their interaction with LLMs in regional languages. Further studies can also explore the effect of different prompting strategies on the performance of LLMs with regional languages.

Our benchmark, HinglishEval, all scripts and generated code-samples are publicly available at https://github.com/mrigankpawagi/HinglishEval to enable reproducibility and further work in this direction.

Acknowledgments. We thank the anonymous reviewers and Dr. Viraj Kumar for their valuable comments and suggestions for improving this paper, the Kotak IISc AI-ML Centre for supporting this work, and Om Prakash Choudhary, Pratham Gupta and Adithya K Anil for their help in validating the translations.

References

1. Achiam, J., et al.: GPT-4 Technical Report. arXiv: 2303.08774 (2023)
2. Agarwal, V., et al.: "Which LLM should I use?": evaluating LLMs for tasks performed by undergraduate computer science students in India. arXiv: 2402.01687 (2024)
3. Alaofi, S., Russell, S.: Computer terminology test for non-native English speaking CS1 students. In: Australasian Computing Education Conference (2022)
4. Anil, R., et al.: Gemini: a family of highly capable multimodal models. arXiv: 2312.11805 (2023)
5. Athiwaratkun, B., et al.: Multi-lingual evaluation of code generation models. In: International Conference on Learning Representations (2023)
6. Austin, J., et al.: Program synthesis with large language models. arXiv: 2108.07732 (2021)
7. Balse, R., et al.: Evaluating the quality of LLM-generated explanations for logical errors in CS1 student programs. In: COMPUTE (2023)
8. Bang, Y., et al.: A multitask, multilingual, multimodal evaluation of ChatGPT on reasoning, hallucination, and interactivity. In: International Joint Conference on Natural Language Processing and Conference of the Asia-Pacific Chapter of the Association for Computational Linguistics (2023)
9. Chen, M., et al.: Evaluating large language models trained on code. arXiv: 2107.03374 (2021)
10. Chen, Y., et al.: Item response theory–a statistical framework for educational and psychological measurement. arXiv: 2108.08604 (2021)
11. Gabbay, H., Cohen, A.: Combining LLM-generated and TestBased feedback in a MOOC for programming. In: Learning @ Scale (2024)
12. Guo, P.J.: Non-native English speakers learning computer programming: barriers, desires, and design opportunities. In: Conference on Human Factors in Computing Systems (2018)
13. Guzman, C.N., Xu, A., Raj, A.G.S.: Experiences of non-native English speakers learning computer science in a US university. In: SIGCSE Technical Symposium (2021)
14. Hendrycks, D., et al.: Measuring coding challenge competence with APPS. In: Neural Information Processing Systems (2021)
15. Jiang, A.Q., et al.: Mistral 7B (2023). arXiv: 2310.06825
16. Jiang, J., et al.: A survey on large language models for code generation. arXiv: 2406.00515 (2024)
17. Jordan, M., Ly, K., Raj, A.G.S.: Need a programming exercise generated in your native language? ChatGPT's got your back: automatic generation of non-English programming exercises using OpenAI GPT-3.5. In: SIGCSE Technical Symposium (2024)
18. Kazemitabaar, M., et al.: How novices use LLM-based code generators to solve CS1 coding tasks in a self-paced learning environment. In: International Conference on Computing Education Research (2023)
19. Khandelwal, A., et al.: Do moral judgment and reasoning capability of LLMs change with language? A study using the multilingual defining issues test. In: Conference of the European Chapter of the Association for Computational Linguistics (2024)
20. Language Census Data. https://language.census.gov.in/showLanguageCensusData
21. Li, Y., et al.: Competition-level code generation with AlphaCode. Science (2022)

22. Liu, F., et al.: Exploring and evaluating hallucinations in LLM-powered code generation. arXiv: 2404.00971 (2024)
23. Liu, J., et al.: Is your code generated by ChatGPT really correct? Rigorous evaluation of large language models for code generation. In: Neural Information Processing Systems (2024)
24. Liu, Y., et al.: Datasets for large language models: a comprehensive survey. arXiv: 2402.18041 (2024)
25. Lyu, W., et al.: Evaluating the effectiveness of LLMs in introductory computer science education: a semester-long field study. In: Learning @ Scale (2024)
26. Myung, J., et al.: BLEnD: a benchmark for LLMs on everyday knowledge in diverse cultures and languages. arXiv: 2406.09948 (2024)
27. Nema, N., Chawla, J.K.: The dialectics of Hinglish: a perspective. Appl. Linguist. Pap. **25**(2), 37–51 (2018)
28. Nijkamp, E., et al.: A conversational paradigm for program synthesis. arXiv: 2203.13474 (2022)
29. Kalliamvakou, E.: Research: quantifying GitHub Copilot's impact on developer productivity and happiness. https://github.blog/news-insights/research/research-quantifying-github-copilotsimpact-on-developer-productivity-and-happiness/ (2022)
30. Reynolds, L., McDonell, K.: Prompt programming for large language models: beyond the few-shot paradigm. In: Conference on Human Factors in Computing Systems (2021)
31. Spiess, C., et al.: Calibration and correctness of language models for code. arXiv: 2402.02047 (2024)
32. The world's most widely adopted AI developer tool (2024). https://github.com/features/copilot
33. Touvron, H., et al.: LLaMA 2: open foundation and fine-tuned chat models. arXiv: 2307.09288 (2023)
34. Understanding Item Analyses (2024). https://www.washington.edu/assessment/scanning-scoring/scoring/reports/item-analysis
35. Virk, Y., Devanbu, P., Ahmed, T.: Enhancing trust in LLM-generated code summaries with calibrated confidence scores. arXiv: 2404.19318 (2024)
36. Wang, L.: The impacts and challenges of artificial intelligence translation tool on translation professionals. In: SHS Web Conference (2023)
37. Yong, Z.X., et al.: Prompting multilingual large language models to generate code-mixed texts: the case of south east Asian languages. In: Computational Approaches to Linguistic Code-Switching (2023)
38. Yu, H., et al.: CoderEval: a benchmark of pragmatic code generation with generative pre-trained models. In: International Conference on Software Engineering (2024)
39. Zhao, J., et al.: LLaMA beyond English: an empirical study on language capability transfer. arXiv: 2401.01055 (2024)
40. Zhao, Y., et al.: How do large language models handle multilingualism?. arXiv: 2402.18815 (2024)

Challenges and Outcomes of Organizing an Open Discussion Forum for Building the CSEd Research Community

Neeraj Goel[1](✉), Bhumika Shah[2], Mrityunjay Kumar[3], Ritwik Murali[4], and Ruchika Gupta[5]

[1] Department of Computer Science and Engineering, IIT Ropar, Rupnagar, India
neeraj@iitrpr.ac.in

[2] Department of Computer Science, Gujarat University, Ahmedabad, Gujarat, India

[3] Palash, Delhi, India

[4] Department of Computer Science and Engineering, Amrita School of Computing, Coimbatore, Amrita Vishwa Vidyapeetham, Coimbatore, India
m_ritwik@cb.amrita.edu

[5] Department of CSE, Chandigarh University, Chandigarh, India
ruchikae7396@cumail.in

Abstract. In India, there are concerns about the learning quality and the skill set of the graduates, as only 47% are estimated to be employable. It is a large and significant problem that needs to be researched and addressed by a community of Indian CS educators and researchers (CSEd). To foster such a community, we have been running a paper-reading activity for sixteen months. This paper reports on the experience of running such an open-group research discussion forum and investigates the impact on the CSEd research community-building process. Every month, this activity begins by selecting a paper based on specific criteria and inviting interested participants to an online discussion session. Major activities during the discussion are recorded for further analysis. To understand the impact of the activity better, we also conducted a survey of community members at the end of this period. The paper shows that the primary challenge is to get unique community members to join the session; a participant who stayed for a few minutes attended the entire session. We find that the factors for keeping the discussion engaging while promoting active participation included starting the discussion with a paper briefing, the presence of domain experts, and having the paper's author present during the discussion. The survey respondents mostly agreed that the activity is important and should be continued. They also provided useful suggestions to make the sessions more effective for the participants, including making it easy for those who didn't read the paper before joining.

Keywords: Open Discussion Forum · Effective Engagement · Community of Practice · CSEd India

M. Kumar—Independent Consultant.

A. Karkare et al. (Eds.): COMPUTE 2024, CCIS 2400, pp. 30–43, 2025.
https://doi.org/10.1007/978-3-031-84391-4_3

1 Introduction

According to the All India Council for Technical Education (AICTE), the certification body for technical education in India, more than 5500 institutions offer engineering courses across the nation [2]. These colleges graduate about nine hundred thousand (900K) students in various engineering disciplines, about a third of whom graduate in Computer Science (CS) and allied disciplines [17]. Many non-CS graduates also enrol in CS courses and take up Information Technology (IT) jobs upon graduation. Even though we have such a large number of engineering graduates, there are concerns about their quality; some estimates [16] suggest that the employability of these graduates is at 47% which is a concerningly low number.

This is a uniquely Indian problem that requires investigation and research by a community of Indian educators and researchers focusing on CS Education (CSEd). It is not easy for CSEd educators to become researchers because trained engineers face multiple cognitive difficulties when learning educational research methods [4]. In general, Engineering Education Research (EER) is new for Indian engineering educators [14]. One way of expediting the process of training teachers to be researchers is to build a community that helps each other learn faster, a Community of Practice (CoP). Wenger defined a CoP as a joint enterprise (as understood and continually renegotiated by its members) consisting of the relationships of mutual engagement that bind members into a social entity and a shared repertoire of communal resources (routines, sensibilities, artefacts, vocabulary, styles, etc.) that members have developed over time [26].

We aim to create and sustain a Community of Practice (CoP) of CSEd researchers in India. There are many ways of fostering such a CoP. Fincher and Tenenburg described a bootstrapping activity that consists of two workshops a year apart and tasks for the participants to perform during the year in their classroom, with a mid-year check-in during a conference [7]. GO-GN research community-building process centres around a conference and online activities, including monthly webinars, social media use, and newsletters [25]. Multi-year experience involvement in building a Teacher Leadership Research Community is another effective method [3]. Our suggested approach for community building, namely, '*Open-group Research Discussion*', spanned several months of activity and meaningful data collection. Over sixteen months, we held monthly discussions on pre-selected papers with defined selection criteria from reputed CSEd conferences and journals.

This paper reports on how this activity has impacted the research community-building process. We frame our research question as follows:

RQ: How does an open-group research discussion impact the CSEd research community-building process?

Section 2 describes the process we used to run the activity of open-group research discussion. Section 3 reports the results of analyzing the attendance data. We also conducted a survey of the community members, and Sect. 4 reports on the results from this survey. Given that the authors were active participants in this activity, Sect. 5 shares the personal observations of each of the authors about the activity. Section 6 outlines the key challenges and opportunities we found through the observations and analyses presented in the previous sections. Section 7 concludes the paper with a summary of our findings and pointers to the next steps for us and the community.

2 Material and Methods

Open group research discussion starts with selecting one paper to be read and discussed. Criteria for selecting the paper are (a) the paper should be recent (b) the paper should be relevant to the computer science education area; (c) the paper should have been published in a top conference or journal in the CSEd area, and (d) the paper should have potential to get discussion points. Since some of the criteria are subjective in nature, a designated team reviewed the papers primarily based on the abstract, and a quick skimming through provided their opinions. The paper with the most votes was selected for the discussion. This process is repeated monthly to select and finalize the paper for the upcoming discussion.

To ensure regularity and larger participation, the discussion is scheduled to occur online using a fixed google meet link[1], on last Tuesday of month at 7:30PM (India time). Since in academia the schedule is weekly based, the specific weekday is fixed rather than a specific date every month. Details about the discussion forum, including the paper title, are shared via email and social media, along with the manuscript copy. Attendees were recommended to read the paper, though it was not mandatory. In each discussion, a few attendees volunteer to discuss their understanding of the paper with the rest of the group, followed by an elaborate discussion on each aspect of the paper, including motivation, methods, and evaluation methods. Discussion is usually moderated by one of the regular attendee. During the discussion, attendees also correlate with their teaching experiences, current practices, and possibly adapting the research findings in the teaching setup. In most cases, possible future research directions, particularly in the Indian context.

Table 1 lists the discussed papers with relevant descriptions. It can be observed that the selected papers were published between 2022 and 2024. Out of sixteen papers, 9 papers (56.25 %) were published in the SIGCSE TS conference, the flagship conference in computing education. Other venues include ICER (1 paper), ITiCSE (3 papers), CIKM (1 paper), ACM TOCE (1 paper), and Compute (1 paper). The activity spanned sixteen months, and at the end, a survey was collected based on the feedback form.

3 Observations

Observation is broadly categorized into the following two categories: Quantitative and Qualitative. Quantitative observation is assessed from the attendance data and its correlation with the topics, engagement, retention, etc. Qualitative observations are mainly based on personal experience.

[1] Google meet link: meet.google.com/huv-gijp-umh.

Table 1. Paper Description including Titles, Topic, Venue, and year of publication. Topics are encoded as ASM: Assessment, PRO: Programming, FDP: Faculty Training, AI: Artificial Intelligence, CUR: Curriculum, DSA: Data Structure and Algorithms, ENG: Engagement, DATA: Data Mining, ALGO: Algorithm

Sr. No.	Title of the Paper	Topic	Venue	Year
1	Preventing Cheating in Hands-on Lab Assignments [24]	ASM	SIGCSE TS	2022
2	Training Computing Educators to Become Computing Education Researchers [5]	FDP	SIGCSE TS	2022
3	Conversing with copilot: Exploring prompt engineering for solving cs1 problems using natural language [6]	AI, PRO	SIGCSE TS	2023
4	Automatic Generation of Programming Exercises and Code Explanations Using Large Language Models [21]	AI, ASM	ICER	2022
5	Mastery Learning with Specs Grading for Programming Courses [23]	PRO, ASM	SIGCSE TS	2023
6	Learning Transfer in Novice Programmers: A Preliminary Study [13]	PRO	ITiCSE	2021
7	On Students' Usage of Tracing for Understanding Code [10]	PRO	SIGCSE TS	2023
8	Psychometric Evaluation of the Cybersecurity Curriculum Assessment. [11]	ASM, CUR	SIGCSE TS	2023
9	Studied Questions in Data Structures and Algorithms Assessments [8]	ASM, DSA	ITiCSE	2023
10	Resilience and Effective Learning in First-Year Undergraduate Computer Science [20]	ENG	ITiCSE	2020
11	Does Bilingual Specification impact students' comprehension of problems in Introductory Programming? [9]	ASM	Compute	2023
12	Exploring multi-objective exercise recommendations in online education systems. [12]	ASM, DATA	CIKM	2019
13	Automated Assessment in Computer Science Education: A State-of-the-Art Review [18]	ASM	ACM TOCE	2022
14	Mining Jewels Together: Debating about Programming Threshold Concepts in Large Classes [22]	PRO	SIGCSE TS	2024
15	How do Undergraduate Students Reason about Ethical and Algorithmic Decision-Making [1]	ALGO	SIGCSE TS	2022
16	Teaching Algorithm Design: A Literature Review [15]	ALGO	SIGCSE TS	2024

3.1 Quantitative Observation Based on Attendance Data

Monthly discussions were conducted using the online meeting platform - Google Meet. After every meeting, Google Meet provides attendance data about each participant: name, email ID (partially masked), joining time, exit time, and attendance duration.

- Name
- Partially masked email id
- Time of joining
- Exit time
- Duration for which participant was present

Since this is an automated email generated by Google Meet, we received this information in fourteen out of sixteen instances due to technical issues. Figure 1 shows the summary of attendance data. It may be noted that data on meeting IDs 9 and 11 is missing since Google Meet has not provided the data on these meetings due to some technical glitch. The figure shows the number of attendees in each meeting and the duration of each meeting.

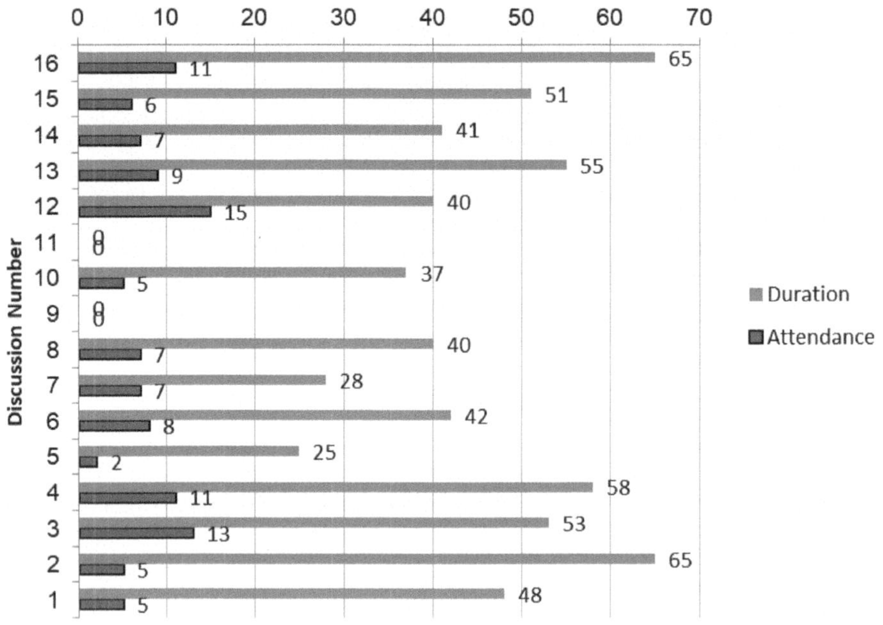

Fig. 1. Attendance and Duration of the Discussion Forum

The correlation between attendance and duration is 0.36. A positive correlation shows that the meeting duration depends on the number of attendees and related factors. The topic of the discussion is another important factor that impacted the interest. For example, Discussion '2', focused on training educators to become computer science education researchers, and '16', focusing on how to teach algorithms, are the two longest sessions. The use of LLMs (discussion '3' and '4') in programming also triggered much interest.

We also observed that a total of 46 unique attendees attended these discussions. Table 2 shows the details. Out of 46 attendees, at least 17 attended it again, thus showing the benefit they are getting. On the negative side, it is also observed that 29 out of 46 (63%) attended the discussion forum only once. The discussion host tried to engage with first-time attendees. In most cases, they were undergraduate students who attended due to curiosity but had no interest in computer science education.

Table 2. Repeated Attendance in Discussion Forum

Number of meetings attended	Number of attendees
More than 5	5
More than or equal to 3	5
Equal to 2	7
Equal to 1	29

Figure 2 shows how much percentage of time attendees were present in the discussion. The graph is generated using 111 attendees across 14 discussions. It can be observed that only ten attendees attended a meeting for less than 10% duration of the meeting. On the other hand, 81 attendees attended more than 80% of the meeting. This shows the bimodal behaviour distribution; that is, an attendee either joins the discussion and leaves in the initial few minutes or stays for most of the duration. The figure also shows the retention of an attendee for a given meeting is 79.7%. In practice, power and Internet failure also contributed to attendees leaving the discussion in the middle.

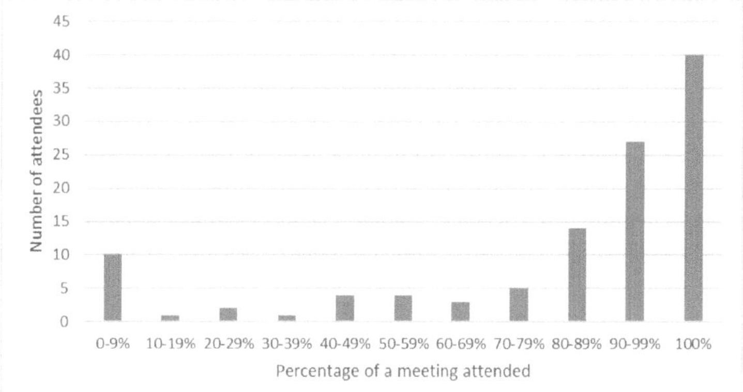

Fig. 2. Percentage Time in a Meeting Attended by an Attendee

3.2 Qualitative Observation Based on Experience

Qualitative observations are broadly based on the experience of the meetings, highlighting the importance of paper selection, the presence of domain experts, and the effectiveness of discussion starting with a paper summary.

a. **Observation based on Selection of Paper:** This includes the participant's information about the relevance of the paper discussed, including their familiarity with the subject matter and previous exposure to similar topics. It is observed that 10 people attended more than 60% of the total 16 sessions and found it interesting, irrespective of the paper. They are considered more focused on the broader domain than the specific paper. Two newcomers were observed to be selective in attending the discussion based on the paper selection related to their current work's research problem.

b. **Observation based on Active Participation in Discussion:** This observation metric focuses on the participation and engagement level during the discussion. It includes an assessment of their involvement throughout the session by sending comments/emoticons and asking questions. Since Google Meet does not record the number of comments or emoticons sent during a meeting, we manually tracked such cases. On average, 70% of attendees participated by sending chat messages or using relevant emoticons based on the ongoing discussion. This parameter was observed to be one of the crucial parameters in classifying the attendee's experience with active participation. Additionally, we observed that initially, passive attendees became more active participants after the paper's key points were summarized.
c. **Observation based on Expert Presence:** This parameter examines the impact of the involvement of subject matter experts during the discussion. We observed the highest attendance during sessions '3', '4', '12', and '16' when a domain expert was present, and participants were informed of this beforehand. Attendees found these sessions more enriching due to the expert's presence and were more engaged during the Q&A segment, actively participating in discussions.
d. **Presence of Authors**: We observe that in the session '3' and '11', authors of the selected research papers were also present during the discussion. Though we have limited concrete data on session '11', based on recall, it is observed that both sessions triggered good attendance as well as good participation.
e. **Mode of discussion**: For discussion 16, the mode of discussion was modified; instead of a summary from all the participants, one of the participants explained the paper in the first 20 min. Discussion afterwards was based on more crisp questions regarding the paper rather than holding a general discussion.

4 Survey Results

To gain feedback regarding the open-group research discussion, a survey was shared at the end of the discussion series requesting all interested participants (including even those who had not attended sessions) to respond. The feedback survey was crafted to understand the participants' aims and objectives while encouraging them to rate their experience. This included identifying the factors that contributed to participants' interest in joining the discussions, the challenges faced towards being available consistently for all meetings and obtaining their suggestions related to the discussion format. Additionally, some questions explored the demographic of the participants concerning their educational qualifications (Masters lever/PhD), current employment (Teaching/Industry/Research), and any teaching experience they might have had (with a focus on the subjects taught). The results showed that 55% of respondents already have a PhD while 45% are either pursuing a PhD or a masters level education. 82% of respondents are faculty members, and only 18% of the respondents are from the industry or are full-time research scholars.

According to the survey results, 'Data Structures & Algorithms' and 'Programming' were the most frequently taught courses, followed by 'Database Management Systems' and 'Artificial Intelligence'. Other courses such as 'Software Development, 'Computer Security', 'Computer Networks', and 'Automata Theory' were also mentioned, but less frequently.

The survey form also collected the reason for not joining the discussion, and 80% of attendees (attending <30% of the sessions) had chosen their occupancy with 'other commitments/conflicting meeting time'.

Further, based on the feedback responses, the participant's interests in attending the meetings are classified into 4 categories: Community building, Research, Professional development, and 'Interested, but unable to attend'. Interestingly, these categories also correlated with regularity in attendance, interest in the activity, and suggestions. The participants interested in developing a CS education community were the most frequent attendees, closely followed by those interested in research. The ones interested in professional development were mostly those currently involved in academic administration. A few responders could not attend due to conflicting meeting schedules or a very busy workload. It is also interesting to note that almost all participants agreed that the paper reading exercise was beneficial. Suggestions for further paper reading ranged from research on pedagogy in general to papers on very specific subjects. The collated themes are showcased in Fig. 3.

Finally, to make the paper reading activity more useful for the community, the respondents suggested that it would be good to summarize the results and

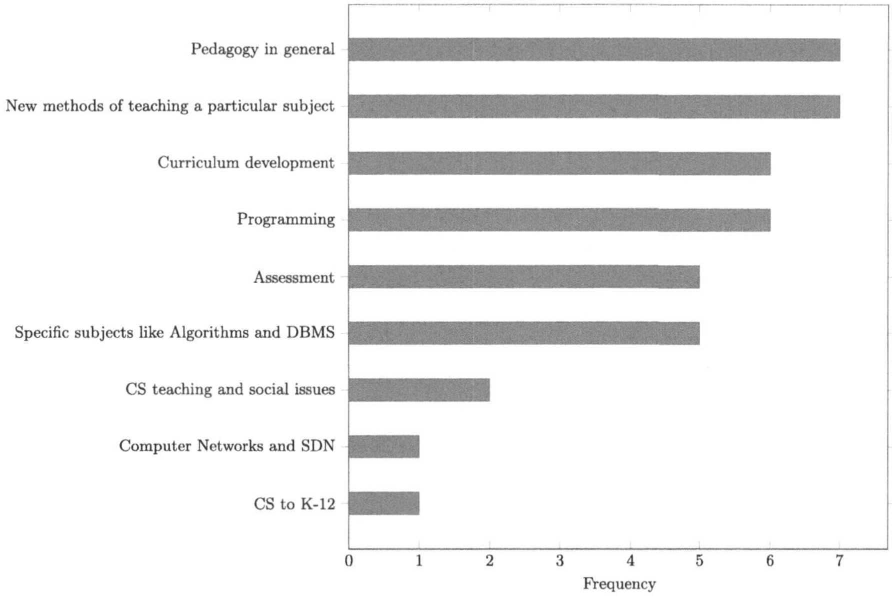

Fig. 3. Suggested Themes for Future Paper Reading Activity

share them to allow more people to understand the outcome of the discussion and encourage them to attend future meetings. There were also suggestions on encouraging the creation of specific discussion forums for specific purposes such as 'writing papers as a collaborative effort', 'providing mentorship', and so on.

5 Personal Observations

This section captures the authors' experiences during their active participation in more than 70% of total sessions. These narratives aim to present the personal evaluation of this year-long activity of individual authors. Their insights are presented as follows, organized in no particular order.

5.1 Author A

In a series of sixteen monthly meetings, we observed that starting the discussion with an introduction of the paper's major contents and findings effectively engaged attendees, including those unfamiliar with the content or unable to review the paper beforehand due to other commitments. Domain experts added depth and made the discussion more engaging. This format successfully sparked interest among new researchers in the field of CSEd. Additionally, the discussion forum dispelled myths and raised awareness about CSEd as a viable area for doctoral research. I find the sessions valuable, as they provide networking opportunities and foster community among participants. Alongside enhancing my knowledge base, I now have a scholar who started working on CSEd research. The scholar was initially invited to these sessions and later chose CSEd as their doctoral research area, motivated by the discussions.

5.2 Author B

Throughout the year-long activity of paper reading to strengthen the CS education community, I attended almost all the paper reading sessions, and I observed that the people who attended the activity certainly gained insights into each of the paper readings. For instance, when we discussed the paper related to pedagogy building [5], the participants saw the advantage in curriculum development and building their lesson plans. Secondly, when we discussed the paper on teaching methodologies, participants were able to try different methods for student engagement and certainly received positive feedback on general subject conduct. I often tried different student engagement activities in my class and received a positive response. Assessment papers [6,21] also helped us try different assessment methodologies and peer assessment models for large classrooms. The paper reading activity certainly helps academicians conduct their class with more insight and see it from learners' perspectives. Hence, I can say that the paper reading activity certainly benefits the community; however, low attendance remains a concern, which may be due to the workload or other prior commitments. The future goal would be to take the community towards the LLMs and discuss large language models and generative programming tools more. The community can help with teacher training and ensure that the education system can align with industry standards.

5.3 Author C

From my perspective, the paper discussion activity is an opportunity to identify and explore good-quality research papers. As a teaching faculty member with a high teaching/administrative workload, I find the time available for research to be minimal. This activity allowed me to identify good quality research in the CS education field. In addition, having a regular time fixed for the discussion also allowed me to be more disciplined in the research. Even if I could not read the paper thoroughly before the discussion, the open and inviting nature of the community allowed me to understand the nuances of the paper by merely following the discussions.

Additionally, with the diverse demographics of the papers and their authors, the discussions often resulted in the attendees exploring the feasibility of implementing such techniques and studies in the Indian context. Consequently, the advantage of such a community is the possibility of collaborating with like-minded individuals to solve problems that impact the daily aspects of the education community. However, the challenge of trying to build such a community still remains. In most cases, many interested individuals cannot be active and attend most meetings due to dynamic administrative requirements. There is also a hesitancy to attend the meetings without adequate preparation (i.e., reading the paper in advance) despite multiple explicit statements that it is not required. The possible cause for this may be the social stigma/embarrassment associated with making mistakes on a public platform. Nevertheless, the paper reading & discussion exercise have expanded my understanding of CS education research and allowed me to connect with amazing individuals excited about meaningful research. I shall continue attending the sessions and encourage others to attend these sessions as well.

5.4 Author D

The paper discussion activity provides a good opportunity to read a quality research paper, discuss it with the community, and engage with peer researchers. During the discussion, we hear different perspectives and understand things that cannot be understood alone. In some cases, even without reading the paper, I could understand the paper just by attending the discussion.

These discussions also lead to many lateral advantages. (a) Almost every discussion ended with new research problems that can be solved in the Indian scenario. Indian scenario presents unique challenges, like classrooms with fixed section sizes but large numbers of sections, where each section is taught by a different faculty, in comparison to large classrooms that are quite common in other countries. (b) These discussions offer opportunities for collaboration and to work together. As a diverse country, India provides enough opportunities for multi-institutional studies that can be done with the help of such a framework. The challenging part is noting new ideas generated during discussions, following up on them, and executing them. Engaging with new audiences was sometimes challenging.

5.5 Author E

I attended most of the monthly discussions and also voted on which paper to select for the month. We started this activity by helping each other write papers we could submit to conferences like COMPUTE. However, the sessions have helped me by encouraging me to read many more papers and learn from the discussions. I benefitted immensely from the insights from the educators about how easy or hard it will be to adapt a given technique from the paper in their classroom. It was also insightful for me to understand how the problems in our classrooms, as articulated by these instructors, could be very different and unique to the Indian higher education ecosystem. Although attendance remained low, the discussions were engaging and productive. One problem I faced was remembering the exact date and time of the sessions, given that they were not scheduled as a calendar event. One surprising thing for me was that even though the events were announced on LinkedIn in advance and got reasonable engagement (as evidenced by Likes and Shares), they didn't translate into many first-time visitors. We also tried to help the potential attendees by reminding them not to read in advance to attend the session, but that didn't seem to help bring new attendees. These should be looked at, and new methods should be devised to attract more first-time attendees. This has been a great experience, and I will continue attending it.

6 Challenges and Opportunities

One of the primary challenges in organizing the CSEd Open Discussion forum is ensuring attendees' consistent participation. The varying levels of familiarity with the topic discussed impact participation consistency. Technical glitches, power failures, and server errors are some of the challenges that are difficult to address.

Moreover, open discussions offer notable opportunities to foster a collaborative environment, where researchers share valuable insights, identify existing gaps and emerging trends, and a platform to mentor scholars in the CSEd field. By providing a platform for open dialogue with a common selected research problem and solution, the sessions boost the knowledge base, promote interdisciplinary research collaboration, and strengthen the CSEd research community.

The survey respondents offered many suggestions for making the sessions more effective, and we want to implement some of these suggestions in the next iteration of this activity. Almost everyone agreed that this was a beneficial activity and should continue.

7 Conclusion and Next Steps

The need of the hour is to have a community of CSEd researchers in India who can focus on local challenges and evolve solutions collaboratively at the national scale. We report on our experience running an open-group research discussion activity over the last sixteen months. Even though the event registered low participation (only 37% of 46 unique attendees attended more than one session), the participation data suggests the event was useful and engaging. This is also corroborated by the survey results, which showed that the activity was beneficial and should continue. Survey results also showed a few distinct categories of participants - community builders, researchers, and professionals - and what they needed from the activity to be engaging and useful. This allows us to design the next iteration of the activity. Survey participants also provided useful suggestions for improving the utility of the sessions: a) providing a discussion summary after every session and b) creating specific discussion forums for specific purposes, such as collaborating to write a paper. This allows us to design the next iteration of the activity to be targeted towards specific initiatives like paper writing, giving and receiving mentorship, etc. Fincher and Tenenburg [7] suggest workshops twice a year with classroom tasks for members throughout the year, which is an idea we will consider for these initiatives.

Data suggests that this activity is of value to attendees and organizers alike. It is important that we continue to build and grow the community. Wenger [26] says, "Members of a community (of practice) are informally bound by what they do together ... and by what they have learned through their mutual engagement in these activities". To build our CoP, we must increase the types of activities we do and ensure members engage and learn through them. The first tip that Parry et al. [19] offer from their experience building the GARNet plant science community is to provide incentives for community participation initially to enhance wider participation and a chance for demonstrating value. Given the low repeat participation we saw, it is important for us to identify incentives that we can offer and how we can demonstrate the value we provide.

Our next steps include a) designing and launching the next iteration of this activity, b) reaching out to more CS educators during conferences and encouraging them to join the community, c) identifying specific problems that we can work on as a community, and d) designing and launch more community-building activities.

References

1. Aggarwal, A., Ranjan, S.: How do undergraduate students reason about ethical and algorithmic decision-making? In: Proceedings of the 53rd ACM Technical Symposium on Computer Science Education, vol. 1, pp. 488–494 (2022)
2. AICTE: All India council for technical education (2024). https://www.aicte-india.org/
3. Berg, J.H., Carver, C.L., Mangin, M.M.: Building a research community, developing a coherent field of study. Int. J. Teach. Leadersh. **9**(1), 9–32 (2018)

4. Borrego, M.: Conceptual difficulties experienced by trained engineers learning educational research methods. J. Eng. Educ. **96**(2), 91–102 (2007)
5. Carver, J.C., Heckman, S., Sherriff, M.: Training computing educators to become computing education researchers. In: Proceedings of the 53rd ACM Technical Symposium on Computer Science Education, vol. 1, pp. 724–730 (2022)
6. Denny, P., Kumar, V., Giacaman, N.: Conversing with copilot: exploring prompt engineering for solving CS1 problems using natural language. In: Proceedings of the 54th ACM Technical Symposium on Computer Science Education, vol. 1. pp. 1136–1142 (2023)
7. Fincher, S., Tenenberg, J.: Using theory to inform capacity-building: bootstrapping communities of practice in computer science education research. J. Eng. Educ. **95**(4), 265–277 (2006)
8. Gaber, I., Kirsh, A., Statter, D.: Studied questions in data structures and algorithms assessments. In: Proceedings of the 2023 Conference on Innovation and Technology in Computer Science Education, vol. 1, pp. 250–256 (2023)
9. Grover, S., Raman, A., Banati, H.: Does bilingual specification impact students' comprehension of problems in introductory programming? In: Proceedings of the 16th Annual ACM India Compute Conference, pp. 66–71 (2023)
10. Hassan, M., Zilles, C.: On students' usage of tracing for understanding code. In: Proceedings of the 54th ACM Technical Symposium on Computer Science Education, vol. 1, pp. 129–136 (2023)
11. Herman, G.L., Huang, S., Peterson, P.A., Oliva, L., Golaszewski, E., Sherman, A.T.: Psychometric evaluation of the cybersecurity curriculum assessment. In: Proceedings of the 54th ACM Technical Symposium on Computer Science Education, vol. 1, pp. 228–234 (2023)
12. Huang, Z., et al.: Exploring multi-objective exercise recommendations in online education systems. In: Proceedings of the 28th ACM International Conference on Information and Knowledge Management, pp. 1261–1270 (2019)
13. Izu, C., Mirolo, C.: Learning transfer in novice programmers: a preliminary study. In: Proceedings of the 26th ACM Conference on Innovation and Technology in Computer Science Education, vol. 1, pp. 178–184 (2021)
14. Kittur, J., Coley, B.C., Kellam, N.N.: Understanding how novice Indian faculty engage in engineering education research. In: 2020 ASEE Virtual Annual Conference Content Access (2020)
15. Liu, J., Poulsen, S., Chen, H., Williams, G., Gertner, Y., Franklin, D.: Teaching algorithm design: a literature review. In: Proceedings of the 55th ACM Technical Symposium on Computer Science Education, vol. 2, pp. 1722–1723 (2024)
16. Mercer | Mettl: India's graduate skill index 2023 (2023). https://pages.mettl.com/indias-graduate-skill-index
17. MoE: All India survey on higher education 2021-22 (2022). https://bit.ly/3Lhfrkz
18. Paiva, J.C., Leal, J.P., Figueira, Á.: Automated assessment in computer science education: a state-of-the-art review. ACM Trans. Comput. Educ. (TOCE) **22**(3), 1–40 (2022)
19. Parry, G., et al.: How to build an effective research network: lessons from two decades of the garnet plant science community. J. Exp. Bot. **71**(22), 6881–6889 (2020)
20. Prickett, T., Walters, J., Yang, L., Harvey, M., Crick, T.: Resilience and effective learning in first-year undergraduate computer science. In: Proceedings of the 2020 ACM Conference on Innovation and Technology in Computer Science Education, pp. 19–25 (2020)

21. Sarsa, S., Denny, P., Hellas, A., Leinonen, J.: Automatic generation of programming exercises and code explanations using large language models. In: Proceedings of the 2022 ACM Conference on International Computing Education Research, vol. 1, pp. 27–43 (2022)
22. Selva, M., Broquedis, F.: Mining jewels together: debating about programming threshold concepts in large classes. In: Proceedings of the 55th ACM Technical Symposium on Computer Science Education, vol. 1, pp. 1189–1195 (2024)
23. Tuson, E., Hickey, T.: Mastery learning with specs grading for programming courses. In: Proceedings of the 54th ACM Technical Symposium on Computer Science Education, vol. 1, pp. 1049–1054 (2023)
24. Vykopal, J., Švábenský, V., Seda, P., Čeleda, P.: Preventing cheating in hands-on lab assignments. In: Proceedings of the 53rd ACM Technical Symposium on Computer Science Education, vol. 1, pp. 78–84 (2022)
25. Weller, M., Farrow, R., Pitt, B.: GO-GN: lessons in building an open research community (2019)
26. Wenger, E., et al.: Communities of practice: learning as a social system. Syst. Thinker **9**(5), 2–3 (1998)

Exploring the Effectiveness of a Multilingual Generative AI Programming Chatbot for Vernacular Medium CS Students

Avval Halani, Prajish Prasad(✉), and Aamod Sane

School of Computing and Data Sciences, FLAME University, Pune, India
{prajish.prasad,aamod.sane}@flame.edu.in

Abstract. The integration of Generative Artificial Intelligence into education has the potential to revolutionize the way vernacular medium students engage with and learn complex subjects such as programming where most available material is in English. This exploratory study is the first step of the Sanganmitra project, where we investigate the effectiveness of a Generative AI-powered programming chatbot for Vernacular Medium with English Materials (VMEM) students. The chatbot was designed to assist students with programming challenges without providing direct solutions. Students were presented with 3 programming problems and could interact with the tool in either English or Marathi.

We conducted a study with 42 VMEM students to understand how they interacted with the tool. We also explored if there are differences in the usage between students who use it in English or Marathi. Our findings show that 21% of students conversed with the chatbot in Marathi, a significant number considering the predominance of English in STEM. A slightly higher percentage of Marathi users asked conceptual or relevant questions. However, in general students merely asked for the full solution by repeating the question. We discuss some implications of these patterns for future studies.

Keywords: LLM · Generative AI · Vernacular Education · Chatbot · CS Education · Native Language Education · NNES · VMEM

1 Introduction

Although English is the global shared language in STEM academia, there is a growing recognition that students in non-English speaking countries can find technical education in regional languages empowering. More than three-fourths of the world's population does not speak English, especially in developing countries.

In 2021, the Government of India launched engineering degree courses in regional languages and allowed 14 engineering colleges across the country to run B. Tech programmes in 11 native languages—Hindi, Marathi, Tamil, Telugu,

A. Karkare et al. (Eds.): COMPUTE 2024, CCIS 2400, pp. 44–57, 2025.
https://doi.org/10.1007/978-3-031-84391-4_4

Kannada, Gujarati, Malayalam, Bengali, Assamese, Punjabi and Odia [1]. A recent news report shows that around 2,500 seats are being offered in local languages by 22 engineering colleges across the country [2]. Since most currently available educational material is in English, it is necessary that such efforts should also create material in the vernacular medium at scale.

Our study concerns VMEM – "Vernacular Medium with English Materials" students in non-English societies, versus NNES – "Non-native English Speakers" in English speaking developed countries. Prior research has concentrated mostly on NNES students in Western countries. A survey conducted by Guo [3] revealed that 78% of NNES students reported a lack of good materials in their native language, leading to issues such as lower confidence levels [4], increased anxiety related to programming assignments [5], and difficulty in choosing and understanding keywords and identifiers [6]. A lack of resources in students' native languages caused significant mental issues and hindered their academic progress. Another concern is regarding providing feedback, because NNES students often do not feel comfortable approaching an instructor or a teaching assistant for help in English [7]. We believe that the concerns of VMEM and NNES students have a great deal of overlap, often because English proficiency is valued in non-English speaking developing countries. Future work can validate whether the distinction matters, but at present we use NNES/VMEM interchangeably.

We believe that some of these VMEM/NNES problems can be addressed using Generative AI technologies. Generative AI, with its ability to comprehend and execute complex language related tasks, holds some promise for bridging the language gap. Generative AI has been put to many uses in Computer Science education [8–13] and its uses in education have been widely discussed [14]. We address a new problem in the context of using regional languages in Computer Science education.

In this paper, we present the first step of the Sanganmitra project, the Sanganmitra chatbot[1] designed to help students with programming problems in Marathi, an Indian language. Sanganmitra was designed to help students understand the programming problem statement in Marathi and English and ask questions to the chatbot in their preferred choice of language in real time.

We conducted a study with 42 students in Pimpri-Chinchwad College of Engineering (PCCOE), in Pune, India, that offers engineering degrees in Marathi. For students enrolled in these programs, the medium of instruction is in Marathi, and the teaching/study material provided is in English. During the study, students were asked to solve 3 programming questions, interacting with the chatbot for assistance. Our research questions are:

1. How are students utilizing a Generative AI-powered Marathi chatbot to solve programming problems?
2. What are differences in the usage patterns and educational outcomes of students using the tool in English and Marathi?

---

[1] Except where it matters, we will also call the bot 'Sanganmitra'.

We begin by looking at related work (Sect. 2), present the design of our tool (Sect. 3), our methodology (Sect. 4), and then present our results in Sect. 5. The findings are discussed in Sect. 6, followed by a consideration of limitations and future work in Sect. 7. We conclude (Sect. 8) by summarizing our contributions.

2 Related Work

2.1 Challenges Faced by NNES Students in Computer Science Education

Guzman et al. surveyed NNES students who were studying computer science at a US University [4]. They asked students to fill out a weekly online reflection survey that had questions about their learning experiences, the resources they utilized, and the amount of time they spent studying outside of class. This study included over 500 NNES and over 800 Native English Speakers (NES). Their finding revealed that NNES students reported lower confidence levels compared to NES students when asked to rate their confidence in succeeding in the course. Another study by Alaofi and Russell [5] was conducted on first-year students in China and Saudi Arabia in order tried to understand and assess the impact of anxiety on their performance in English-based computer science courses. The results showed that NNES students experienced higher anxiety levels, however, the difference was not statistically significant. Another interesting study that focuses on NNES was by Guo [3] which revealed that 78% of NNES respondents cited lack of materials in their native language as a major issue.

Collectively, these studies highlight the significant challenges NNES students face in learning programming and how these obstacles can impede their academic success. This clearly highlights the need for a tool for students to assist them in their native language.

2.2 Generative AI in Programming Education

Generative AI has been used in the education domain for a multitude of reasons including generating content, providing feedback, and assisting students [9–13]. One application of Generative AI is the development of chatbots which interact with students. For example, CodeHelp [15] is a chatbot that uses Generative AI to help students with programming. It provides on-demand assistance without revealing the solution to the problem. The tool uses guardrails to ensure that the chatbot does not provide the solution to the problem but rather guides the student to the solution, thus mitigating the over-reliance trap that direct use of LLMs may cause. Results show that 65% of students who used CodeHelp found it to be helpful. Another example of a chatbot being used in programming education is CodeAid [16]. CodeAid focusses on providing technical assistance by generating pseudocode and explanations for programming problems rather than direct code solutions.

However, such tools have been developed for the English-speaking world, and for the needs of NNES students, but not for content in regional languages.

Our study aims to address this gap by exploring the impact of a Generative AI powered multilingual chatbot for VMEM students.

2.3 Language and Education

The choice for the language of education is difficult especially in India, where many speak one language at home, another in their locality, a third as a national language, and expect to use English with their global customers. While there are studies on the effect of language in education [17–20], the results are tentative. Among linguists, whether and how different languages influence thinking – called linguistic relativity – is still being studied [21–24]. Dijkstra opined in [25] that "mastery of one's native tongue is the most vital asset of a competent programmer". Anecdotally, instructors have seen vernacular medium students being more fluent and thoughtful in classroom discussions in the native language, but it is an open question whether this behavior generalizes to an automated tool. In the Sanganmitra project, we see ourselves as exploring this domain.

3 Sanganmitra-Bot: The Generative AI Powered Chatbot for Programming

3.1 Tool Design

Sanganmitra is a Generative AI-powered chatbot designed to provide students with on-demand programming assistance in their native language. The goals of the tool are: (1) help students with their programming problems, (2) provide them with hints and guidance to solve the problem, (3) not provide them with the solution to the problem and (4) provide answers in Marathi. It is designed to understand and respond to student queries in multiple languages, including English and Marathi based on the language preference of the user.

A snapshot of the tool is shown in Fig. 1. The tool has two main sections, the chatbot and question navigation on the left and the questions and IDE on the right. Students could navigate to any question and start attempting them in any order. Students could choose to see the output in English or Marathi and this was recorded for analysis as well. We set the output to be provided in Marathi by default, as we hypothesized that students would prefer to see the output in Marathi. (see Fig. 1).

The underlying Generative AI model used was GPT-3.5 turbo with temperature set to 0. Python was chosen for building this tool because of its simplicity and the availability of many libraries that can be used to build the tool. Python was used for the frontend and API calls to the GPT model. The tool was built using Streamlit[2] for the user interface and Langchain[3] for making calls to the GPT model. We used MongoDB to store the student conversations with the chatbot and their submissions.

[2] https://streamlit.io/.
[3] https://www.langchain.com/.

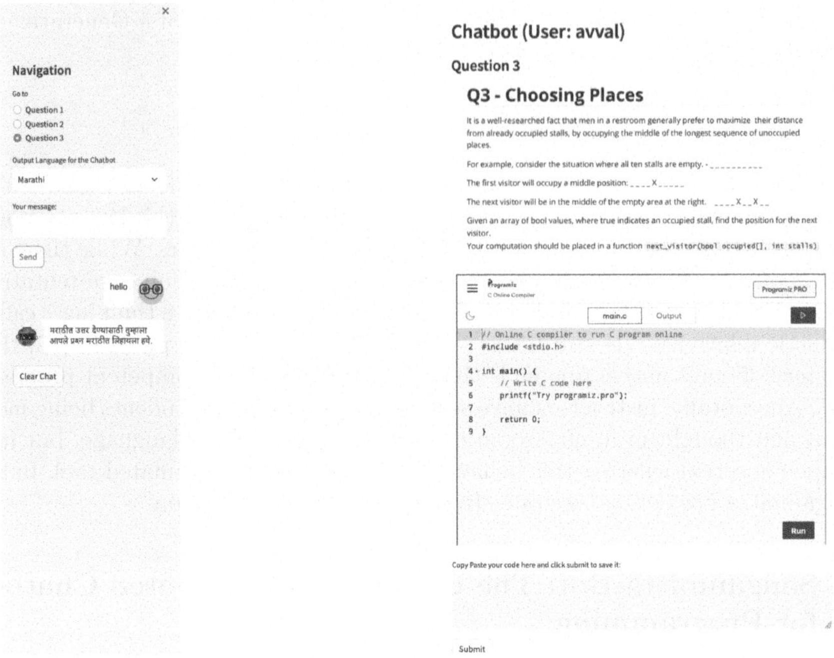

Fig. 1. Screenshot of the chatbot

3.2 Prompt Design

Our prompt had to be designed in a way so that it addressed the following needs:

- Give Hints and Guidance: We wanted the chatbot guide students so that they could solve the problem on their own. Thus our prompt instructs the underlying LLM to not provide the solution to the problem but remain limited to showing hints and guidance to the student using the question description and the student's question as the prompt.
- Only provide answers if it is related to the question: Our prompt instructs the LLM to detect relevant and irrelevant interactions from the student, relating them to the actual problem description.
- Provide the answer in Marathi: Our tool sets the LLM to provide answers in Marathi by default, but allows switching to English. Note that technical terms are not translated to Marathi – they remain in English.

After some prompt engineering, we were able to achieve our goal by using the prompt as shown in Fig. 2. No additional training was done to the model to generate Marathi text, as GPT-3.5 turbo was trained on multilingual text and could generate text in Marathi as well. Based on the user's preference for the output language (left portion of Fig. 1), the chatbot provided the answer in the selected language.

```
if language == 'Marathi':
    chat = ChatOpenAI(model_name="gpt-3.5-turbo", temperature=0)
    messages = [
        SystemMessage(content=f"{SystemPrompt}"),
        HumanMessage(content=
                    f"""
                    You are mentoring a student who is trying to solve the following programming problem:\n\"{question_description
                    [question]}\"\n"
                    The student will ask questions related to the problem. DO NOT OUTPUT THE SOLUTION OF THE ENTIRE PROBLEM. You can
                    provide hints and suggestions to their questions. If they have questions related to programming concepts, you can
                    answer them by providing snippets of code.\n
                    Only provide answers if it is related to the question.\n
                    Provide the answer in Marathi\n
                    The student's question is: {input_user}
                    """),
    ]
elif language == 'English':
    chat = ChatOpenAI(model_name="gpt-3.5-turbo", temperature=0)
    messages = [
        SystemMessage(content=f"{SystemPrompt}"),
        HumanMessage(content=
                    f"""
                    You are mentoring a student who is trying to solve the following programming problem:"{question_description[question]}
                    The student has to write code in C. The student will ask questions related to the problem. DO NOT OUTPUT THE SOLUTION
                    OF THE ENTIRE PROBLEM. You can provide hints and suggestions to their questions. If they have questions related to
                    programming concepts, you can answer them by providing snippets of code.\n
                    Only provide answers if it is related to the question.\n
                    The student's question is: {input_user}
                    """),
    ]
```

Fig. 2. The prompt used in the Generative AI chatbot

4 Methodology

4.1 Research Questions

The research questions guiding the study are

1. How are students utilizing a Generative AI-powered Marathi chatbot to solve programming problems?
2. What are differences in the usage patterns and educational outcomes of students using the tool in English and Marathi?

4.2 Study Procedure

The study was conducted with 42 s year computer science and engineering students at Pimpri-Chinchwad College of Engineering (PCCOE), in Pune, India, that offers engineering degrees in Marathi. Students were required to solve 3 programming problems in the C language. All students had prior experience with programming in C as it was taught in their first year. Each question had a problem description and a few test cases. We also ensured that the questions were displayed as a JPEG image to discourage students from copying the question text directly and provide it to the chatbot.

The set of 42 students consisted of 2 groups, one group whose medium of instruction was English and the other group whose medium of instruction was Marathi. Participation in this study was voluntary and students were informed that their participation would not affect their grades and that they could withdraw from the study at any time. To ensure that consent was given, students were asked to fill out a consent form before the study began.

We initially explained the main goals of the study to students and how the tool would help them with their programming problems. A demo of the tool was then given to students so that they could understand how to use the tool. The participants interacted with the tool at their own pace and were asked to solve the programming problems using the tool. We did not interfere while students were solving the problems, but we were present in the lab to answer any questions that students had.

4.3 Data Sources and Analysis

The main data source used was the logs of the chatbot which were stored in the database. The logs consisted of each student's language preference, the conversations with the chatbot, and their final code submissions.

To answer the first research question (usage of the chatbot), we analyzed the language preference of the users as well as the logs of the chatbot to understand how students were using the tool. In addition, we also analyzed the questions which they asked the chatbot and categorized them. For the second research question (difference between English and Marathi users), we compared the number of chats, and the average duration of submissions based on the language preference of the users.

5 Findings

5.1 Research Question 1: How Are Students Utilizing a Generative AI-Powered Marathi Chatbot to Solve Programming Problems?

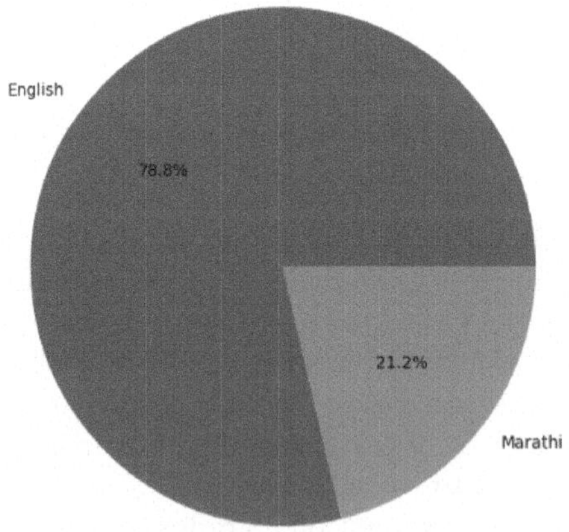

Fig. 3. Language preference of students using the tool

We first looked at the language preference of students using the tool. We found that 78.8% of students preferred to see the output in English, while 21.2%

of students chose Marathi as the preferred output (see Fig. 3). In order to understand what students actually used the chatbot for, we analyzed each prompt which the student provided to the chatbot. There were a total of 96 prompts provided to the chatbot. The categories and number of prompts in each category is shown in Fig. 4. The categories are as follows:

- **Direct Answer:** The student asked the chatbot for the direct answer to the problem (Example: *"give solution of this problem"*). This was the dominant category, accounting for 42% of the total prompts to the tool. Even though it was mentioned to students that the tool will not give the answer, we hypothesize that students wanted to test whether this was the case.
- **Not Related:** The student asked the chatbot a question that was not related to the problem or concepts required to solve the question (Example: *"Give me client server code of TCP ip in JAVA"*). This was the next dominant category with 24% of the prompts belonging to this category.
- **Questions about the problem statement:** 15% of the prompts were related to the problem or concepts required to solve the problem (Example: *"explain me the question"*)
- **Exact problem statement** (5%): In this category, students provided the exact problem statement to the chatbot.
- **Questions about their code** (4%): In this category, students asked the chatbot questions about the code they wrote (Example:*"is there error in my code"*).
- **Questions on the generated code** (4%): In this category, students asked questions about the code generated by the chatbot (Example: *"code given by you contains many mistakes.plz correct them all"*)
- **Just code** (3%): In this category, students just pasted code as part of their prompt without providing any other question to the chatbot.
- **Conceptual programming questions** (3%): In this category, students asked questions related to programming concepts (Examples: *"how to initialize array"*, *"what is destructor"*).

Another interesting observation was that students chose to stick with their choice of language, and did not switch between English and Marathi output. This is an interesting finding as we hypothesized that students would switch between English and Marathi output based on the type of question they were asking, however, this was not the case. Manual evaluation of some of the chatbot responses revealed that the Marathi output was not always accurate and grammatically correct.

One metric that we used to understand whether students using the chatbot actually showed an improvement compared to their counterparts was the use of average duration between submissions. We used 4 conversations as the threshold to differentiate between users who used the chatbot and those who did not. We used 4 conversations as the threshold because we noticed that most students who used the chatbot (when asked this question in the feedback) had more than 4 conversations with the chatbot.

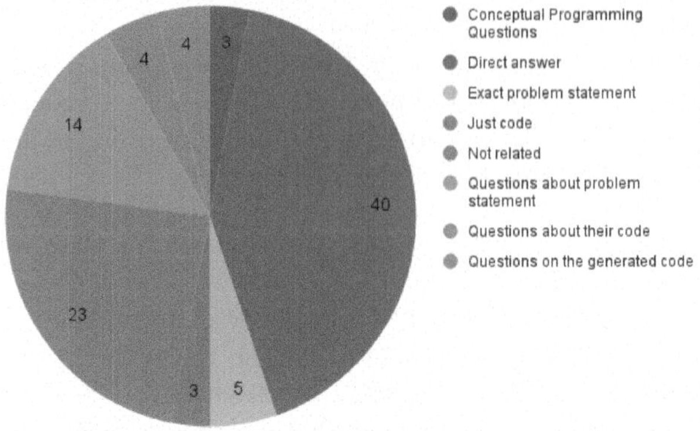

Fig. 4. Categorisation of the questions asked to the chatbot

We observed that the average duration for users that have more than 4 chats is 221.6 s, while the average duration for other users is 297.5 s. This shows that students who used the chatbot had a lower average duration between submissions compared to students who did not use the chatbot. This could be because students who used the chatbot were able to get help with their programming problems quickly and were able to solve the problems faster than students who did not use the chatbot.

5.2 Research Question 2: Differences in the Usage Patterns of Students Using the Tool in English and Marathi

To answer the second research question, we divided students into two groups based on their preferred language of communication with the chatbot. We refer to these groups as English users and Marathi users. There were a total of 96 prompts provided to the chatbot, of which 79 prompts were provided in English and 17 prompts were provided in Marathi. We compared the number of chats between the English and Marathi users, and found that the mean number of chats for Marathi users was higher than the mean number of chats for English users. Marathi users had a mean number of chats of 2.6, while English users had a mean number of chats of 1.6.

Using the student prompt categories from RQ 1, we examined the differences between the prompt categories between English and Marathi users. This is summarized in Table 1. Due to the large difference in the number of prompts between the two groups, we compared the percentages of prompts between the groups rather than the actual numbers. We observed that the most common category in both languages is asking for a direct answer to the question (around 41% for both groups). Questions about understanding the problem statement was the second dominant category for Marathi users (23.5%), and the third dominant category for English users (12.7%). A significant portion were unrelated questions in both languages (17.6% for Marathi users and 25.3% for English users).

Questions about their own code or on the code the chatbot provided were relatively uncommon in both (<10%). Marathi users had a slightly higher percentage of asking conceptual programming questions and asking questions about their code, compared to English users. English users had more instances of copying the exact problem statement and asking the chatbot.

Table 1. Prompt categories of Marathi and English users and their percentages.

Prompt Category	Marathi Users (%)	English Users (%)
Direct answer	41.2	41.8
Questions about the problem statement	23.5	12.7
Not related	17.6	25.3
Questions about their code	5.9	3.8
Conceptual programming questions	5.9	2.5
Just code	5.9	2.5
Exact problem statement	0	6.3
Questions on the generated code	0	5.1

6 Discussion

The main goal of this study was to characterize how non-native English speaking students would use Sanganmitra. From the first research question, we see that the majority of students interacted with the tool in English. Discussions with faculty from the institute regarding this finding gave us some insights to this matter. First, although students are not fluent in speaking and writing English, they were fluent in reading English, as their textbooks and other materials are in English. In their classes, the material used is English and the medium of instruction is in Marathi. Second, many students believe that having a strong command of technical English can benefit their future employability prospects in the IT industry, where English is widely used as the common language for communication. By using English for coding, students can improve their proficiency in technical English. Hence, they might have preferred to use English rather than Marathi for solving the programming problems. Third, from our analysis, we found that some of the Marathi output was difficult to read and grammatically incorrect. We noticed there were a few instances where technical terms were literally translated into Marathi. Hence, students may not be able to understand the Marathi translation of these technical terms, and hence would have preferred English.

The above speculated reasons provide interesting future directions for research in understanding the effects of providing technical education in regional languages. Supporting student aspirations to master the English language for future prospects, along with providing effective instruction and feedback in their regional language to aid in conceptual understanding is a tricky balancing act. This requires understanding the perspectives of students, instructors and administrators in colleges which offer these programs, which can lead to better guidelines on how such programs should be taken forward. Second, providing relevant and accurate content in regional languages, while maintaining technical terms in English is a challenge for current Generative AI tools. Hence, research as well as development of tools which address these challenges can provide effective learning material, as well as on-demand feedback for students in regional languages.

Based on the categorisation of the questions which students provided to the chatbot, we observe that a majority of the questions were not the desired type of questions we wanted students to ask (e.g. Directly asking for the answer, Questions not related to the problem, and asking the exact problem statement.). These categories accounted for around 71% of the total number of questions. Marathi users ask more questions about the problem statement (23.5% vs 12.7%). They had longer chats, and also asked more conceptual and explanatory questions (5.9% vs 2.5%), however, this difference is smaller than we anticipated. Our expectation was that students would feel freer to ask conceptual questions, and help on the code they have written or on the code generated by the chatbot. Tool redesign that encourages more conceptual interactions, and more training of students might help in this case. In future iterations of this work, we plan to interview students to reveal reasons that can lead to improvements in the tool.

7 Limitations and Future Work

This study has limitations that we plan to address in future work. The study was conducted with 42 students and this may not be representative of a larger student population. Future studies can be conducted with a larger sample size.

Now that GPT-4 and other advanced models, as well as India specific tools like Bhashini [26] are available, we can improve the accuracy of the Marathi output. This is particularly important as the Marathi output was inaccurate and grammatically incorrect in some cases. Future studies can explore whether using a more advanced model can improve the accuracy of the Marathi output.

The study was conducted around the time of the final exams and this may have affected the results. Future studies can be conducted at a different time to ensure that the results are not affected by the timing of the study. We also did not analyze and compare the correctness of the program submissions of English and Marathi users. This can be done in future studies to understand the differences between the two groups. Finally, the study was conducted with only second-year students. Future studies can be conducted with students from different years to ensure that the results are generalizable across different years.

As we discussed in Sect. 2.3, we have anecdotal experience of greater participation in classroom discussions when the native language was used. The percentage of students asking conceptual questions in Marathi is also higher

(5.9% vs 2.5%), however since such students are a small fraction of the total, in subsequent studies we plan to verify whether this effect truly exists.

8 Conclusion

We have reported on a preliminary study of developing an LLM based chatbot to support vernacular learners of programming. That 1 out 5 students did use it seems interesting; as the quality of the bot improves it is plausible that more students will find it useful. Students appear to use the tool more mechanically, and we need to understand how to nudge them to use it as a discussion partner.

This is a first step in the Sanganmitra project, where we plan to develop the bot as well as other material in native languages as we move towards making computing education inclusive for everyone, especially for vernacular medium students.

Acknowledgments. We would like to thank Dr. Rachana Patil, Associate Professor &Head Department of Computer Engineering (Regional Language), and Dr. K. Rajeswari, Professor (Computer Engineering) & Dean Academics, Pimpri Chinchwad College of Engineering, Pune, for the support extended towards conducting the study at their institute.

References

1. Press release: Press information bureau. https://pib.gov.in/PressReleaseIframePage.aspx?PRID=1737462. Accessed 01 Aug 2024
2. Engineering in local language? Slow start but uptick in students in up, Tamil Nadu, Andhra. https://indianexpress.com/article/education/engineering-in-local-language-slow-start-but-uptick-in-students-in-up-tn-andhra-9287283/. Accessed 01 Aug 2024
3. Guo, P.J.: Non-native English speakers learning computer programming: barriers, desires, and design opportunities. In: Proceedings of the 2018 CHI Conference on Human Factors in Computing Systems, pp. 1–14 (2018)
4. Guzman, C.N., Xu, A., Gerald Soosai Raj, A.: Experiences of non-native English speakers learning computer science in a us university. In: Proceedings of the 52nd ACM Technical Symposium on Computer Science Education, pp. 633–639 (2021)
5. Alaofi, S., Russell, S.: The influence of foreign language classroom anxiety on academic performance in English-based CS1 courses. In: Proceedings of the 2022 Conference on United Kingdom & Ireland Computing Education Research, pp. 1–7 (2022)
6. Becker, B.A.: Parlez-vous Java? bonjour la monde!= hello world: barriers to programming language acquisition for non-native English speakers. In: PPIG (2019)
7. Gao, Z., Heckman, S., Lynch, C.: Who uses office hours? A comparison of in-person and virtual office hours utilization. In: Proceedings of the 53rd ACM Technical Symposium on Computer Science Education (SIGCSE 2022), vol. 1, pp. 300–306 (2022). https://doi.org/10.1145/3478431.3499334

8. Lau, S., Guo, P.: From "ban it till we understand it" to "resistance is futile": how university programming instructors plan to adapt as more students use AI code generation and explanation tools such as chatgpt and github copilot. In: Proceedings of the 2023 ACM Conference on International Computing Education Research, vol. 1, pp. 106–121 (2023)
9. Becker, B.A., Denny, P., Finnie-Ansley, J., Luxton-Reilly, A., Prather, J., Santos, E.A.: Programming is hard-or at least it used to be: educational opportunities and challenges of AI code generation. In: Proceedings of the 54th ACM Technical Symposium on Computer Science Education, vol. 1, pp. 500–506 (2023). https://doi.org/10.1145/3545945.3569759
10. Finnie-Ansley, J., Denny, P., Becker, B.A., Luxton-Reilly, A., Prather, J.: The robots are coming: exploring the implications of OpenAI codex on introductory programming. In: Australasian Computing Education Conference, pp. 10–19 (2022)
11. Sarsa, S., Denny, P., Hellas, A., Leinonen, J.: Automatic generation of programming exercises and code explanations using large language models. In: Proceedings of the 2022 ACM Conference on International Computing Education Research, vol. 1, pp. 27–43 (2022)
12. Leinonen, J., et al.: Using large language models to enhance programming error messages. In: Proceedings of the 54th ACM Technical Symposium on Computer Science Education, vol. 1, pp. 563–569 (2023)
13. Leinonen, J., et al.: Comparing code explanations created by students and large language models. In: Proceedings of the 2023 Conference on Innovation and Technology in Computer Science Education, ITiCSE 2023, vol. 1, pp. 124–130. Association for Computing Machinery, New York (2023). https://doi.org/10.1145/3587102.3588785
14. Baidoo-Anu, D., Ansah, L.O.: Education in the era of generative artificial intelligence (AI): understanding the potential benefits of chatgpt in promoting teaching and learning. J. AI **7**(1), 52–62 (2023)
15. Liffiton, M., Sheese, B.E., Savelka, J., Denny, P.: Codehelp: using large language models with guardrails for scalable support in programming classes. In: Proceedings of the 23rd Koli Calling International Conference on Computing Education Research, pp. 1–11 (2023)
16. Kazemitabaar, M., et al.: Codeaid: evaluating a classroom deployment of an LLM-based programming assistant that balances student and educator needs. In: Proceedings of the CHI Conference on Human Factors in Computing Systems, pp. 1–20 (2024)
17. Shepard, C., Rose, H.: English medium higher education in Hong Kong: linguistic challenges of local and non-local students. Lang. Educ. **37**(6), 788–805 (2023)
18. Cho, D.W.: English-medium instruction in the university context of Korea: tradeoff between teaching outcomes and media-initiated university ranking. J. Asia TEFL **9**(4) (2012)
19. Guo, L., He, Y., Wang, S.: An evaluation of English-medium instruction in higher education: influencing factors and effects. J. Multilingual Multicultural Dev. 1–18 (2022)
20. Chen, Y.-L.E., Kraklow, D.: Taiwanese college students' motivation and engagement for English learning in the context of internationalization at home: a comparison of students in EMI and non-EMI programs. J. Stud. Int. Educ. **19**(1), 46–64 (2015)
21. Gumperz, J.J., Levinson, S.C.: Rethinking Linguistic Relativity, no. 17. Cambridge University Press (1996)

22. Rosch, E.: Linguistic relativity. In: Human Communication, pp. 95–121. Routledge (2015)
23. Levinson, S.C.: Language and cognition: the cognitive consequences of spatial description in Guugu Yimithirr. J. Linguist. Anthropol. **7**(1), 98–131 (1997)
24. Lucy, J.A.: Linguistic relativity. Annu. Rev. Anthropol. **26**(1), 291–312 (1997)
25. Dijkstra, E.W.: How do we tell truths that might hurt? ACM Sigplan Notices **17**(5), 13–15 (1982)
26. Bhashini, harnessing technology to bridge language barriers. https://bhashini.gov.in

Assessment and Evaluation

Scaling Evaluation of Non-objective Assessments Using AI-Based Solutions

Harsha Chaturvedi[1,2], Gowri Srinivasa[2,4](✉), Akarsh Hegde[1,3], Ananya Adiga[1,2], Anwesha Paul[1,3], M. Poornachandra[1,3], and Tejas R. Simha[1]

[1] 4gd.ai, PES University, Bengaluru 560085, India
harshachaturvedi@pes.edu,
{akarshh,ananya,anweshap,poornachandra,tejas}@4gd.ai

[2] Department of Computer Science and Engineering, PES University, Bengaluru 560085, India
gsrinivasa@pes.edu

[3] Department of Electronics and Communication Engineering, PES University, Bengaluru 560085, India

[4] PES Center for Pattern Recognition, PES University, Bengaluru 560085, India

Abstract. Evaluation of student answer scripts for multiple in-semester and end-semester assessments is beset with the challenges of scale, fairness and timeliness of providing meaningful feedback to students to facilitate their learning. The time-consuming and biased nature of manual evaluation has necessitated the development of automated grading systems. This work presents a solution that incorporates automated and near real-time digital evaluation of students' descriptive answer scripts utilizing multi-modal Large Language Models (LLMs) across various university courses. The methodology involves a three-stage sequential process: setting up Retrieval Augmented Generation (RAG), context-aware rubric generation, and context-aware evaluation. We use RAG to provide context to the LLMs to automate the rubric composition for a question and perform an evaluation of answers submitted in hybrid mode (handwritten or digitally keyed in) in near-real time. The incorporation of inputs from one or more course instructors on the LLM-generated rubric vouchsafes meaningful feedback for students to facilitate learning. The results demonstrate the efficacy of our workflow on multiple undergraduate and graduate courses offered to students majoring in several Engineering courses, thus offering a promising solution to the challenge of providing scalable, automated assessments with feedback that facilitates learning.

Keywords: automated evaluation · Large Language Models (LLMs) · Rubric · Retrieval Augmented Generation (RAG) · Optical Mark Recognition (OMR) · Generative Pre-trained Transformer (GPT)

1 Introduction

Objective assessments typically encompass questions that have one correct answer and include gap-fill questions, multiple-choice questions, etc. In recent

A. Karkare et al. (Eds.): COMPUTE 2024, CCIS 2400, pp. 61–73, 2025.
https://doi.org/10.1007/978-3-031-84391-4_5

years, research on the automated evaluation of short answers and coding assignments has demonstrated the efficacy of automated systems that have been well-received both by students and instructors [18,20,21]. These studies encourage the design of automated grading systems to promote efficiency and fairness in the evaluation of non-objective assessments [17]. Another key benefit of automated grading systems is that course instructors can use the substantial time previously spent on manual grading to focus on curriculum design, personalized student support, professional development, and research. This shift in focus can lead to an overall improvement in the quality of education and research [6]. The product utilizes AI to assist in grading, giving the professors a different perspective to evaluation instead of mimicking the manual evaluation process. While embedding rubrics in learning management systems has been a popular option for automating the evaluation of descriptive answers [2], the time and manual effort needed to design robust systems for individual courses has been a longstanding challenge, one that is further compounded when the responses include block diagrams, equations, graphs, etc. [11]. The advent of LLMs has made it possible to employ rubrics to grade students' answers, with clear criteria and expected responses outlined for each performance level [10]. However, the requirement of a large volume of annotated data and pipelining of techniques to handle different data classes continues to be a widely reported challenge, that we envisage to address in this work.

Contributions of this Work: The digital drive of over a decade now at PES University affords us a large volume of scanned answer scripts that have been evaluated. Leveraging this vast retrospective data and working with course instructors for ongoing courses, we present a pipeline for the automated evaluation of descriptive assessments using LLMs. Incorporating Retrieval-Augmented Generation (RAG) with Large Language Models (LLMs), with the support of cloud-based infrastructure and distributed processing, our solution can process both digitally keyed-in responses and scanned handwritten answers with complex elements like block diagrams, equations, and graphs, yielding a solution that is robust and scalable. This ability to handle multiple types of input extends the scalability of the AI assistant beyond large volumes of student responses to a large variety of courses offered in the University across numerous majors. In the following section, we summarize some of the relevant literature on harnessing the power of LLMs for automated evaluation followed by the detailed design of our AI assistant with some experimental results.

2 Related Work

The application of LLMs in automated evaluation and scoring has seen significant advancements, demonstrating the reliability, accuracy, and scalability of these systems, with the possibility of providing detailed feedback to learners.

Chain-of-thought prompting with LLMs for evaluating students' formative assessment responses has reported an improvement in accuracy, with the additional benefit of providing detailed feedback [3,4,12]. These approaches require complex prompt engineering. Rubric-based evaluation systems have been proposed [15]. Further, augmenting rubric-based evaluation with Retrieval-Augment-ed Generation (RAG) has been used to assess the relevance of information in responses [5,8]. The results demonstrate that RAG-LLM-based rubric enhances precision but requires fine-tuning and depends on the quality of retrieval.

Literature also reports the evaluation of LLM models and metrics [7,16]. Another study investigates the calibration of LLM-based evaluators to align with human preferences, demonstrating that novel calibration techniques can significantly improve alignment and outperform baseline models [13]. Scalability is another dimension that has been explored through LLM-based grading for Massive Open Online Course (MOOCs), achieving high accuracy for large-scale online education [9]. Different LLM prompting strategies to discern learner-created computational artifacts have been reported to enhance evaluation accuracy and feedback quality [19]. With the learnings from predecessor work and building on the digital evaluation effort in the University, we present a scalable, AI-based solution for non-objective assessments.

3 Methodology: Design of the AI Assistant

Our product is an AI assistant that guides the course instructors in the consistent and efficient evaluation of non-objective assessments that include descriptive, numerical, creative, diagrammatic and coding-based data classes. The proposed methodology is a three-stage sequential process: setting up RAG, context-aware rubric generation and context-aware evaluation.

In the first stage, relevant data is collected and provided as knowledge-base to the RAG, from which the relevant context is retrieved and stored in a vector database to provide additional context during rubric generation and evaluation. The second stage involves generating rubrics based on provided questions, model solutions, and contextual data from RAG. The final stage utilizes these rubrics to generate an AI score and feedback for each student answer, ensuring a comprehensive and consistent evaluation process.

3.1 Setting Up RAG

This stage includes the collection and storing of data in a vector database (as shown in Fig. 1). This data can be accessed to provide additional context to downstream LLM services, at the time of rubric generation and evaluation.

Fig. 1. Knowledge Base Creation and Vector Database Storing

1. Data Collection: The data collected can be text based or image based and in the form of PDFs, teacher notes, powerpoint presentations, reference text books, case studies and relevant images. These are crucial for the creation of knowledge base.

2. Data Ingestion: The data directory is parsed using a data framework to obtain the content and convert the data into document objects before vectorizing them.
3. Indexing: Text and image embedding models are used to chunk document objects and create the respective vector embeddings. They are indexed and stored as text and image collections in the same vector database [14]. To efficiently manage multiple queries from downstream services without the need to recompute the index for each query, the index is persisted and stored with reference to a specific subject.
4. Storage: The vectors can be stored in a cloud based vector database. Each vector has the metadata containing information about chunk type (image or text), chunk ID, date of creation, source of the chunk (file name, page number, file path), etc.
5. Query Handling: The input query is converted to a vector using a text embedding model. Cosine similarity is used as the metric to calculate the similarity between the vectors in the database and the query. The retrieved chunks are used as context by an LLM to synthesize a context aware response as illustrated in Fig. 2.

3.2 Rubric Generation

This stage generates a rubric for a given question from a particular subject, provided the knowledge base exists. A rubric is an evaluation criteria used by the downstream evaluation service to generate AI score and feedback. The rubric is generated based on the provided question, model solution and additional context from the RAG system and total marks allotted for that respective question.

1. Data Collection: The dataset consists of questions and model solutions stored as a combination of image and text based data per question-solution pair.
2. Data Pre-processing: The images are converted to Base64 format and the text based data is stored as strings. Each question is classified into a combination of the following data categories based on the type of expected answer: (i) creative (ii) matrix operations (iii) numerical (iv) generic text (v) code (vi) graph (vii) table (viii) sequence diagram or flowchart.
3. Handling Rubric generation: The text component of the question is sent to the RAG system for context. Depending on the combination of image and text-based data sent to the rubric generation service, a prompt with XML tags is dynamically generated at run time [1]. The prompt template is populated dynamically for rubric generation as follows:

```
<role>
To assign a role in a particular subject
(example: you are an expert at Image processing)
</role>

<action>
Prompt to generate a rubric
```

```
(a rubric here means an evaluation criteria) to
assess student answers for the given question
and model solution and additional context.
Additional prompt is added to optimize the
rubric to be utilized by another downstream LLM
service for evaluating the student answer. The
total marks for the question is {total_points}
</action>

<context>RAG response based on the question
string</context>
{dynamically generated question block consisting
of question text and question image}
{dynamically generated model solution block
consisting of model solution text and model
solution image}

<Expected_output>
Specify the expected output
</Expected_output>
```

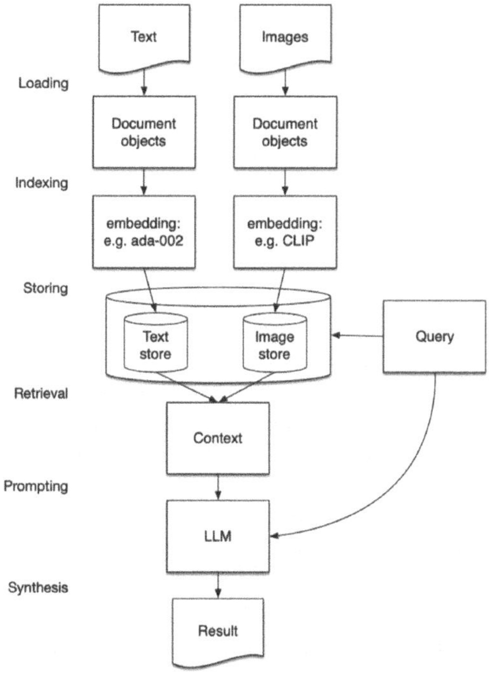

Fig. 2. RAG architecture [14]

The generated rubric, the action block and RAG response for each question is stored in a database. These steps are summarized in Fig. 3.

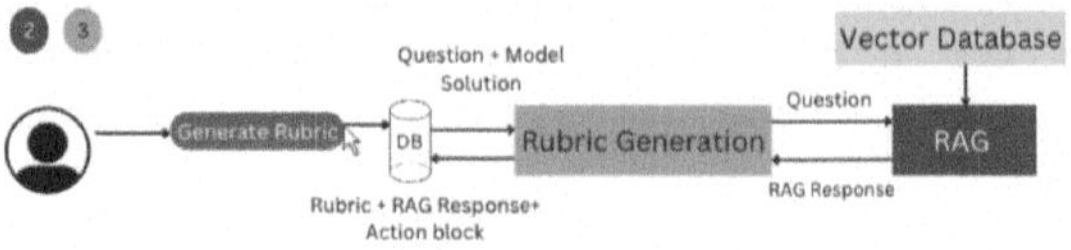

Fig. 3. Rubric Generation

3.3 Evaluation

This stage (summarized in Fig. 4) generates an AI score and feedback that provides the reasoning for the score provided.

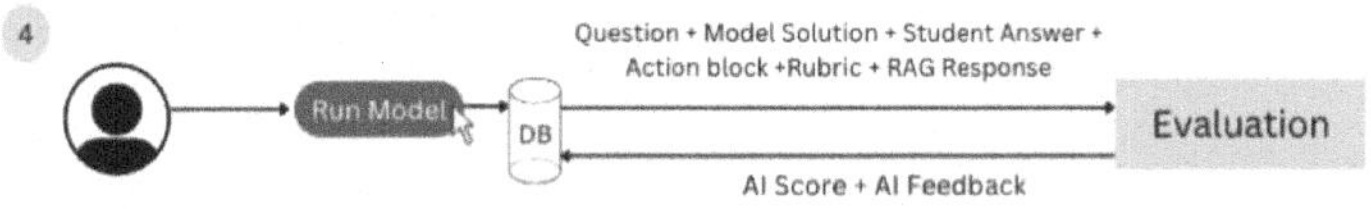

Fig. 4. Evaluation

1. Data collection: The student answers collected can be scanned images of the handwritten answers on a sheet containing Optical Mark Recognition (OMR) markings to identify the questions or the answer can be digital texts.
2. Data preprocessing:
   (a) OMR segregation: The student's booklet is meticulously organized, with each page featuring a designated space at the top for the student to indicate the question number and section letter corresponding to their answer on that page. Our current workflow involves organizing student answers by question number and section letter. Each page has a designated space for indicating this information. A deep learning approach, with an object detection model was implemented to isolate the sections designated for the question number and section letter markings. Crops were obtained for the two classes, and a LLM was utilized to accurately recognize the marked bubbles in each case. This information was then employed to appropriately classify and move the images into their respective folders. Clear markings yield 100% accuracy. However, if two bubbles are marked for a category or markings bleed from previous pages, the model may fail. In such cases, images are moved to an "uncertain" folder. Images with no markings go to a "none" folder. The student answer images are stored as base64 strings and the text based data as strings.

(b) Processing in text format: All the data from images is extracted into text as LLMs provide mature responses in text processes. The previously generated rubric and action block per question should be validated before evaluating by a subject matter expert.

3. Generating AI score and feedback: Depending on the combination of image and text based data sent to the evaluation service, a prompt with XML tags is dynamically generated at run time. The prompt template is populated dynamically for evaluation:

```
<role>
To assign a role in a particular subject
(example: you are an expert at Image processing)
</role>
{dynamically generated action block unique to
each question type to help the LLM understand
how to use the given rubric and model solution
and context when evaluating the student answer}

<context>RAG response based on the question
string </context>
{ dynamically generated question block
consisting of question text and question image}
{ dynamically generated model solution block
consisting of model solution text and model
solution image}
{ dynamically generated student answer block
consisting of student answer text and student
answer image}

<Expected_output>
Specify the expected output format of the AI
score and AI feedback
</Expected_output>
```

The generated AI score and feedback is stored in the database.

4 Experimental Results

Various engineering university courses were considered as a part of this study. We report the evaluation results for Image Processing and Computer Vision (IPCV) and Operating Systems (OS), run in a pilot study as well as the full-scale deployment on Database Management Systems (DBMS) (in Table 1) to illustrate the efficacy of the AI-based evaluation. We observe that the agreement in grades between the AI-assistant and human evaluator (also referred to as 'teacher') is the highest for both courses when both rubric and RAG context are used. While the questions in IPCV were more objective (numericals or specific points were expected), yielding a match of 91%, those in OS were generally more open-ended and included sequence diagrams, explaining a match of 67% in the grades. The score per question differs by 1 or 2 points only when mismatched. For the full-scale deployment, we have retained the AI-based rubric with RAG and tested scalability on high volumes of data across two campuses of the University, exemplified by the result for DBMS.

4.1 Ablation Studies: Accuracy of Grade Matching Between the AI and the Human Evaluator

The post-analytic results of the independent manual evaluation and AI assistant scores show the extent of matching between grades for three scenarios on the pilot study on two courses.

Table 1. Results of automated evaluation on the pilot study for Image Processing and Computer Vision (IPCV), Operating Systems (OS) and on the full-scale deployment for Database Management Systems (DBMS)

Subject	Case Scenario	#Students	#Matches	Match (%)	#Grades higher by AI	#Grades lower by AI
IPCV	AI Rubric and RAG context	31	28	91	0	3
	Without RAG context	31	26	84	0	5
	With manual rubric	31	21	68	1	9
OS	AI Rubric and RAG context	36	24	67	0	12
	Without RAG context	36	18	50	0	18
	With manual rubric	36	17	48	1	18
DBMS	AI Rubric and RAG context	1549	1045	67	336	168

1. **Evaluation with both Rubric and RAG context** combines both the rubric and RAG context for AI evaluation. As observed in Fig. 5a, the grade distributions in this setup yields the highest alignment with the teacher grades, underscoring the combined effectiveness of a rubric and contextual information in enhancing AI grading accuracy.
2. **Evaluation without the RAG context** shows the grade distribution in the event that the AI evaluation is carried out without making use of the RAG context. The findings in Fig. 5b, highlight the significance of context in

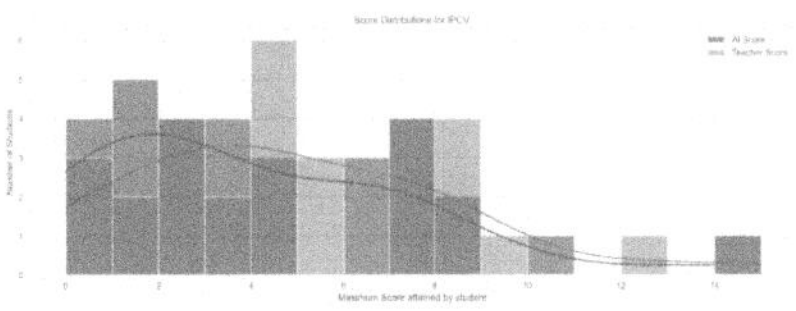

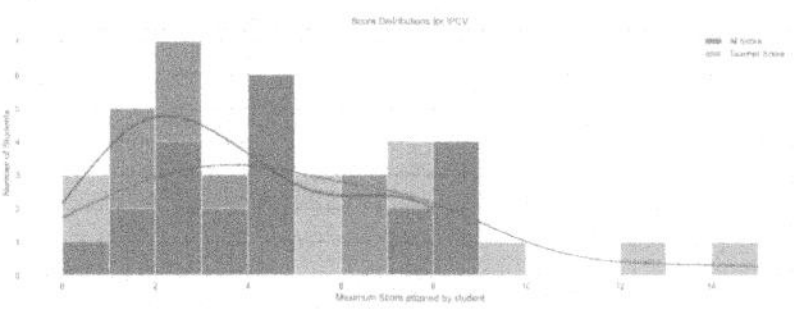

(a) Evaluation done with both rubric and RAG context. (b) Evaluation without RAG context.

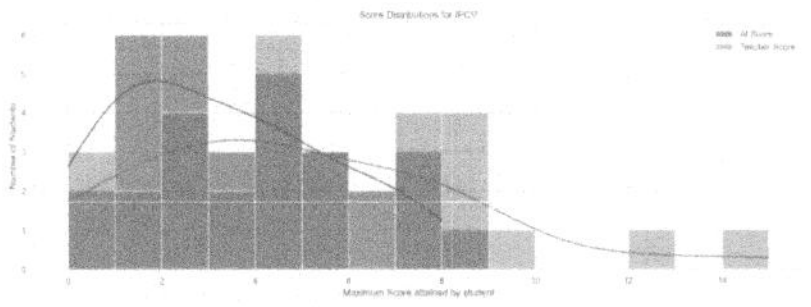

(c) Evaluation without rubric.

Fig. 5. Ablation studies for the course on Image Processing and Computer Vision (a) with both rubric and RAG context, (b) without RAG context and (c) without rubric.

enhancing AI accuracy through a substantial difference between the AI and teacher grades.

3. **Evaluation with manual rubric** represents the results of AI evaluation when AI uses a rubric provided by the evaluator (i.e., the rubric is not AI generated unlike the foregoing scenarios). With significant differences between AI and instructor evaluations, we note the distribution of scores in Fig. 5c indicates that the rubric is essential for the AI evaluation to coordinate better with manual grading.

4.2 AI Assistant Opens Up the 'Evaluation Black-Box'

Table 2 presents the teacher score, along with the AI score and AI feedback for student answers for the course on Machine Learning (ML). These serve as a proof of concept for the AI-based evaluation's handling of scanned handwritten text and problems that involve equations and numerals. While human evaluators can provide written feedback for small classes, it is infeasible to provide the reason points are deducted for each answer to each student across multiple assessments and large classes. Further, the results of the AI evaluator are reproducible, making any errors in the evaluation systemic. Consequently, the feedback also helps the teacher course-correct the AI assistant in case of any error.

4.3 Consistency in AI Evaluation

To assess the consistency of the AI evaluation system, we compared scores for similar student responses; we allude again to Table 2 to exemplify how AI evaluation can be better than manual evaluation. The question requires students to compute the average accuracy and F1 score from a confusion matrix. While both

Table 2. Sample student answers with evaluation scores and AI feedback for Machine learning.

Student Answers	Teacher Score	AI Score	AI Feedback
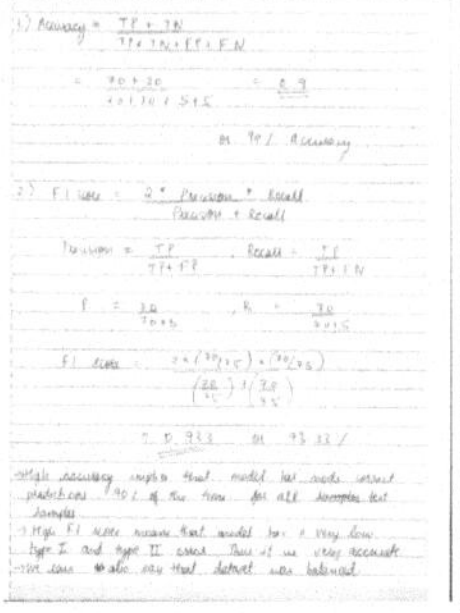	3	4	The student correctly calculated both accuracy and F1 score, demonstrating understanding of the formulas and their application. The explanations also correctly interpret the scores, highlighting the model's strong performance in terms of accuracy and balance between precision and recall. While the student's explanation could be more detailed, it effectively conveys the meaning of the calculated metrics.
	4	4	The student correctly calculated accuracy and F1 score, demonstrating understanding of the formulas and their application. The explanation for both metrics is also accurate and clear, indicating a good comprehension of their meaning in the context of model performance.

student answers are similar, the AI is consistent in the scores awarded to the students. This helps eliminate bias or inconsistency inherent in human evaluation, particularly, when there are multiple evaluators for a question.

4.4 Time-Saving Analysis and Scalability

Table 3 represents the time taken for each stage of the AI evaluation. From tuning the design of the AI-based evaluator on 31 and 36 students on two courses in the pilot study phase, we scaled to over 1500 students in sixteen courses during the first production of the AI evaluator.

5 Role of the Instructor

In contrast to manual evaluation, which could be affected by fatigue, etc., AI offers consistent results and insightful feedback for every student response. This feedback enables the instructor to identify systemic biases or errors, if any. There is provision in the design to override the AI score with that of manual evaluation. Thus, the pipeline expedites evaluation over manual evaluation of all answer scripts and facilitate evaluators to make better decisions that guarantee students

Table 3. Time-saving analysis at every step of evaluation on deployment.

Course	#Student Answers	RAG context generation	OMR answer segregation	OCR on student answer images	AI evaluation
DBMS	5988	10 min for around 5000 pages of textbook	36 min for 27000 answer images	20 min for 5988 images	15 min for 5988 students
MCSE	5988	10 min for around 5000 pages of textbook	36.76 min for 27570 answer images	20 min for 5988 images	15 min for 5988 students
ML	5792	10 min for around 5000 pages of textbook	36.6 min for 27,493 answer images	20 min for 5988 images	15 min for 5792 students

receive the points they are due. While we emphasize *automating* the evaluation, the course instructor plays a key role in setting up and employing the AI assistant for their course. The instructor

1. provides the data resources for creation of the knowledge-base for the RAG,
2. validates the AI-generated rubrics before the AI evaluation and
3. post the evaluation by the AI assistant, takes the final decision to retain the AI score or to override that with the score from manual evaluation.

6 Conclusion

We have demonstrated the efficacy of AI in automated evaluation for IPCV, OS, DBMS and ML—undergraduate courses for a Computer Science and Engineering major—as a proof of concept. Our evaluation of the AI assistant on other courses spanning various data classes has proved to be consistent in rubric generation and evaluation, along with providing reasoning for the evaluation. We will continue to improve the system on handling open-ended questions and different data classes accurately by incorporating better prompts and training data.

Disclosure of Interests. The authors have no competing interests to declare that are relevant to the content of this article.

References

1. Anthrop: Prompt engineering: Use xml tags to structure your prompts (2024). https://docs.anthropic.com/en/docs/build-with-claude/prompt-engineering/use-xml-tags. Accessed 29 July 2024

2. Atkinson, D., Lim, S.L.: Improving assessment processes in higher education: student and teacher perceptions of the effectiveness of a rubric embedded in a LMS. Australas. J. Educ. Technol. **29**(5) (2013)
3. Cohn, C., Hutchins, N., Le, T., Biswas, G.: A chain-of-thought prompting approach with LLMs for evaluating students' formative assessment responses in science. In: Proceedings of the AAAI Conference on Artificial Intelligence, vol. 38, pp. 23182–23190 (2024)
4. Desmond, M., Ashktorab, Z., Pan, Q., Dugan, C., Johnson, J.M.: EvaluLLM: LLM assisted evaluation of generative outputs. In: Companion Proceedings of the 29th International Conference on Intelligent User Interfaces, pp. 30–32 (2024)
5. Dietz, L.: A workbench for autograding retrieve/generate systems (2024). https://arxiv.org/abs/2405.13177
6. Dreher, C., Reiners, T., Dreher, H.: Investigating factors affecting the uptake of automated assessment technology. J. Inf. Technol. Educ. Res. **10**(1), 161–181 (2011)
7. Farzi, N., Dietz, L.: Exam++: LLM-based answerability metrics for IR evaluation. In: Proceedings of LLM4Eval: The First Workshop on Large Language Models for Evaluation in Information Retrieval (2024)
8. Farzi, N., Dietz, L.: Pencils down! automatic rubric-based evaluation of retrieve/-generate systems. In: The 10th ACM SIGIR/The 14th International Conference on the Theory of Information Retrieval (2024)
9. Golchin, S., Garuda, N., Impey, C., Wenger, M.: Grading massive open online courses using large language models. arXiv preprint arXiv:2406.11102 (2024)
10. González-Calatayud, V., Prendes-Espinosa, P., Roig-Vila, R.: Artificial intelligence for student assessment: a systematic review. Appl. Sci. **11**(12), 5467 (2021)
11. Kovacic, Z.J., Green, J.: Automatic grading of spreadsheet and database skills. J. Inf. Technol. Educ. Innov. Pract. **11**, 53 (2012)
12. Lee, G.G., Latif, E., Wu, X., Liu, N., Zhai, X.: Applying large language models and chain-of-thought for automatic scoring. Comput. Educ. Artif. Intell. **6**, 100213 (2024)
13. Liu, Y., et al.: Calibrating LLM-based evaluator. arXiv preprint arXiv:2309.13308 (2023)
14. LlamaIndex: Multi-modal retrieval using GPT text embedding and clip image embedding for Wikipedia articles (2024). https://docs.llamaindex.ai/en/stable/examples/multi_modal/multi_modal_ret-rieval. Accessed 29 July 2024
15. Senanayake, C., Asanka, D.: Rubric based automated short answer scoring using large language models (LLMs). In: 2024 International Research Conference on Smart Computing and Systems Engineering (SCSE), vol. 7, pp. 1–6. IEEE (2024)
16. Shankar, S., Zamfirescu-Pereira, J., Hartmann, B., Parameswaran, A.G., Arawjo, I.: Who validates the validators? Aligning LLM-assisted evaluation of LLM outputs with human preferences. arXiv preprint arXiv:2404.12272 (2024)
17. Siddiqi, R., Harrison, C.J., Siddiqi, R.: Improving teaching and learning through automated short-answer marking. IEEE Trans. Learn. Technol. **3**(3), 237–249 (2010)
18. Singh, A., Karayev, S., Gutowski, K., Abbeel, P.: Gradescope: a fast, flexible, and fair system for scalable assessment of handwritten work. In: Proceedings of the Fourth ACM Conference on Learning@ Scale, pp. 81–88 (2017)
19. Tian, X., et al.: Examining LLM prompting strategies for automatic evaluation of learner-created computational artifacts (2024)

20. Watt, S., Simpson, C., McKillop, C., Nunn, V.: Electronic course surveys: does automating feedback and reporting give better results? Assess. Eval. High. Educ. **27**(4), 325–337 (2002)
21. Wilcox, C.: The role of automation in undergraduate computer science education. In: Proceedings of the 46th ACM Technical Symposium on Computer Science Education, pp. 90–95 (2015)

Leveraging ChatGPT-3.5 for Automated Evaluation of Time Complexity in Programming Assignments

Raja Kumar, Sushant Phalke, Deependra Singh Rajput, and Sujith Thomas(✉)

BITS Pilani, K K Birla Goa Campus, Goa, India
{h20230059,h20230069,h20230044,sujitht}@goa.bits-pilani.ac.in

Abstract. The test-case-based approach is widely used for automated evaluation of students' lab submissions in Data Structures and Algorithms (e.g., HackerRank, CodeChef). However, this method has key limitations: distinguishing between O(log n) and O(n) time solutions requires large test cases, and even optimal solutions fail sometimes under high server load conditions. As a result, an alternative method for evaluating time complexity is necessary. This study explores the potential of using a Large Language Model (LLM), specifically ChatGPT-3.5, for determining the time complexity of student programs. Using a dataset from four DSA lab problems with 259 student submissions, we compared ChatGPT-3.5's predictions with the manually calculated ground truth. Our findings demonstrate that the ChatGPT-3.5-based approach achieves an average accuracy of 99.6% in correctly identifying time complexity. This suggests that an LLM-based method can effectively replace the large test cases typically required to determine the time complexity of submitted solutions.

Keywords: Automated Grading · Time Complexity Evaluation · Data Structures and Algorithms (DSA) · Large Language Models (LLMs) · ChatGPT-3.5

1 Introduction

Several efforts have been made to utilize AI in the education sector [1]. The emergence of ChatGPT is considered one of the most significant outcomes of AI technology. ChatGPT, created by OpenAI, is an advanced language model based on the GPT (Generative Pre-trained Transformer) architecture [2]. The model utilizes prompts, which are instructions or questions to generate a specific type of response. When formulating effective prompts for models, it is crucial to consider context, precision, and clarity to enable the model to generate the most relevant and helpful answer [3]. Our research primarily focuses on using ChatGPT for data structures and algorithm labs specific to time complexity evaluations of submitted codes. The study of prompt engineering emphasizes the significance of designing prompts in maximizing the utility of conversational LLMs and aims to improve communication and interaction with users. With the help of well-defined prompts, we can draw out expected results from LLMs [4].

A. Karkare et al. (Eds.): COMPUTE 2024, CCIS 2400, pp. 74–82, 2025.
https://doi.org/10.1007/978-3-031-84391-4_6

Study on prompt engineering by Jules White et al. helped to understand the LLM model's critical behavior according to slight prompt modification [4]. The ChatGPT models are highly proficient in programming tasks and offer valuable insights to the AI community, especially to academics [5] and developers [6]. We are utilizing ChatGPT LLM as our AI assistant for these reasons. Integrating advanced technologies such as GPT for content generation, prompt engineering for personalization, and autonomous computing for session management, reducing human effort and time [7]. We can use LLMs (ChatGPT) for automatic grading systems and enable them with AI [8]. Above study highlights the impression of AI in different sectors viz. Educational, Automatic grading, Development, Content writing etc. Our proposed study focuses on the automation of determining time complexity of programs with ChatGPT 3.5-Turbo, analyzing its effectiveness and reliability on DSA assignments.

Time complexity analysis is a fundamental aspect of evaluating program efficiency in Data Structures and Algorithms (DSA) labs. It quantifies the amount of time a computer takes to run a program by counting the number of operations an algorithm performs [9]. Traditional methods, such as test-case-based approaches, are commonly used to automate the evaluation of program efficiency in DSA labs. Online coding platforms like *CodeChef*, *HackerRank*, and others employ this approach, providing students with instant grading and feedback [10–12].

While this method is generally effective, distinguishing between a program with $\Theta(n)$ time complexity and one with $\Theta(\log n)$ time complexity often requires very large test cases. As computer speeds continue to increase, the size of the test cases needed to differentiate between $\Theta(n)$ and $\Theta(\log n)$ solutions will also grow. In competitive programming, factors such as server performance and resource contention during high-load scenarios can further complicate grading, sometimes causing optimal solutions to fail by exceeding time limits [13]. These challenges highlight the need for an alternative approach to determine the time complexity of code submissions.

In this study, we explore the use of Large Language Models (LLMs) for estimating the worst-case time complexity of student code submissions. To simplify the process, we assume that a student's program will have one of the following worst-case time complexities: $O(\log n)$, $O(n)$, $O(n \log n)$, $O(n^2)$, or $O(n^3)$. This assumption is reasonable, as most efficient solutions to DSA lab problems fall into one of these five categories. We designed a prompt for ChatGPT-3.5 to predict one of these five time complexities for each student's submission. We then compared ChatGPT-3.5's predictions with time complexities determined through manual evaluations by four independent reviewers. Our findings show that ChatGPT-3.5 provides highly accurate time complexity predictions, allowing us to use smaller test cases to assess whether a student's solution is optimal.

2 Experiments

We conducted experiment to evaluate the effectiveness of the ChatGPT 3.5-Turbo model in predicting the time complexity of student submissions in Data Structures and Algorithms (DSA) lab assignments. The primary objective was to assess the model's performance against manual evaluations by human experts and to explore its reliability across different experimental scenarios.

2.1 Dataset

The dataset used in this experiment comprised submissions from four different DSA lab assignments, each containing 259 student submissions written in C++. A boilerplate code for lab submission was given to the students. The boilerplate code read input from a test case file and passed the input to a `Solve` function, which was defined in a separate file. The students were asked to modify and submit only the file containing the `Solve` function. This allowed us to check whether the `Solve` function takes the desired optimal time even though reading the input would take O(n) time. We obtained informed consent from the students that their anonymized code submissions will be used for research purposes.

The assignments were designed to assess various algorithmic approaches, including divide-and-conquer, two pointers, and hashing techniques. By focusing on this diverse set of problems, we ensured that the time complexity predictions made by ChatGPT 3.5-Turbo were not biased toward a single type of algorithm, but rather spanned a broad range of algorithmic techniques. Although ChatGPT may possess prior knowledge of standard algorithms, our experiment aimed to evaluate its ability to generalize and predict the time complexity of different student implementations. The four DSA lab assignments are described below:

- *Finding the Peak Element in an Array*: This problem involves identifying a peak element in a 0-indexed array *A* of size *n*. A peak element is defined as an element at index *i* such that $A[k] \leq A[i] \geq A[j]$, where $0 \leq k \leq i \leq j < n$. Essentially, a peak is an element that is greater than or equal to its neighboring elements, ensuring that it is a local maximum. The problem guarantees that there is exactly one peak in the array.
- *Longest Subarray with Sum K*: Given an array *A* of size *n* and an integer *K*, the objective is to find the maximal length of any contiguous subarray $A[i...j]$ where $0 \leq i \leq j < n$, such that the sum of its elements equals *K*. The expected time complexity for this problem is O(n).
- *Merge Sort Implementation*: This assignment requires students to implement the merge sort algorithm, with an expected worst-case time complexity of O(n log n). The task tests their understanding of divide-and-conquer strategies and recursive function design.
- *Counting Unique Triplets with Zero Sum*: In this problem, students must count all unique triplets in an integer array whose elements sum to zero, ensuring no duplicate triplets are considered. Specifically, given an array A of size n, the goal is to identify and count all sets of three distinct elements $(A[i],A[j],A[k])$ where $i \neq j \neq k$ and $A[i] + A[j] + A[k] = 0$. A key focus of this problem is eliminating duplicate triplets from the final count, with an expected worst-case time complexity of $O(n^2)$.

2.2 Experimental Settings

This section outlines the setup and configuration used to integrate the ChatGPT API for time complexity analysis. We describe the roles, parameters, and input-output mechanisms involved in the experiment to ensure reproducibility and accuracy.

Integration of ChatGPT API. Our experiment's fundamental feature is the incorporation of the ChatGPT API for a time complexity study. We selected the ChatGPT

3.5-Turbo model for our research due to its cost-effectiveness. We set the temperature to 0.0 in the API settings to guarantee deterministic responses. We also limited the maximum number of tokens to 10 in order to control the model's output length. To ensure the model generates more likely and coherent responses, we adjusted the top-p parameter to 0.9, which limits the model to considering only the top 90% of the most probable outcomes when making predictions.

We established two discrete roles in our evaluation system: the user and the system, as shown in Table 1. The system role included all of the parts that were in charge of creating messages and interacting with the ChatGPT API, which made communication and data sharing easy. In contrast, the user role served as a representation of the interface that allowed users to interact with the system by entering data and getting predictions in

Table 1. Code used for the Experiment

```
system_message = """
You are a smart code evaluator. Your task is to identify
the worst-case time complexity of given code out of the
following complexities:
    O(log n), O(n), O(n log n), O(n^2) and O(n^3)
Output format will be (Fill time complexity of given
code at #):
    Time Complexity=#
Note: Output format to be strictly followed.
"""


def generate_prompt(file):
    prompt = f""" SolutionCode: {file}."""
    return prompt

def get_answer(solution):
    messages=[
        {"role":"system",'content': system_message},
        {"role":"user",'content': generate_prompt(file)}
    ]
    completion=client.chat.completions.create(
        model="gpt-3.5-turbo",
        messages=messages,
        temperature=0.0,
        max_tokens=10
        top_p=0.9
    )
    return completion.choices[0].message.content
```

return. Table 1 shows the `system_message` which defines the system role and `generate_prompt()` function which acts as a user role. The `generate_prompt()` function takes the student code as input for time complexity analysis.

Input and Output format. A CSV file with student code submissions served as the source of input data for the time complexity analysis. The string corresponding to a student code submission formed one column and the roll number of students formed another column in the CSV file. Each row in the CSV file represented a single student submission. The predicted time complexity, as determined by the ChatGPT 3.5-Turbo model, was added as the third column in the output CSV file.

3 Proposed Methodology

This section outlines the approach taken to evaluate time complexity predictions of student code submissions, combining manual evaluations with the ChatGPT 3.5-Turbo model. We describe the steps involved in the manual checking process, followed by the use of ChatGPT for time complexity analysis. Additionally, the methodology includes a detailed experiment-wise validation of the model's accuracy and reliability in various scenarios, ensuring comprehensive assessment of the results.

3.1 Manual Checking of Codes

For establishing the ground truth of the student submitted codes, a manual evaluation process was conducted. Four human evaluators were given submitted codes to determine the time complexity. As mentioned earlier, we have assumed that the student program submission can have one of the following five time complexities: O(log n), O(n), O(n log n), $O(n^2)$ and $O(n^3)$. For each student program submission, a human evaluator selected one of the above five time complexities.

The evaluators determined the time complexity by analyzing the code structure, loops, recursive calls, and any other relevant computational patterns. To ensure the reliability of the manual evaluations, we calculated the inter-rater reliability using Cohen's kappa coefficient. The Cohen's kappa coefficient value was found to be 0.92, which indicates a high level of agreement among the human evaluators. For each student program, the time complexity selected by the majority of the evaluators was deemed to be the correct time complexity of the student's program. The correct time complexity obtained by the above method was compared against the time complexity predictions made by ChatGPT 3.5-Turbo. We want to stress that the manual evaluators only determined the time complexity of each student program; they did not check the correctness of each program. Correctness must be checked using the traditional test-case-based approach.

Table 2 shows the assignment wise data of the number of student codes that do not meet the expected optimal time complexity (when checked manually). It shows on an average 12% students are not submitting the solution with optimal time complexity. As mentioned earlier, a student program may have the expected time complexity but fail to pass one or more test cases. We want to use ChatGPT 3.5-Turbo only to predict the time complexity of a student program and not whether the program is correct.

Table 2. Submissions without optimal time complexity

Assignment no	Expected Optimal Time complexity	No. of Student codes having other than expected time complexity (out of 259 students in each assignment)
1	O(log n)	30
2	O(n)	25
3	O(n log n)	42
4	$O(n^2)$	28
		Avg. ~32 (12.3%)

3.2 Time Complexity Analysis with ChatGPT 3.5-Turbo

The assignment data was collected and organized into a CSV file, as previously described. For each student submission, the code was analysed to determine its time complexity using the ChatGPT 3.5-Turbo model. The predicted time complexities were recorded, and these results were compared against the manually calculated time complexities. The results were then summarized, where a value of 1 indicated a match between the ChatGPT prediction and the manual evaluation, and 0 indicated no match.

Upon cross-checking, we found that ChatGPT correctly predicted the time complexity for all student submissions, achieving 100% accuracy in this experiment. To further test for any potential hallucination, we repeated the experiment five times, obtaining accuracy rates of 100%, 99.6%, 98.8%, 100%, and 100%, respectively. Overall, the average accuracy for time complexity prediction across the five trials was 99.6%.

Reliability Testing and Experimental Validation. We carried out further tests to determine the reliability of our results. We used a subset of the student submissions to check the effect of function name modification and presence of commented code. We evaluated the model's overall performance and dependability on the four assignment problems mentioned above.

Original Dataset Evaluation. As mentioned earlier, we were able to obtain an average accuracy of 99.6% on our dataset.

Function Name Modification. In this test, we modified the function names in student code to check whether this would affect the model's performance. In many student programs, the function name (e.g. *Binary_Search*) indicated the approach they had taken. We wanted to see if renaming the function names would affect the predictions made by the GPT model. We chose 75 student codes at random from each of the four assignment submissions (making a total of 300 codes). The function names in these codes were modified such that the names do not indicate the algorithmic approach the student has taken. The ChatGPT 3.5-Turbo model achieved accuracies of 99.5%, 100%, 98.8%, 99.5%, and 99.6% across five iterations, resulting in an average accuracy of 99.9%. This outcome emphasizes that the model focuses on the underlying logic and structure of the code and not the function names.

Commented Code Evaluation. In this test, we added extra code as comments to 300 student submissions (selected from the previous test), such that if the comments were uncommented, the program's time complexity would change. The goal was to test the model's ability to distinguish between functional code and comments. The model remained very accurate even with the existence of unnecessary information that can change the time complexity of the code when it is uncommented. In this case, the model's accuracy was 100%, 99.8%, 99.7%, 99.8%, 100% over the five iterations respectively, with an average accuracy of 99.8%. This shows that commented code does not affect the model's performance. Figure 1 shows the effect of student code modifications on the model performance.

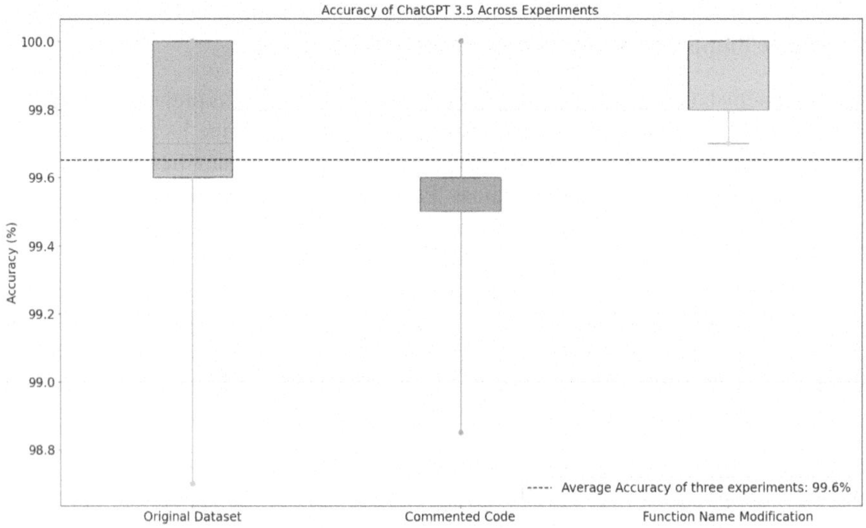

Fig. 1. Accuracy of ChatGPT Across Different Experiments

4 Conclusion

Our findings demonstrate that ChatGPT 3.5-Turbo can predict the time complexity of student code submissions with an accuracy of 99.6%. This approach eliminates the need for large test cases to identify efficient programs. Proposed method along with smaller test cases can be used to determine both the time complexity and correctness of students' code submissions. The predictions made by ChatGPT 3.5-Turbo proved to be robust, even when function names were altered or extra code was added as comments. However, further research is required to assess the reliability of this GPT-based approach across a broader range of DSA lab problems.

5 Limitations of Current Study

There are certain limitations to LLM-based models such as the existence of hallucinations. Also, we have concentrated our research on programs with the five time complexities. Further studies are needed to explore the model's performance for time complexities outside of this set. Our research is only focused on time complexity analysis; correctness of code must be determined using the traditional test-case-based approach. Lastly, our findings are based on only C++ programming language data of four DSA lab problems.

Acknowledgments. We would like to acknowledge the assistance of OpenAI's ChatGPT in helping with proofreading and improving the fluency of this paper. While the core research and content are our own, ChatGPT was used as a tool to enhance the clarity and presentation of the ideas expressed.

Disclosure of Interests. We have no competing interests to declare that are relevant to the content of this article.

References

1. Zhai, X., et al.: A review of artificial intelligence (AI) in education from 2010 to 2020. Complexity, 8812542, 18 (2021). https://doi.org/10.1155/2021/8812542
2. Lund, B.D., Wang, T.: Chatting about ChatGPT: how may AI and GPT impact academia and libraries? Libr. Hi Tech News **40**(3), 26–29 (2023). https://doi.org/10.1108/LHTN-01-2023-0009
3. Jukiewicz, M.: The Future of Grading Programming Assignments in Education: The Role of ChatGPT in Automating the Assessment and Feedback Process (2023). https://doi.org/10.13140/RG.2.2.22103.85924. https://doi.org/10.1016/j.tsc.2024.101522
4. White, J., et al.: A Prompt Pattern Catalog to Enhance Prompt Engineering with ChatGPT (2023). https://doi.org/10.48550/arXiv.2302.11382
5. Coello, C., Alimam, M., Kouatly, R.: Effectiveness of ChatGPT in coding: a comparative analysis of popular large language models. Digital **4**, 114–125 (2024). https://doi.org/10.3390/digital4010005
6. Alshami, A., Elsayed, M., Ali, E., Eltoukhy, A.E.E., Zayed, T.: Harnessing the power of ChatGPT for automating systematic review process: methodology, case study, limitations, and future directions. Systems **11**, 351 (2023). https://doi.org/10.3390/systems11070351
7. Jin, J., Kim, M.: GPT-empowered personalized elearning system for programming languages. Appl. Sci. **13**, 12773 (2023). https://doi.org/10.3390/app132312773
8. Aldriye, H., Alkhalaf, A., Alkhalaf, M.: Automated grading systems for programming assignments: a literature review. Int. J. Adv. Comput. Sci. Appl. **10** (2019). https://doi.org/10.14569/IJACSA.2019.0100328
9. Phalke, S., Vaidya, Y., Metkar, S.: Big-O time complexity analysis of algorithm. In: 2022 International Conference on Signal and Information Processing (IConSIP), Pune, India, pp. 1–5 (2022). https://doi.org/10.1109/ICoNSIP49665.2022.10007469
10. Skalka, J., Drlík, M., Obonya, J.: Automated Assessment in Learning and Teaching Programming Languages using Virtual Learning Environment, pp. 689–697 (2019). https://doi.org/10.1109/EDUCON.2019.8725127
11. Douce, C., Livingstone, D., Orwell, J.: Automatic test-based assessment of programming: a review. J. Educ. Resour. Comput. **5** (2005). https://doi.org/10.1145/1163405.1163409

12. Gonzalez Calatayud, V., Prendes, P., Roig-Vila, R.: Artificial intelligence for student assessment: a systematic review. Appl. Sci. **11**, 5467 (2021). https://doi.org/10.3390/app11125467
13. https://usaco.guide/general/intro-cp?lang=cpp. Accessed 30 June 2024

RECE: A Family of Explainable Rubrics for Autograding Refute Problems

Viraj Kumar(✉)

Indian Institute of Science Bangalore, Bengaluru, Karnataka, India
viraj@iisc.ac.in

Abstract. A Refute problem provides students with (1) a programming *task* and (2) a *buggy solution* (typically, a function) for that task. A student answers a Refute problem by specifying an input on which the function does *not* return the expected result (as per the task). This paper makes three contributions. First, by identifying inconsistencies in scores to Refute problems produced manually by Computer Science faculty, we demonstrate that it is challenging to manually score such problems. Second, we identify a key category of *near-correct* responses whose importance seems to be under-appreciated by faculty in our study. Together, these findings indicate a need for rubrics that can support automated grading and are easy to explain. As a third contribution, we propose RECE (rhyming with *peace*), a family of simple rubrics for autograding Refute problems. RECE rubrics reward near-correct responses from the above category, but they otherwise align with the scores suggested by faculty. We believe that these contributions will aid faculty in introducing Refute problems as assessment items in programming courses.

Keywords: Refute Problems · Rubrics · Autograding · Programming

1 Introduction

Refute problems [12] have been proposed by Computer Science (CS) education researchers as one way to simultaneously develop two key abilities of novice programmers: task comprehension and code comprehension [1]. While developing these abilities has always been important in CS education, it is particularly so at a time when students have easy access to code generation tools that can produce plausible but not necessarily correct code [1,5]. For example, the chapter on *Generative AI and the Curriculum* in the ACM/IEEE-CS/AAAI Computer Science Curricula (CS2023)[1] notes the following (emphasis added):

> It seems likely that *reading programs will see a sharpened focus* and the idea of learning to program by writing, and reliance on learning syntax, will change towards learning to program by prompting, *comprehending*, verifying, editing, modifying, adapting, and testing code.

[1] https://csed.acm.org/wp-content/uploads/2024/04/4.3-Generative-AI-and-the-Curriculum.pdf.

A. Karkare et al. (Eds.): COMPUTE 2024, CCIS 2400, pp. 83–96, 2025.
https://doi.org/10.1007/978-3-031-84391-4_7

To illustrate how Refute problems align with these curricular directions, consider the example shown in Fig. 1. For the given task specification, GitHub Copilot (a popular code generation tool) has created a buggy solution (Fig. 1, left). This code may be too complex for novice programmers to comprehend. Hence, our Refute problem is based on a much simpler (but also buggy) solution for the same task (Fig. 1, right).

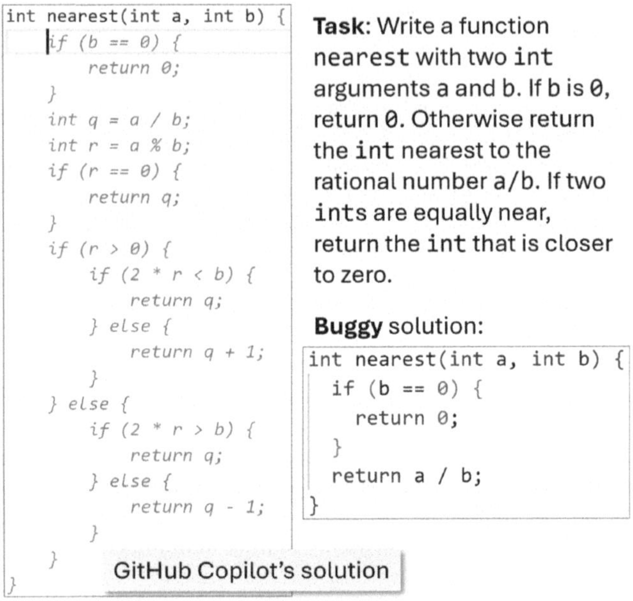

Fig. 1. (*Left*). A buggy solution suggested by GitHub Copilot (shown in grey font). On the input a $= -1$ and b $= 2$, this function returns -1, but the expected result is 0. This is because two integers (0 and -1) are equally near to the rational number $\frac{-1}{2}$, but the former is closer to zero. (*Right*). A simpler buggy solution which correctly returns 0 on the input above, but incorrectly returns 0 when a $= 5$ and b $= 6$. It should return 1, the nearest integer to $\frac{5}{6}$.

A student's solution to a refute problem has three parts. We describe these parts in general, and illustrate them for $f =$ `nearest` (Fig. 1, right).

1. A valid *input* x. This requires the student to comprehend the function's argument types. For the example above, student S_1 may choose the input $x_1 = (5, 6)$ (i.e., a $= 5$ and b $= 6$) whereas student S_2 may choose the input $x_2 = (0, 0)$. An input $x_3 = (0.5, 0)$ would be *invalid* for this problem.
2. The *expected* result $e(x)$ on the chosen input x. This requires the student to comprehend the task. For the example above, $e(x_1)$ should be 1 and $e(x_2)$ should be 0.

3. The value $r(x)$ *returned* by the buggy function f on input x. This requires the student to accurately trace the execution of the code (a simple form of code comprehension [11]) on this input. For the example above, both $r(x_1)$ and $r(x_2)$ should be 0.

Note that the input x_1 is a *counterexample* i.e., it demonstrates why the function is buggy. However, a student's solution may contain errors. For example, while student S_1 may correctly state that $e(x_1)$ is 1, they may incorrectly state that $r(x_1)$ is also 1 i.e., they may fail to realise that their input x_1 refutes the buggy function. In contrast, student S_2's input is *not* a counterexample. Thus, even if S_2 accurately states the values $e(x_2)$ and $r(x_2)$, this solution is deficient because it fails to refute the given function. The question motivating this study is: how should *partial* scores be assigned to partially correct solutions such as the ones above?

2 Related Work

The development of fair rubrics that instructors can use in reliable ways has been of interest to the CS education research community since the 1980s, particularly in the context of code-writing tasks [10,15]. With the growing usage and development of autograding techniques, it is increasingly evident that meaningful rubrics can also assist students by making it clear what they should aim to achieve, and by quickly providing helpful feedback [2]. Such feedback can also help students better understand the progress they are making [3].

Refute problems present students with intentionally buggy solutions to code-writing tasks. Griffin identifies six theories from cognitive psychology that "support the idea that intentional errors can promote learning" [8]. Refute problems were originally proposed as an alternative to Explain-in-Plain-English (EiPE) problems [12]. For EiPE problems, Chen et al. have developed and validated a 7-point rubric [4]. Further, Weeda et al. have developed a rubric that can be used to provide feedback on EiPE problems in formative assessment contexts [17]. A variety of autograding techniques have been proposed for EiPE problems, with some systems capable of producing scores similar to trained teaching assistants when trained on large volumes of problem-specific human-labeled data [7]. More recent work has eliminated this need for training data via Code Generation Based Grading [16], using large language models (LLMs) to automatically translate student explanations into testable code.

In the specific context of Refute problems, we previously showed that such problems can be autograded as either correct or incorrect [12] without the need for any training data. Subsequently, we proposed *partial correctness* characteristics of solutions to Refute problems [14] by assigning up to three tags to each solution as per the following rules[2]:

[2] While these details were presented orally at our SIGCSE workshop [14], this paper is the first time they are appearing in a peer-reviewed publication.

Tag c This tag is assigned to the solution if the input x specified by the student is a counterexample. This can be determined automatically by executing both the buggy function f and a model solution m on input x and checking whether $f(x) \neq m(x)$.

Tag e This tag is assigned to the solution if the value $e(x)$ specified by the student is the correct expected value on input x (as per the task). This can be determined automatically by checking whether $e(x) = m(x)$.

Tag r This tag is assigned to the solution if the value $r(x)$ specified by the student is the correct value returned by the buggy function on input x. This can be determined automatically by checking whether $r(x) = f(x)$.

Since each of the three tags **c**, **e**, and **r** can either be assigned or unassigned, there are $2^3 = 8$ categories of responses to a Refute problem. We will refer to solutions with all three tags assigned as **cer**-solutions. In our prior work [14], we assigned the maximum possible score to **cer**-solutions since they correctly refute the given buggy code. At the other extreme, we assigned the minimum possible score to solutions with *no* tags. (For clarity, we will refer to these as **n**-solutions.) However, we did not propose any grading rubric for the remaining six categories of partially correct solutions, and no such rubric has been proposed to date. We view the lack of such a rubric as a barrier to the effective usage of Refute problems as assessment items in programming courses.

3 Research Study

In an attempt to address this research gap, we designed and conducted a study to understand how Computer Science faculty score Refute problems. Our study was part of a 3-day Faculty Development Programme (FDP) on C Programming at a large private Indian university outside the top-tier[3]. A total of 56 faculty participated in this FDP. These faculty were introduced to Refute problems on Day 1. On Day 2, a two-hour session was devoted to solving Refute problems (with immediate correct/incorrect feedback) and discussing various partially correct solutions. (The discussion was led by the author, who conducted this FDP.) Finally, faculty were given one hour to evaluate 3 Refute problems, each with 8 solutions (one solution from each category described in Sect. 2). These problems were presented in order, but the order of solutions was jumbled as shown in Table 1. Note that the buggy implementations span a range of argument types and programming concepts.

While some participants chose to work on these problems individually, others organized themselves into teams of 2 or 3 faculty. We collected team responses anonymously and sought consent from each team to use their responses. Specifically, each team was asked to choose exactly one of the following statements:

- *All* members of our team grant consent for our anonymized responses to be used for research purposes.

[3] The university ranks outside the top 100 Engineering institutions, as per NIRF 2023: https://www.nirfindia.org/Rankings/2023/EngineeringRanking150.html.

Table 1. Three Refute problems and 8 solutions presented in jumbled Tag order (as in our study). Each solution has an input x, expected value $e(x)$, and return value $r(x)$. For problems 1 and 2, the x component is a pair representing the two function arguments. The RECE score (out of 4 points) is calculated by setting $w_r = w_e = 1$ and $w_{ce} = 2$ in Eq. 2.

Task specification, programming concept(s), and buggy function.

Problem 1: Write a function `nearest` with two `int` arguments `a` and `b`. If `b` is `0`, return `0`. Otherwise return the `int` nearest to the rational number `a`/`b`. If two `int`s are equally near, return the `int` that is closer to zero.

Concepts: Simple conditionals.

```
int nearest(int a, int b) {
  if (b == 0) {
    return 0;
  }
  return a / b;
}
```

x	$e(x)$	$r(x)$	Tag(s)	RECE score
$(0,0)$	0	0	**er**	2/4
$(5,6)$	1	1	**ce**	3/4
$(6,5)$	2	1	**r**	1/4
$(6,5)$	2	2	**n**	0/4
$(-1,2)$	0	-1	**e**	1/4
$(4,5)$	1	0	**cer**	4/4
$(4,5)$	0	1	**c**	0/4
$(4,5)$	0	0	**cr**	1/4

Problem 2: Write a function `max_odd` with two arguments: a non-`NULL` `int` array `a` and its `int` length `n`. Return the maximum odd `int` in the array. If there are no odd integers, return `0`.

Concepts: Iteration; Complex conditionals.

```
int max_odd(const int *a, int n) {
  int result = 0;
  for (int i = 0; i < n; i++) {
    if (a[i] % 2 != 0 && a[i] > result) {
      result = a[i];
    }
  }
  return result;
}
```

x	$e(x)$	$r(x)$	Tag(s)	RECE score
$(\{7\},1)$	7	0	**e**	1/4
$(\{-7\},1)$	-7	0	**cer**	4/4
$(\{-7\},1)$	0	-7	**c**	0/4
$(\{-7\},1)$	0	0	**cr**	1/4
$(\{-7\},1)$	-7	-7	**ce**	3/4
$(\{3,5\},2)$	3	5	**r**	1/4
$(\{3,5\},2)$	3	3	**n**	0/4
$(\{3,5\},2)$	5	5	**er**	2/4

Problem 3: Write a function `num_digits` with one argument: a non-`NULL` string `s`. Return the number of decimal digits in `s`.

Concepts: Recursion; Pointer arithmetic

```
int num_digits(const char *s) {
  int result = 0;
  if (s[0] != '\0') {
    if (s[0] >= '0' && s[0] <= '9') {
      result++;
    } else {
      result += num_digits(s + 1);
    }
  }
  return result;
}
```

x	$e(x)$	$r(x)$	Tag(s)	RECE score
"a2"	1	0	**e**	1/4
"23"	2	1	**cer**	4/4
"23"	1	2	**c**	0/4
"23"	1	1	**cr**	1/4
"23"	2	0	**ce**	3/4
"2a"	1	1	**er**	2/4
"2a"	2	1	**r**	1/4
"2a"	2	0	**n**	0/4

- At least one member of our team does *not* grant consent.

Only one faculty member (working individually) withheld consent. Thus, this study is based on responses from 55 faculty working in 21 teams (average team size: 2.6 faculty). These faculty have taught the C programming course an average of 3.3 times (minimum: 0, maximum: 10, median: 2, mode: 1).

As part of our study design, we chose to hide the tags indicating the category of each solution. Hence, faculty were obliged to manually assess whether each component of each solution was correct or not, and accordingly assign scores. This process is time-consuming, and it greatly limits the number of Refute problems faculty can evaluate within the available time. However, this design choice allows us to eliminate scores assigned by teams who either misunderstood certain Refute problems or did not attempt the grading task with adequate rigour. Specifically, for each Refute problem, we determine whether the 8 (not necessarily distinct) scores assigned by a team for the 8 solutions to that problem satisfy four natural[4] checks for consistency:

C1 The **n**-solution is assigned the minimum score and the **cer**-solution is assigned the maximum score, where the latter is strictly larger than the former.
C2 The **ce**-solution's score is at least the maximum of the scores given to the **c**- and **e**-solutions.
C3 The **cr**-solution's score is at least the maximum of the scores given to the **c**- and **r**-solutions.
C4 The **er**-solution's score is at least the maximum of the scores given to the **e**- and **r**-solutions.

3.1 Research Questions

We are interested in understanding whether teams of CS faculty can score Refute problems *consistently* and, if so, what *patterns* are discernible among consistent scores. More precisely, our two research questions are:

RQ1 How consistently can teams of CS faculty manually score Refute problems (as per consistency checks **C1** to **C4**)?
RQ2 For responses that are consistently scored, what patterns are observed among the scores for the 6 categories of partially correct responses?

4 Results

4.1 RQ1: Grading Consistency

Recall that 21 teams granted consent for their submissions to be used for research purposes. Table 2 summarizes the consistency of teams across all three Refute

[4] There is a natural partial order on the set of 8 solution categories: $s_1 \preceq s_2$ iff solution s_2 includes all the tags that solution s_1 contains. Our consistency checks ensure that score(s_1) $\leq$ score(s_2) whenever $s_1 \preceq s_2$.

problems. Unfortunately, only four teams were able to produce consistent scores for Problem 1. In the discussion immediately following the one-hour grading exercise, several FDP participants reported that wording for Problem 1's Task (see Table 1) was confusing. In particular, several faculty misunderstood "If two `int`s are equally near ..." as referring to the two integers `a` and `b`, whereas we meant the two `int`s closest to the rational number `a/b`.

While no such misunderstanding was reported for Problems 2 and 3, more than one in every three faculty teams was unable to score these problems consistently. These results provide evidence that grading Refute problems manually can be challenging.

Table 2. Team consistency for each Refute Problem (✓ indicates that the team's score satisfied *all* consistency checks **C1** to **C4**). Otherwise, we list all violated consistency checks. The final row totals the number of teams that scored each problem consistently.

Team ID	Problem 1	Problem 2	Problem 3
1	C1	C1, C2	C1, C3
2	C1	C1, C2	C1, C2, C3
3	C1, C3, C4	✓	✓
4	✓	✓	✓
5	C1, C2, C3, C4	✓	✓
6	C1, C2, C3	✓	✓
7	C1, C2, C3, C4	✓	✓
8	C1, C2	C1, C2	C1, C2
9	C1, C2, C3	✓	✓
10	C3	C1	C1
11	C1	C1, C2	C1
12	✓	✓	✓
13	✓	C1, C2, C4	✓
14	C1, C3	✓	✓
15	C1, C3	C1	C3
16	C1, C3	✓	✓
17	✓	✓	✓
18	C1, C2	✓	C1, C2, C3
19	C1, C2, C4	✓	✓
20	C1, C2, C3, C4	C1, C2, C4	C1, C2
21	C1, C3	✓	C1, C3
Total consistent	4	13	12

4.2 RQ2: Grading Patterns for Partially Correct Solutions

For each Refute problem, teams were asked to self-select the maximum score a solution could earn (a positive integer), and to assign non-negative integer scores to each of the 8 solutions given (see Table 1). In order to identify patterns among *consistent* scores (see Table 2), we first normalized these assigned scores as follows. Since the assigned scores satisfy consistency check **C1**, the **n**-solution has the minimum score m among the scores assigned to this problem, and the **cer**-solution has the maximum score $M > m$. We normalized each integer score s to a rational number between 0 and 1 as:

$$\text{Normalized}(s) = \frac{s - m}{M - m} \tag{1}$$

Finally, we computed the mean values of the normalized scores across each of the six categories of partially correct responses. Since the number of teams who submitted consistent responses is small (particularly for Problem 1), we used the bootstrap method [6] with 1,000 samples to compute 95% confidence intervals for the mean values. These values are shown in Fig. 2.

The small number of consistently scored responses in our study prevent us from determining whether any of the following patterns are statistically significant. Nevertheless, as a first study of this type, we believe these patterns are worth noting.

P1 For each **er**-solution, the score is approximately the sum of the scores for the corresponding **e**-solution and **r**-solution. For Problems 2 and 3, we have sufficiently many consistent scores to observe this pattern in both the average scores (Fig. 2b and Fig. 2c) as well as the per-response scores (Fig. 3). We only have 4 consistent scores for Problem 1, but the pattern appears to hold for average scores (Fig. 2a).

P2 For all three Refute problems, the average scores of these partially correct solutions are in strictly increasing order: **c**-solutions (lowest average), **r**-solutions, **cr**-solutions, **er**-solutions (highest average).

P3 Between the near-correct **ce**- and **er**-solutions, the former receive a lower score on average than the latter. As we discuss in Sect. 5.2, we find this pattern worthy of attention.

5 Proposed Rubric Family

We now propose a family of simple rubrics for autograding Refute problems. As noted previously, the applicability of tags **c**, **e**, and **r** can be determined automatically for any solution. For each such tag **t**, we define the indicator variable **[t]** as 1 if the solution has tag **t**, and as 0 otherwise. Each rubric in our family is based only on the indicator variables **[r]**, **[e]**, and **[ce]**. Accordingly, we name this family of rubrics RECE. The score for any solution to a Refute problem is given by a simple formula that is easy to explain to students:

$$\text{Score} = w_r \cdot [\mathbf{r}] + w_e \cdot [\mathbf{e}] + w_{ce} \cdot [\mathbf{ce}] \tag{2}$$

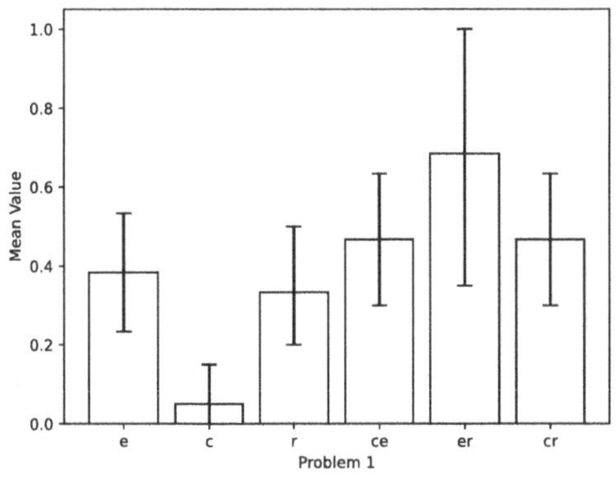

(a) Problem 1: **nearest**

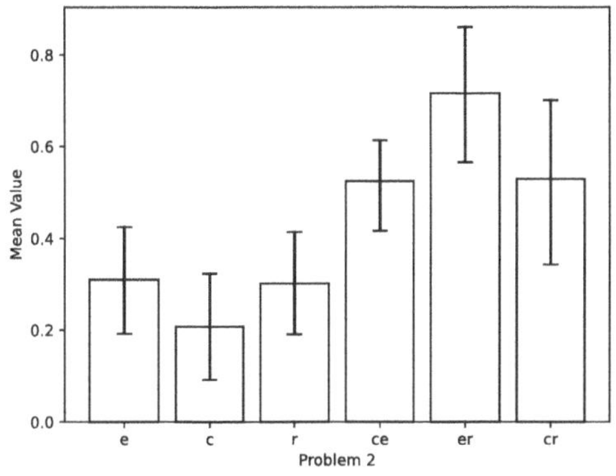

(b) Problem 2: **max_odd**

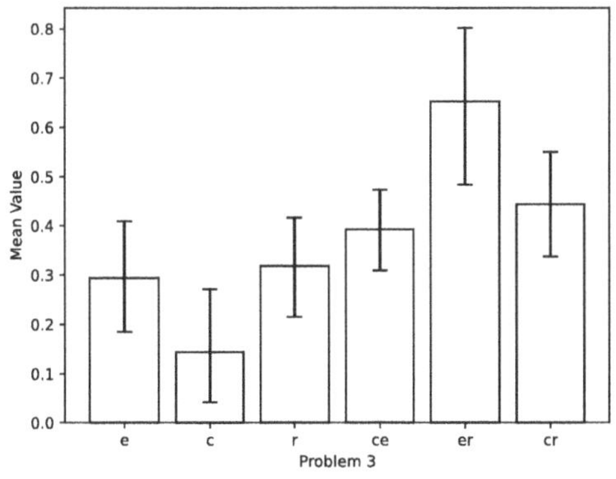

(c) Problem 3: **num_digits**

Fig. 2. Consistent scores for the six partially correct solution categories, normalized using Eq. 1. The average and 95% confidence intervals are shown.

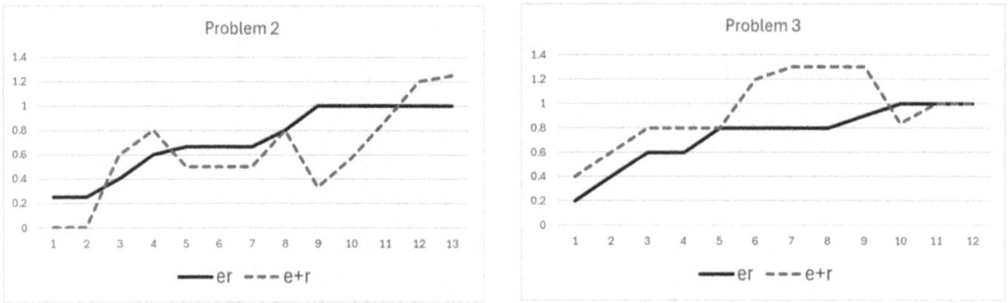

Fig. 3. A comparison of the normalized **er** score vs. the sum of normalized **e** and **r** scores, for each consistent response to Problems 2 and 3.

The weights w_r, w_e, and w_{ce} are non-negative values that sum up to the maximum score for this problem. Instructors must determine this maximum score and break it up into these three weights. For instance, if instructors believe that students will struggle to trace the buggy function's execution on some input x (i.e., to determine $r(x)$ accurately), they can increase the weight w_r. Note that when $w_r = w_e$, Eq. 2 reflects the pattern **P1** observed in Sect. 4.2.

5.1 Pattern P2

The simplest RECE rubric is when all weights are equal e.g., $w_r = w_e = w_{ce} = 1$. In this case, the maximum score is 3. This rubric aligns to almost all aspects of the observed pattern **P2**: it assigns the score 0 to **c**-solutions, score 1 to **r**-solutions, and score 2 (the highest integer score possible for an incorrect solution) to **er**-solutions.

However, whether the assigned weights w_r, w_e, and w_{ce} are equal or not, our rubrics *always* violate one aspect of pattern **P2**: they assign the same score to an **r**-solution and a **cr**-solution, even though the latter satisfies the additional partial correctness characteristic associated with tag **c**. To justify this, consider a **cr**-solution where the input x is a counterexample. Since the expected result $e(x)$ is incorrect, the student who has authored this solution has (at best[5]) refuted the given function relative to a *misunderstood* task. Thus, we see no justification for a **cr**-solution to outscore an **r**-solution: both score w_r for correctly tracing the return value on input x. Similarly, our rubric assigns the score 0 to **c**-solutions.

5.2 Pattern P3

We now focus our attention on pattern **P3**, which contrasts scores for **ce**- and **er**-solutions. In the context of our study, it is perhaps unsurprising that faculty gave the highest score (among partially correct solutions) to **er**-solutions: it is fairly easy for faculty to manually check that, for the student's input x, the value $e(x)$ is

[5] This best case would occur when the incorrect value $e(x)$ differs from the value $r(x)$. This does not occur in our study, since $e(x) = r(x)$ for each **cr**-solution in Table 1.

as per the task and the value $r(x)$ is returned by the buggy function. (We expect faculty to be reasonably proficient at tracing code [13].) For similar reasons, faculty may find it easy to penalize **ce**-solutions, since they can confirm that the $r(x)$ component of the student's solution is incorrect. However, we believe that a **ce**-solution $(x_1, e(x_1), r(x_1))$ deserves *at least* as much credit as an **er**-solution $(x_2, e(x_2), r(x_2))$ because the former solution has correctly identified a counterexample input x_1. At this point, "all" that is needed to confirm that the given function f is buggy is to execute f on input x_1. A student who cannot accurately trace this by hand can at least execute the code on a computer. In contrast, the **er**-solution merely confirms that the function f aligns with the stated task on input x_2, which does not make progress towards refuting the code. In this sense, we find pattern **P3** somewhat disturbing. Hence, our rubric explicitly rewards **ce**-solutions. For the simplest RECE rubric (i.e., $w_r = w_e = w_{ce} = 1$), both **ce**- and **er**-solutions earn a score of 2 out of 3. For our paper-based assessments, we often choose the weights $w_r = w_e = 1$ and $w_{ce} = 2$ to ensure that **ce**-solutions receive a higher score (3 out of 4) than any other partially correct solution. This RECE rubric is applied to the solutions in Table 1.

6 RECE Rubrics in Practice

If students can execute code on a computer during an assessment, the weight w_r should be decreased. On such assessments, we typically discard the $r(x)$ component of the solution and set $w_r = 0$ in Eq. 2. We have also used RECE rubrics to efficiently and objectively evaluate paper-and-pen solutions to Refute problems on high-stakes summative assessments. Prior to such assessments, we explain our rubric using the weights w_r, w_e, and w_{ce} we will actually use for grading. We also demonstrate how the rubric assigns partial credit for **e**-, **r**-, and **er**-solutions, even when students are unable to determine a counterexample. Finally, we alert students that incomplete or otherwise invalid responses will be scored as 0. However, we have occasionally found it necessary to allow problem-specific exceptions to this rule. An example is shown in Fig. 4, where `int` values were expected for the three components of the input, the expected result, and the return value. Our autograder enforced this expectation, and therefore assigned the score 0 to this student's attempt. After the graded assessment was returned, the student sent us the following query:

> Just before the end I realised that c had to be smallest and I thought somehow zero isn't allowed. I didn't have time to change a and b but my logic is basically correct, no?

We concurred with this student and manually scored this as a **cer**-solution.

We have also adapted RECE rubrics to provide formative feedback. Instead of computing a score for a solution $(x, e(x), r(x))$, we test the following sequence of conditions. If all conditions hold, we print a "Success!" message. Otherwise, we provide feedback corresponding to the *first* failing condition[6]:

[6] An example of such a problem is available at: https://codecheck.io/files/24092811215i9915eslgy1copaexwjfdsi2.

Problem 3 [4 marks]. Refute the following *buggy* function for computing the median of three integers *a*, *b*, and *c*.

```
def median(a: int, b: int, c: int) -> int:
    if a <= b <= c:
        return b
    if b <= a <= c:
        return a
    return c
```

a	b	c	Expected result	Return value
2	1	~~3~~ 0.5	~~2~~ 1	~~1~~ 0.5

Fig. 4. A Refute problem on a high-stakes assessment. The student's solution is *invalid* since the input `c` and return value are not of the expected type (`int`).

1. Is the input x valid? If not, we clarify the input and output types.
2. Is $e(x)$ the expected result? If not, we clarify the task using simpler language or with an example. Similar to the Examplar system [18], we avoid revealing the expected answer for input x.
3. Is $r(x)$ the correct return value? If not, we encourage students to use tools like PythonTutor [9] to trace the code on their input x.
4. Are the values $e(x)$ and $r(x)$ different? If not, we remind students that they have *not* provided a counterexample.

7 Limitations and Future Work

Our study has provided initial evidence that Refute problems can be challenging for faculty to score manually. While we have attempted to include several programming concepts in our problems, two key limitations are: (1) a small set of only 3 Refute problems in only one programming language (C), and (2) a small number of consistent scores. Larger studies would need to be conducted to better understand how faculty score Refute problems. The design of such studies, particularly if conducted in linguistically diverse countries such as India, should also note the importance of ensuring that faculty find the task statements clear. In retrospect, we should have added clarifying examples for each of our Refute problems.

Despite these limitations, we believe that the patterns we have identified and the family of rubrics we have proposed will be valuable for faculty to start using Refute problems as assessment items in order to develop the ability of their students to critique code [1], and to gather sufficient data to validate such rubrics [4].

Acknowledgments. We thank the Kotak-IISc AI-ML Centre for supporting this research. We gratefully acknowledge the contributions of all faculty in this study. Finally, we thank the anonymous reviewers for multiple constructive comments.

References

1. Agarwal, N., Kumar, V., Raman, A., Karkare, A.: A bug's new life: creating refute questions from filtered CS1 student code snapshots. In: Proceedings of the ACM Conference on Global Computing Education. CompEd 2023, vol. 1, pp. 7–14. Association for Computing Machinery, New York (2023). https://doi.org/10.1145/3576882.3617916
2. Becker, K.: Grading programming assignments using rubrics. In: Proceedings of the 8th Annual Conference on Innovation and Technology in Computer Science Education, p. 253 (2003)
3. Black, P., Wiliam, D.: Developing the theory of formative assessment. Educ. Assess. Eval. Accountability (formerly: J. Pers. Eval. Educ.) **21**, 5–31 (2009)
4. Chen, B., Azad, S., Haldar, R., West, M., Zilles, C.: A validated scoring rubric for explain-in-plain-English questions. In: Proceedings of the 51st ACM Technical Symposium on Computer Science Education. SIGCSE '20, pp. 563–569. Association for Computing Machinery, New York (2020). https://doi.org/10.1145/3328778.3366879
5. Denny, P., Kumar, V., Giacaman, N.: Conversing with copilot: exploring prompt engineering for solving CS1 problems using natural language. In: Proceedings of the 54th ACM Technical Symposium on Computer Science Education. SIGCSE 2023, vol. 1, pp. 1136–1142. Association for Computing Machinery, New York (2023). https://doi.org/10.1145/3545945.3569823
6. Efron, B.: Bootstrap methods: another look at the jackknife. Ann. Stat. **7**(1), 1–26 (1979). https://doi.org/10.1214/aos/1176344552
7. Fowler, M., Chen, B., Azad, S., West, M., Zilles, C.: Autograding "explain in plain English" questions using NLP. In: Proceedings of the 52nd ACM Technical Symposium on Computer Science Education. SIGCSE '21, pp. 1163–1169. Association for Computing Machinery, New York (2021). https://doi.org/10.1145/3408877.3432539
8. Griffin, J.M.: Designing intentional bugs for learning. In: Proceedings of the 2019 Conference on United Kingdom & Ireland Computing Education Research. UKICER '19. Association for Computing Machinery, New York (2019). https://doi.org/10.1145/3351287.3351289
9. Guo, P.J.: Online python tutor: embeddable web-based program visualization for CS education. In: Proceeding of the 44th ACM Technical Symposium on Computer Science Education, pp. 579–584 (2013)
10. Hamm, R.W., Henderson Jr, K.D., Repsher, M.L., Timmer, K.M.: A tool for program grading: the jacksonville university scale. In: Proceedings of the Fourteenth SIGCSE Technical Symposium on Computer Science Education, pp. 248–252 (1983)
11. Izu, C., et al.: Fostering program comprehension in novice programmers - learning activities and learning trajectories. In: Proceedings of the Working Group Reports on Innovation and Technology in Computer Science Education. ITiCSE-WGR '19, pp. 27–52. Association for Computing Machinery, New York (2019). https://doi.org/10.1145/3344429.3372501
12. Kumar, V.: Refute: an alternative to 'explain in plain English' questions. In: Proceedings of the 17th ACM Conference on International Computing Education Research. ICER 2021, pp. 438–440. Association for Computing Machinery, New York (2021). https://doi.org/10.1145/3446871.3469791

13. Kumar, V., Karkare, A.: Instructor performance on progressively complex programming tasks: a multi-institutional study from India. In: Proceedings of the 26th ACM Conference on Innovation and Technology in Computer Science Education. ITiCSE '21, vol. 1, pp. 561–567. Association for Computing Machinery, New York (2021). https://doi.org/10.1145/3430665.3456384
14. Kumar, V., Raman, A.: Helping students develop a critical eye with refute questions. In: Proceedings of the 54th ACM Technical Symposium on Computer Science Education. SIGCSE 2023, vol. 2, p. 1181. Association for Computing Machinery, New York (2023). https://doi.org/10.1145/3545947.3569636
15. Miller, N.E., Peterson, C.G.: A method for evaluating student written computer programs in an undergraduate computer science programming language course. ACM SIGCSE Bull. **12**(4), 9–17 (1980)
16. Smith, D.H., Zilles, C.: Code generation based grading: evaluating an auto-grading mechanism for "explain-in-plain-English" questions. In: Proceedings of the 2024 on Innovation and Technology in Computer Science Education. ITiCSE 2024, vol. 1, pp. 171–177. Association for Computing Machinery, New York (2024). https://doi.org/10.1145/3649217.3653582
17. Weeda, R., Izu, C., Kallia, M., Barendsen, E.: Towards an assessment rubric for EiPE tasks in secondary education: identifying quality indicators and descriptors. In: Proceedings of the 20th Koli Calling International Conference on Computing Education Research. Koli Calling '20. Association for Computing Machinery, New York (2020). https://doi.org/10.1145/3428029.3428031
18. Wrenn, J., Krishnamurthi, S.: Executable examples for programming problem comprehension. In: Proceedings of the 2019 ACM Conference on International Computing Education Research. ICER '19, pp. 131–139. Association for Computing Machinery, New York (2019). https://doi.org/10.1145/3291279.3339416

Interactive Tools, Visualizations and Learning Analytics

JestViz: Towards Supporting Novice Web Developers Debug JavaScript

Shriram Shanbhag(✉) and Sridhar Chimalakonda

Research in Intelligent Software & Human Analytics (RISHA) Lab, Department of Computer Science and Engineering, Indian Institute of Technology Tirupati, Chindepalle, India
{cs20s503,ch}@iittp.ac.in

Abstract. JavaScript is one of the most preferred programming languages for web development and many novice programmers use it for learning programming through web development. JavaScript programmers often rely on browser *devTools* to debug their programs. The error messages in web browsers get logged into the web console, which is a part of the *devTools*. However, novice programmers often find it difficult to understand and interpret the error messages. Therefore, we propose *JestViz*, a tool aimed at helping novice web developers through the modification of the error reporting mechanism and visualization of the stack trace from error messages as a function call graph. We conjecture that these improvements provide novice programmers with a better interpretation of program errors, leading to faster debugging. Our evaluation of *JestViz* with 20 novice programmers involving the task of comprehending and debugging an erroneous JavaScript program showed that those who used *JestViz* took 46% lesser time to debug the program and gained an improved understanding of the inputs and nested function calls that produced the errors.

Keywords: Error messages · Debugging · Novice programmers · Javascript · Browser

1 Introduction

Novice programmers often find it challenging to interpret error messages [3, 5,37]. Reading error messages is a cognitively demanding task comparable to reading source code [2]. Error messages are often not user-friendly [26]. For novice programmers, error messages can be a source of frustration and pose a barrier to their learning process [6]. Researchers have proposed several approaches to help novice programmers deal with the issue of cryptic error messages [1,4,16,22, 31,35]. However, the focus has remained primarily on programming languages such as *Java* [4,16,31], *Python* [11,22,35] and *C* [1,15]. JavaScript is one of the most popular programming languages for web browsers [18]. According to the Stack Overflow developer survey 2024, JavaScript has been ranked as the

A. Karkare et al. (Eds.): COMPUTE 2024, CCIS 2400, pp. 99–112, 2025.
https://doi.org/10.1007/978-3-031-84391-4_8

most popular programming language for the ninth year in a row, with over 65% of the developers using it in their projects[1]. Despite the popularity of web development as a means to introduce students to programming [28], helping novice web developers with error messages has received little attention. So, as a step towards helping novice web developers, we present our tool *JestViz* as a Google Chrome extension.

To support web developers, all major browsers include web development tools (also called *devTools*[2]) that contain features to help programmers test and debug their code. *DevTools* provide users with a wide range of features such as editing the HTML and the DOM, profiling the web-page, accessing the network information and debugging JavaScript. The JavaScript errors are logged into the *console* tab of the browser *devTools* which can be used for debugging. However, unlike IDEs, the *devTools* lack the mechanism to automatically hint the users about their program running into an error. To view error messages, users must manually open the *devTools* and navigate to the console tab each time they suspect that their JavaScript program has encountered an error. Since novice developers have to simultaneously deal with the challenges of learning the syntax, problem solving, navigating through programs, reading and interpreting errors etc. when they start their programming journey, an unfriendly error reporting mechanism would add to the existing challenges.

Improving the error feedback mechanism to make it more "live" is shown to have helped novice programmers [17]. "Liveness" has two dimensions [33]. One dimension corresponds to the immediacy of semantic feedback. The other dimension corresponds to whether the feedback is obtained automatically or obtained upon explicit request. In the case of IDEs, an explicit request corresponds to hitting the "run" button which would normally give semantic feedback. In the case of a JavaScript code that runs on browsers, merely hitting the "run" button to open the browser does not provide the users with the semantic feedback present in the *console* tab of the *devTools*. Changing the error reporting mechanism and error presentation have shown to substantially impact the programming experience and behaviour of novices [5,19,29]. The tool *JestViz* is our first step towards improving the error reporting and the error presentation in web browsers.

Enhancing the compiler error messages has been found to decrease the incorrect understanding and thereby reduce the cognitive load on novice programmers [30]. Even cosmetic changes in the presentation of error messages have been found to lead to substantial improvements in their comprehension and resolution [10]. Studies on the impact of enhanced compiler errors have shown that the enhancements could lead to significantly shorter debugging time [9]. Enhancing the compiler error messages has been a popular theme among methods aimed at helping novices [4,5,16,31,35]. However, these methods have ignored the stack trace from the error messages. A stack trace is generated when the program crashes because of an exception or an error. It contains a report of a sequence

[1] https://stackoverflow.blog/2024/07/24/developers-want-more-more-more-the-2024-results-from-stack-overflow-s-annual-developer-survey/.

[2] Google Chrome - https://bit.ly/3nuugBS, Mozilla Firefox - https://mzl.la/39ls7mZ.

of functions called before the program encountered the error. Our motivation for enhancing the stack trace is that stack traces and call graphs can benefit developers in program comprehension, which is a fundamental step in debugging [21,23]. Program comprehension through stack trace visualization is shown to have improved the performance of developers in accomplishing tasks, both in terms of time and correctness [8]. It has also been a very popular feature [27,36] in environments designed for novice programmers.

JestViz stands for **J**avascript **E**rror **S**tack **T**race **Vi**suali**z**er. *JestViz* is a Google Chrome extension that attempts to improve the presentation of JavaScript error messages in web browsers in two ways.

1. It provides feedback to the users about the errors as and when they are encountered without having to open the *devTools*.
2. It provides a visual representation of the stack trace from the error messages in the form of a function call graph with the aim of helping the users trace the root of the error, thereby improving its comprehension.

In the current version of *JestViz*, we have decided to target a specific set of JavaScript errors. JavaScript programs throw *Error objects* when runtime errors occur. JavaScript comes with a few default error types[3] that represent the context in which those errors were thrown. Stack trace comes as a part of these runtime error messages. *JestViz* visualizes stack traces from four different types of runtime errors, namely, *EvalError*, *RangeError*, *ReferenceError*, and *TypeError*. The description of each of these error types is shown in the Table 1.

Table 1. Description of JavaScript Errors

Error Type	Description
EvalError	Error resulting from incorrect use of global eval() function
RangeError	Error resulting from values that are not in range or in set of allowed values
ReferenceError	Error resulting from reference to a non-existant variable
TypeError	Error resulting from incorrect type of value for the required operation

We performed both quantitative and qualitative evaluation of *JestViz*. A quantitative evaluation of *JestViz* showed us that programmers who used *JestViz* took 46% lesser time to resolve errors in their program. A qualitative evaluation based on the TAM2 model showed us that the participants found *JestViz* reasonably useful and easy to use. The detailed evaluation and results are explained in

[3] https://developer.mozilla.org/en-US/docs/Web/JavaScript/Reference/Global_Objects/Error.

Sect. 5 and Sect. 6. The tool and the survey results are available in the following GitHub repository[4].

2 Related Work

In this section, we discuss the related work that aimed to help novice programmers by enhancing the representation of error messages. However, the existing literature has not focused on JavaScript runtime errors in web browsers, motivating the need.

2.1 Enhancement of Compiler Errors

Several methods have been proposed to help novice programmers by enhancing error messages [3,4,7,12,16,22,31]. Becker et al. [4] have proposed a Java editor called *Decaf* that enhances compiler error messages. The students who used the editor experienced a reduction in the number of errors [4]. Hristova et al. [16] proposed a tool named *Expresso*, which identifies 20 common errors in Java programs and provides explanations if any of those common errors are detected in the program. *Gild* [31] is a plug-in for Eclipse IDE which provides users with explanations about error messages in plain English text. An evaluation of *Gild* showed that majority of the users found the tool "useful atleast some of the time". Barik et al. [3] have proposed the use of taxonomies for error notifications and their corresponding resolutions. Kohn and Manaris [22] proposed an educational environment called *TigerJython* for novice Python programmers. Apart from enhanced error messages, *TigerJython* had a few modifications to the Python language to overcome learning hurdles, and included a visual debugger. Additionally, *TigerJython* also contained a feature to display error messages in multiple languages to help non-native speakers. The authors hypothesized that their tool might be useful to novice programmers based on its increasing usage [22]. Campbell et al. [7] proposed a tool that uses the method of exploiting the nature of software code to detect the location of errors thereby providing improved error reporting, which can substantially impact the programming experience. Dong et al. [10] measured the impact of cosmetic changes to error messages and found them to have a substantial positive impact on error comprehension and resolution. Li et al. [25] explore the use of machine learning to classify compilation error messages that would help novices asses their readability [29].

Few methods focused on leveraging data from online platforms to provide additional information about error messages and suggest some possible solutions [1,14,35,39]. *Pycee* [35], a plugin for sublime text IDE, enhances error messages for Python and provides a summary of Stack Overflow queries related to the error within the editor. A recommender system is proposed that helps novice programmers debug their code by suggesting the solution that has been used by peers [14]. Watson et al. [39] proposed *Bluefix*, a tool integrated with *BlueJ*[5] that

[4] https://github.com/rishalab/jestviz.

[5] https://www.bluej.org/.

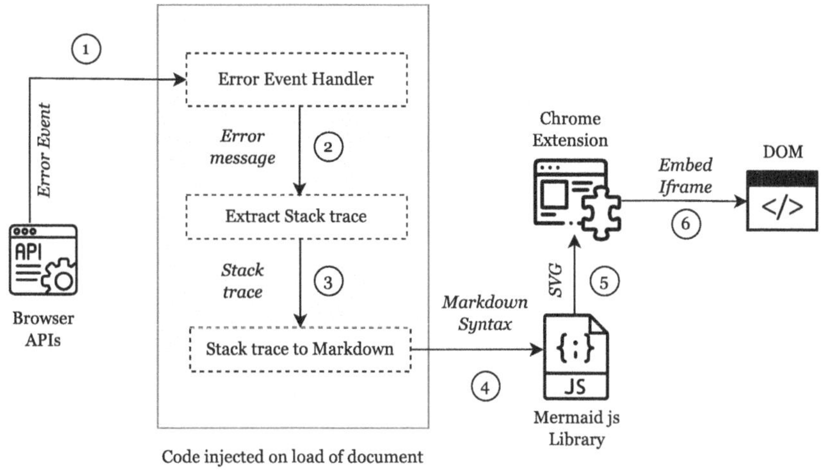

Fig. 1. Working of *JestViz* extension

provides varying levels of crowd-sourced feedback to the users. *TEGCER* uses pre-existing errors classified using supervised classification to generates hints and targeted examples for the errors generated by the C compiler [1].

With the rise of prompt engineering and large language models, their capabilities have also been leveraged and studied to enhance error messages [13,20,24]. Leinonen et al. [24] used Codex model to explain and suggest fixes for Python error messages and found that the model could provide correct explanation for the errors half of the time. Fwa et al. [13] found that utilizing ChatGPT enables instructors to obtain a comprehensive overview of the common errors made by their students.

However, the methods and approaches mentioned above have not focused on leveraging the stack trace, even though it contains valuable information. Besides, the scope of these studies remain restricted largely to the programming languages such as Java, Python and C. The methods have not attempted to improve the presentation of error messages for the code running in web browsers and they remain focused to IDEs.

2.2 Tools to Help Novice Web Developers Through Enhancement of Error Messages

In the context of web programming, Schmoll et al. [32] have developed a tool for novice programmers to detect and visualize errors in HTML code. This tool uses reduced line representation and color-coding of errors based on the severity to improve visual effectiveness [32]. However, their tool only focuses on HTML code and does not help developers with JavaScript errors.

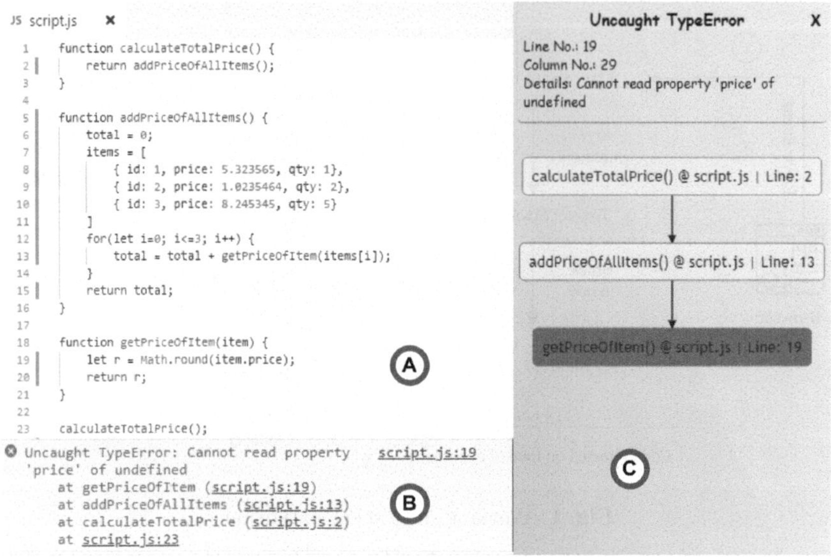

Fig. 2. [A] shows the program that is executed, [B] shows the error message from *devTools* and [C] shows the visualization generated by *JestViz*

3 Design and Development

The main aim behind developing *JestViz* is to help novice developers debug their JavaScript code by improving the reporting and presentation of the errors. We wish to improve the mechanism of reporting the errors by displaying them as and when they occur, without relying on the *devTools.* In order to accomplish this, we display the error messages in a panel in the right corner of the browser window. The panel pops up every time an error is encountered, and disappears when the error gets resolved. In order to improve the presentation of the error messages, we display a formatted version of the error by highlighting the *error type, location of the error in the code,* and the *details* of the error as shown in [C] of Fig. 2. We also leverage the stack trace from the error message and improve its presentation by visualizing a function call graph displayed below the formatted error. We choose to provide visual representation as visualization has been found to reduce the cognitive load on learners of computer programming concepts [40]. A visual representation of stack trace lets the users track the entire sequence of functions called before the program ran into the error. The graph also provides information about the location of each of function calls in the code shown in [C] of Fig. 2.

We have implemented *JestViz* as a Google Chrome extension. The following modules enable the working of *JestViz* as shown in Fig. 1.

- **Error Event Handler**: It monitors the browser devtool console. Whenever an error occurs in the program, an error event is triggered. Upon detecting the error event, the module extracts the error logs from the browser *devTools.*
- **Stack Trace Extractor**: It extracts the stack trace from the error message and gathers the useful data needed to convey the information regarding function calls and error location.
- **Markdown Generator**: It generates a markdown syntax representing the function call graph.
- **Mermaid library**: *mermaidjs*[6] is an external library used to convert the markdown syntax representing the function call graph into an SVG format.
- **Iframe Generation**: The module puts the formatted error message and the function call graph in SVG format on a panel that is displayed to the user.

The *Error Event Handler*, *Stack Trace Extractor*, and the *Markdown Generator* modules are injected into the browser document on the browser window's load to ensure that all error events are captured.

The working of *JestViz* is shown in Fig. 1. When the program running on the browser throws an error, the browser API triggers an error event (1). This error event is detected by *Error event handler* module, which extracts the error logs from the browser *devTools* (2). The *Stack trace extractor* module secures all the data required to generate the function call graph and passes it to the *Markdown generator* (3). The*Markdown generator* produces the markdown syntax (4), which is converted into an SVG format by the *mermaidjs* library (5). This SVG is then rendered on the screen in an Iframe (6).

4 User Scenario

Consider *Moksha*, a novice programmer who is learning web development. *Moksha* runs a JavaScript program, as shown in Fig. 2 [A], on her Google Chrome browser. Her program suffers from a runtime error since the loop on line no. 13 runs four iterations on an array containing three elements. On the fourth iteration of the for loop, the *getPriceOfItem* function gets invoked with a null input. So the program throws an **Uncaught TypeError**. However, the *devTools* give no notification about the error. *Moksha* spends some time looking for the cause and figures out that an error may have occurred. She then manually opens the *console* tab of the *devTools. Moksha* attempts to fix the issue by trying to understand the error message in the *devTools.* But being a beginner, *Moksha* finds it challenging to interpret the error message and the corresponding stack trace seen from the *devTools* shown in Fig. 2 [B]. Later, *Moksha* discovers the *JestViz* extension for Google Chrome. She re-executes the program. This time, the error message gets presented even without opening the *devTools.* She finds the enhanced visual representation of the stack trace in the form of a function call graph, along with a cleaner, formatted **Uncaught TypeError** exception and its location in the program at the top in a panel, as shown in Fig. 2 [C].

---

[6] https://mermaid-js.github.io/mermaid.

Moksha may get a better understanding of how her program ran into an error from the function call graph shown in Fig. 2 [C]. The statement on line no. 2 in *calculateTotalPrice* function invokes *addPriceOfAllItems* function. During the execution of *addPriceOfAllItems* function, the program invokes another function, *getPriceOfItem* on line no. 13. This function throws a ***Uncaught TypeError*** exception on line no. 19, highlighted in a red-colored background in the function call graph.

5 Evaluation

JestViz aims to help novice web developers by improving the error reporting and error presentation in browsers in order to enable better understanding of the error and faster debugging. Tools aimed at similar objective were evaluated using mixed-method involving quantitative analysis followed by a questionnaire for qualitative analysis [34,35]. Hence we decided to follow a similar mixed-method of evaluation. In quantitative analysis, we tried to analyze the tool's impact on measuring the duration of fixing the bugs. A similar quantitative evaluation method has been followed to study the impact of tools or methods aimed at helping programmers debug faster [10,34]. In qualitative analysis, we tried to understand the user experience using a questionnaire.

5.1 Quantitative Analysis

The evaluation involved 20 participants in the age group of 19 to 21 years, with 13 male and 7 female participants. The participants were undergraduate students at the Indian Institute of Technology Tirupati, with prior experience in JavaScript ranging from 2 weeks to 4 months, and could be considered novice programmers. We divided them into experimental and control groups. The experimental group consisted of 10 participants and the control group consisted of 10 participants. We gave the participants from the experimental group a five minute demonstration on how to install and use *JestViz* by debugging an example code snippet. We then asked them to debug a JavaScript code containing two runtime errors that produce a stack trace, using the *JestViz* extension on their Google Chrome browser. The code was provided to them in an online JavaScript editor called JSFiddle[7]. The control group had to debug the code on JSFiddle editor without the extension. We recorded the time taken to fix both the errors for both groups. The participants were monitored throughout the experiment over a video call.

The prototype version of *JestViz* identifies the correct location of the error in the program only for local editors but not for online editors. For the purpose of this evaluation, slight modifications were made to *JestViz* to make sure that it provides correct line numbers of error messages for JSFiddle. The program that the participants were required to debug is provided here[8]. The participants were informed that the errors are present in the JavaScript section of the editor and that the HTML and CSS code should not be modified.

[7] https://jsfiddle.net/.

[8] https://jsfiddle.net/qx63c05k/1/.

5.2 Qualitative Analysis

The main objective of qualitative analysis is to understand the user experience. We asked the experimental group to answer a questionnaire at the end of the survey. Considering the goals of our evaluation, we decided to use a questionnaire based on TAM2 [38] which evaluates Compatibility (C), Perceived Usefulness (PU), Perceived Ease of Use (PEOU), Behavioral Intention to Use (BI), and Actual Use (AU) on a Likert scale. The questions used for qualitative analysis are in Table 2.

Table 2. Qualitative User Survey

Quality Factors	Question/Statement
Compatibility (C1)	Using JestViz is compatible with my debugging style
Compatibility (C2)	The visualization from JestViz is compatible with the way I understand stack trace
Perceived Usefulness (PU1)	JestViz would improve my understanding of function calls that produce errors on certain types of inputs
Perceived Usefulness (PU2)	JestViz would improve my ability to foresee different types of errors that might occur in the future when the same or similar sequence of functions are called
Perceived Usefulness (PU3)	JestViz would help me spot bugs faster when compared to the stack trace
Perceived Ease of Use (PEOU1)	I think learning to use JestViz is easy
Perceived Ease of Use (PEOU2)	I think getting accustomed to JestViz is easy
Behavioral Intention to Use (BI)	Assuming I had JestViz, I intend to use it for reading stack traces
Actual Use (AU)	I would often use JestViz to debug my program

6 Results

6.1 Quantitative Analysis

JestViz has been quantitatively evaluated with 20 volunteers divided into control group of 10 volunteers and an experimental group of 10 volunteers. The results of the quantitative evaluation are shown in Fig. 3. The experimental group took an average of 541.8 s to fix both the errors, while the control group took an average

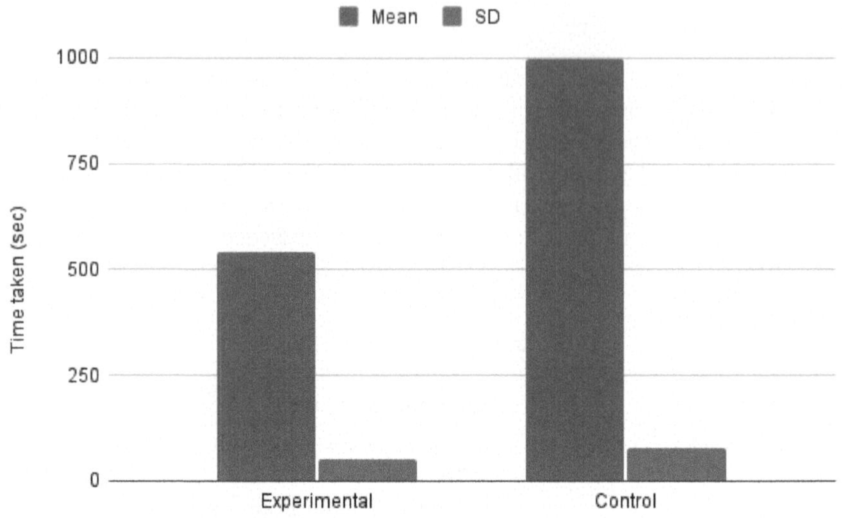

Fig. 3. Mean & SD of time taken by control & experimental groups

of 997.3 s. The standard deviation for the experimental and control groups was 76.15 s and 50.54 s, respectively. We observed that the experimental group took 46% lesser time on average to fix the errors.

6.2 Qualitative Analysis

As a part of qualitative analysis, the experimental group answered a questionnaire based on 5 point Likert scale with *Strongly Agree* being assigned the highest score of 5 and *Strongly Disagree* being assigned the lowest score of 1. The questions are shown in Table 2. The results of the qualitative survey are shown in Fig. 4. The questions corresponding to each factor are shown by the factors' abbreviated form, followed by the question number. We observe that all questions across all factors except BI1 have a mean greater than four and a standard deviation lesser than 1. From the survey, we can deduce that *JestViz* was perceived to be reasonably useful (PU1, PU2, and AU1 have **mean** > **4**) and easy to use (PEOU1 and PEOU2 have **mean** > **4**). It was perceived to be compatible (C1 and C2 have **mean** > **4**). The PU1 quality factor had a mean score of 4.75 indicating that the participants felt that *JestViz* provides a better understanding of the cause of their errors. Participants were also largely in agreement when it comes to their intent to use the tool (BI1 has **mean** > **4**).

7 Discussion and Limitations

JestViz aims to help novice web developers by enhancing the error reporting and presentation in web browsers. The prototype version has a few limitations.

In its current state, even though it can visualize nested function calls, it cannot visualize stack trace from recursive function calls. When not designed carefully, recursive functions can cause the function call stack to exceed the available memory and cause the program to crash, which is called as *stack overflow*. The prototype version does not cover visualizations for stack overflow. In the case of large stack traces that are observed very commonly in JavaScript programs that use external libraries, the function call graphs can get too long, and the users need to scroll through to get information about function calls that led to the error. A modified representation of function call graphs more convenient to the users could be used to overcome this. The current version of *JestViz* provides an accurate location of the errors in the file only for programs written on a local editor. In the case of online IDE, the line numbers of errors and function calls usually have an offset added to them. It happens because of the pre-written code of IDE running on browsers in addition to the code written by the programmer. Offsets could be added for popular online IDEs to overcome this. The display panel that contains the visualization is not customized to smaller screens. This could be made responsive to smaller screens.

Our analysis of the user survey is limited to responses from only 20 participants. However, a future survey with a larger number of participants from a wider range of professional backgrounds could lead to further reliable results.

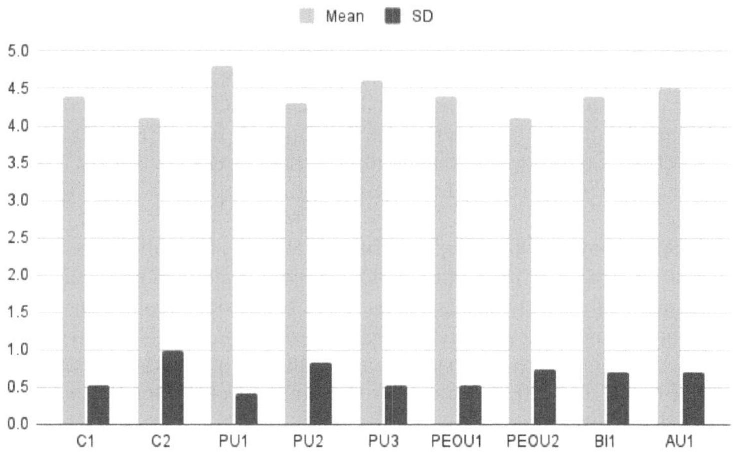

Fig. 4. Mean and standard deviation for factors in TAM 2 questionnaire

8 Conclusion and Future Work

In this paper, we presented *JestViz*, a visualization tool that helps novice web developers. Our tool tries to accomplish it by modifying the error reporting mechanism and providing visualization of stack trace from four different types of JavaScript errors. The tool intends to help novice programmers get a better understanding of error messages and enable faster debugging. The tool shows the stack trace from error messages as a function call graph. We evaluated *JestViz* with 20 novice programmers and found that the programmers who used *JestViz* could debug 46% faster than those who did not. We also found through qualitative evaluation that *JestViz* might provide users a better understanding of the cause of errors in their program.

We plan to extend *JestViz* to other major browsers like Mozilla Firefox. The prototype version supports only four types of JavaScript errors. We plan to include support for the remaining default error types and the custom errors defined by users. *JestViz* could also be extended to visualize stack overflow and recursive functions, and to provide an alternative visual representation to function call graphs. Its visualization could be integrated as a part of *devTools* instead of being displayed on a separate panel. The tool could be extended to support online IDEs. The extension could be extended to support other popular programming languages used in web development, such as Typescript.

Acknowledgments. We extend our gratitude to all the users who participated in our evaluation and for their valuable feedback. We would also like to thank Mr. Chiranjeevi B S for his support in improving the readability of the paper.

References

1. Ahmed, U.Z., Sindhgatta, R., Srivastava, N., Karkare, A.: Targeted example generation for compilation errors. In: 2019 34th IEEE/ACM International Conference on Automated Software Engineering (ASE), pp. 327–338. IEEE (2019)
2. Barik, T., et al.: Do developers read compiler error messages? In: 2017 IEEE/ACM 39th International Conference on Software Engineering (ICSE), pp. 575–585. IEEE (2017)
3. Barik, T., Witschey, J., Johnson, B., Murphy-Hill, E.: Compiler error notifications revisited: an interaction-first approach for helping developers more effectively comprehend and resolve error notifications. In: Companion Proceedings of the 36th International Conference on Software Engineering, pp. 536–539 (2014)
4. Becker, B.A.: An effective approach to enhancing compiler error messages. In: Proceedings of the 47th ACM Technical Symposium on Computing Science Education, pp. 126–131 (2016)
5. Becker, B.A., Denny, P., Prather, J., Pettit, R., Nix, R., Mooney, C.: Towards assessing the readability of programming error messages. In: Australasian Computing Education Conference, pp. 181–188 (2021)
6. Becker, B.A., Murray, C., Tao, T., Song, C., McCartney, R., Sanders, K.: Fix the first, ignore the rest: dealing with multiple compiler error messages. In: Proceedings of the 49th ACM Technical Symposium on Computer Science Education, pp. 634–639 (2018)
7. Campbell, J.C., Hindle, A., Amaral, J.N.: Syntax errors just aren't natural: improving error reporting with language models. In: Proceedings of the 11th Working Conference on Mining Software Repositories, pp. 252–261 (2014)
8. Cornelissen, B., Zaidman, A., van Deursen, A.: A controlled experiment for program comprehension through trace visualization. IEEE Trans. Softw. Eng. **37**(3), 341–355 (2010)

9. Denny, P., Prather, J., Becker, B.A.: Error message readability and novice debugging performance. In: Proceedings of the 2020 ACM Conference on Innovation and Technology in Computer Science Education, pp. 480–486 (2020)
10. Dong, T., Khandwala, K.: The impact of "cosmetic" changes on the usability of error messages. In: Extended Abstracts of the 2019 CHI Conference on Human Factors in Computing Systems, pp. 1–6 (2019)
11. D'souza, R., Zavaleta Bernuy, A., Harrington, B.: PyBuggy: testing the effects of enhanced error messages on novice programmers. In: Proceedings of the 52nd ACM Technical Symposium on Computer Science Education, pp. 1346–1346 (2021)
12. Fujisaka, N., Yamada, M., Ishii, E., Hoshino, Y.: Simplifying compilation messages for beginning programmers: a web-based system proposal. Int. J. ICT Appl. Res. **1**(1), 20–25 (2024)
13. Fwa, H.L.: Experience report: identifying common misconceptions and errors of novice programmers with ChatGPT. In: Proceedings of the 46th International Conference on Software Engineering: Software Engineering Education and Training, pp. 233–241 (2024)
14. Hartmann, B., MacDougall, D., Brandt, J., Klemmer, S.R.: What would other programmers do: suggesting solutions to error messages. In: Proceedings of the SIGCHI Conference on Human Factors in Computing Systems, pp. 1019–1028 (2010)
15. Heinsen Egan, M., McDonald, C.: An evaluation of SeeC: a tool designed to assist novice C programmers with program understanding and debugging. Comput. Sci. Educ. **31**(3), 340–373 (2021)
16. Hristova, M., Misra, A., Rutter, M., Mercuri, R.: Identifying and correcting Java programming errors for introductory computer science students. ACM SIGCSE Bull. **35**(1), 153–156 (2003)
17. Hundhausen, C.D., Brown, J.L.: An experimental study of the impact of visual semantic feedback on novice programming. J. Vis. Lang. Comput. **18**(6), 537–559 (2007)
18. Jensen, S.H., Møller, A., Thiemann, P.: Type analysis for JavaScript. In: International Static Analysis Symposium, pp. 238–255. Springer (2009)
19. Karvelas, I., Li, A., Becker, B.A.: The effects of compilation mechanisms and error message presentation on novice programmer behavior. In: Proceedings of the 51st ACM Technical Symposium on Computer Science Education, pp. 759–765 (2020)
20. Kimmel, B., et al.: Enhancing programming error messages in real time with generative AI. In: Extended Abstracts of the CHI Conference on Human Factors in Computing Systems, pp. 1–7 (2024)
21. Ko, A.J., Myers, B.A.: Finding causes of program output with the Java Whyline. In: Proceedings of the SIGCHI Conference on Human Factors in Computing Systems, pp. 1569–1578 (2009)
22. Kohn, T., Manaris, B.: Tell me what's wrong: a Python IDE with error messages. In: Proceedings of the 51st ACM Technical Symposium on Computer Science Education, pp. 1054–1060 (2020)
23. Krämer, J.P., Karrer, T., Kurz, J., Wittenhagen, M., Borchers, J.: How tools in ides shape developers' navigation behavior. In: Proceedings of the SIGCHI Conference on Human Factors in Computing Systems, pp. 3073–3082 (2013)
24. Leinonen, J., et al.: Using large language models to enhance programming error messages. In: SIGCSE 2023. Association for Computing Machinery, New York (2023). https://doi.org/10.1145/3545945.3569770

25. Li, Z., Sun, F., Wang, H., Ding, Y., Liu, Y., Chen, X.: CLACER: a deep learning-based compilation error classification method for novice students' programs. In: 2021 IEEE 45th Annual Computers, Software, and Applications Conference (COMPSAC), pp. 74–83. IEEE (2021)
26. Marceau, G., Fisler, K., Krishnamurthi, S.: Mind your language: on novices' interactions with error messages. In: Proceedings of the 10th SIGPLAN Symposium on New Ideas, New Paradigms, and Reflections on Programming and Software, pp. 3–18 (2011)
27. Miller, P., Pane, J., Meter, G., Vorthmann, S.: Evolution of novice programming environments: the structure editors of Carnegie Mellon University. Interact. Learn. Environ. **4**(2), 140–158 (1994)
28. Park, T.H., Dorn, B., Forte, A.: An analysis of HTML and CSS syntax errors in a web development course. ACM Trans. Comput. Educ. (TOCE) **15**(1), 1–21 (2015)
29. Prather, J., et al.: First steps towards predicting the readability of programming error messages. In: Proceedings of the 54th ACM Technical Symposium on Computer Science Education. SIGCSE 2023, vol. 1, pp. 549–555. Association for Computing Machinery, New York (2023). https://doi.org/10.1145/3545945.3569791
30. Prather, J., et al.: On novices' interaction with compiler error messages: a human factors approach. In: Proceedings of the 2017 ACM Conference on International Computing Education Research, pp. 74–82 (2017)
31. Rigby, P.C., Thompson, S.: Study of novice programmers using eclipse and gild. In: Proceedings of the 2005 OOPSLA Workshop on Eclipse Technology eXchange, pp. 105–109 (2005)
32. Schmoll, S., Vishwanath, A., Siddiqui, M.A., Subbaiah, B.K., Chua, C.: HTML document error detector and visualiser for novice programmers. In: 2018 IEEE Symposium on Visual Languages and Human-Centric Computing (VL/HCC), pp. 291–292. IEEE (2018)
33. Tanimoto, S.L.: VIVA: a visual language for image processing. J. Vis. Lang. Comput. **1**(2), 127–139 (1990)
34. Tanner, K., Johnson, N., Landay, J.A.: Poirot: a web inspector for designers. In: Proceedings of the 2019 CHI Conference on Human Factors in Computing Systems, pp. 1–12 (2019)
35. Thiselton, E., Treude, C.: Enhancing Python compiler error messages via stack. In: 2019 ACM/IEEE International Symposium on Empirical Software Engineering and Measurement (ESEM), pp. 1–12. IEEE (2019)
36. Topali, P., Mikropoulos, T.A.: Scratch-based learning objects for novice programmers: exploring quality aspects and perceptions for primary education. Interact. Learn. Environ. 1–16 (2021)
37. Traver, V.J.: On compiler error messages: what they say and what they mean. Adv. Hum.-Comput. Interact. **2010** (2010)
38. Venkatesh, V., Bala, H.: Technology acceptance model 3 and a research agenda on interventions. Decis. Sci. **39**(2), 273–315 (2008)
39. Watson, C., Li, F.W., Godwin, J.L.: BlueFix: using crowd-sourced feedback to support programming students in error diagnosis and repair. In: International Conference on Web-Based Learning, pp. 228–239. Springer (2012)
40. Winter, V., Friend, M., Matthews, M., Love, B., Vasireddy, S.: Using visualization to reduce the cognitive load of threshold concepts in computer programming. In: 2019 IEEE Frontiers in Education Conference (FIE), pp. 1–9 (2019). https://doi.org/10.1109/FIE43999.2019.9028612

An Interactive Lambda Calculus Interpreter and Visualization Tool

Bhashithe Abeysinghe[1], Murray Patterson[2], and Rajshekhar Sunderraman[2](✉)

[1] American Institutes for Research, Arlington, VA, USA
[2] Georgia State University, Atlanta, GA, USA
{mpatterson30,rsunderraman}@gsu.edu

Abstract. Lambda Calculus forms the foundational basis for all functional programming languages. In addition, since most other modern programming languages are slowly incorporating functional features such as higher-order functions, lambda expressions, and combinatory logic operators, one can argue that a basic understanding of Lambda Calculus is necessary for modern computer scientists. Typically, Lambda Calculus is introduced in the undergraduate Computer Science curriculum in the Programming Languages Concepts, Programming Paradigms, or Functional Programming courses. In this paper, we present a command-line tool and an interactive Web visualization tool that provide a platform for the student to learn to formulate and evaluate lambda expressions. In the command-line tool, the user can compute free-variables in lambda expressions, perform alpha-reductions and substitutions, and simplify lambda expressions using beta-reductions. This interface is convenient for evaluating lambda expressions to its most reduced form by going through a series of beta-reductions. In the visualization tool, the user inputs a lambda expression and interactively evaluates the expressions, one beta-reduction at a time. The lambda expression is shown in the form of an expression tree, with ready to execute function application nodes shown in green. The student can click on any of these green nodes to perform a beta reduction and the resulting tree is shown. The student can also go back to any of the previous trees to try other beta reductions. The tool was validated in an offering of the Programming Language Concepts class and results from the study are presented in the paper.

Keywords: Lambda Calculus · Visualization · Interactive Tool

1 Introduction

Lambda Calculus [1,13] is a formal model of computation based on two simple ideas: function abstraction and function application. Introduced by Alonzo Church in the early 1930s, this model of computation forms the basis for modern day functional programming languages such as Haskell, OCaml, etc. Lambda Calculus has been proven to be equivalent to the other popular model of Computation, the Turing Machine [12], which forms the basis for modern procedural

A. Karkare et al. (Eds.): COMPUTE 2024, CCIS 2400, pp. 113–125, 2025.
https://doi.org/10.1007/978-3-031-84391-4_9

or state-based programming languages. Procedural or state-based programming languages, such as Python, Java, or Javascript, incorporate many ideas from functional programming, including lambda expressions and higher-order functions. For these reasons, it is important for a Computer Science student to be well versed in the basics of the Lambda Calculus.

Lambda Calculus is usually introduced in a Programming Language Concepts course or in a course on Functional Programming in the undergraduate curriculum, or in a theoretical course on Models of Computation. Lambda Calculus concepts include the (simple) syntax of function abstractions and function applications, and semantics that include concepts such as free and bound variables, α-reductions, substitutions, and β-reductions.

Even though the syntax of Lambda expressions is quite simple, with just two operators, the nested structure of these expressions causes a lot of difficulty in understanding their structure. Having a tool that can automatically produce a visual expression tree for a given Lambda expression will enable students to better understand the nested structures in expressions. Further, the semantics of Lambda Calculus is defined in terms of β-reductions, a transformation that is mathematically defined and which operates on the tree structure of the expressions, thereby causing considerable difficulty for the student in understanding the semantics. Incorporating user interactivity in the visual tool to be able to produce the result of a β-reduction on an existing tree to visualize the next tree in the evaluation can go a long way in improving the student's understanding of semantics. We present such an interactive visual tool that accepts a Lambda expression as input and displays a visual expression tree with cues to apply β-reductions. The user is provided with various options to simplify the expression and can see the workings of the evaluation process. They can also get an understanding of the recursive structures in these expressions. A command line version of the tool is also available and complements the functionalities of the visual tool. The command line version allows users to "execute" lambda expressions all the way to termination, thereby allowing students to test their ability to compose programs from expressions.

The remainder of this paper is organized as follows: Sect. 2 covers basics of Lambda Calculus, including syntax, expression trees, and semantics. Section 3 discusses the command line tool and Sect. 4 describes the interactive visual tool. Section 5 describes an evaluation study of the tool, as well as the results and possible improvements. Section 6 summarizes related work, while Sect. 7 concludes the paper and suggests future work.

2 Lambda Calculus

Lambda Calculus was introduced by Church in the 1930s as a model of computation. The general idea was to define computation as consisting of two main constructs: function definition and function application. This model of computation forms the foundation of modern day functional programming languages such as Haskell, etc.

2.1 Syntax

Definition 1. *A λ-expression is defined inductively as follows:*

1. *A variable is a λ-expression (e.g. x, y, m, n, etc.).*
2. *If M is a λ-expression and x is a variable, then $(\lambda\ x.M)$ is a λ-expression.*
3. *If M and N are λ-expressions then $(M\ N)$ is a λ-expression.*
4. *A number is a λ-expression (e.g. 20, 7.5, -2.22, etc.).*
5. *If M and N are λ-expressions and op is an arithmetic operator such as $+$, $-$, $*$, or $/$, then $(op\ M\ N)$ is a λ-expression.*

In the above definition,

- $(\lambda x.M)$ is called a lambda abstraction; or in programming terminology the definition of a function. Here, x is the input parameter (bound variable) and M is the body of the function. Note that all function definitions in Lambda Calculus take exactly one input parameter.
- $(M\ N)$ is called a function application; or in programming terminology a function call. M is the function being called and N is the actual argument provided as input to M.
- The number and arithmetic operator λ-terms (4. and 5., respectively) are not part of the original Lambda Calculus and are introduced to make it interesting while using the interactive tool.

Here are some examples of λ-expressions:

1. (((λ x. (λ y. (+ x y))) 10) 5)
2. (((λ f. (λ x. (f x))) (λ y. (* y y))) 12)
3. (λ x. (λ y. (λ z. ((x z)(y z)))))
4. ((((λ f. (λ x. ((f x) f))) (λ y. (λ g. (g (* y y))))) 2) (λ a. a))

2.2 Expression Trees

Lambda expressions can be visualized as an expression tree with interior nodes denoting lambda abstractions, function applications, or arithmetic operators and leaves denoting variables or numbers. An example expression tree is shown in Fig. 1 using a screenshot from our system.

2.3 Semantics

The semantics of lambda expressions is defined through a series of formal definitions that follow. To start with, we denote the **scope** of parameter variable x in (λ x.M) to be the body M. The following defines the concept of bound and free variables.

Definition 2. *In the λ-expression $(\lambda x.M)$, the variable occurrence immediately after λ is said to be* **bound**. *In addition, any occurrence of x in M that is not otherwise* **bound** *to another λ-expression within M is said to be* **bound** *to the parameter variable x in $(\lambda\ x.M)$. Any variable that is not bound is said to be* **free**.

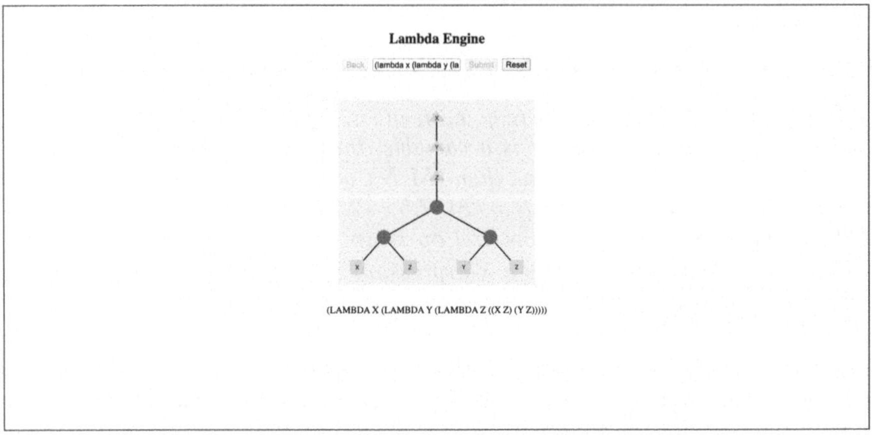

Fig. 1. Expression tree for (λ x.(λ y.(λ z.((x z) (y z))))))

Definition 3. *The set of free variables in M, denoted by FV[M], is inductively defined as follows:*

1. $FV[x] = x$
2. $FV[(\lambda\ x.M)] = FV[M] \setminus \{ x \}$
3. $FV[(M\ N)] = FV[M] \cup FV[N]$
4. $FV[number] = \{ \}$
5. $FV[(op\ M\ N)] = FV[M] \cup FV[N]$

The next concept is that of α-equivalence. Two function abstractions are α-equivalent if the two differ only in the name of the formal parameter/input. This relates to the naming of the formal parameter. For example, the λ-expressions (λ x.x) and (λ y.y) are essentially the same. Renaming the bound variable does not change the function abstraction. More formally,

Definition 4. $(\lambda\ x.M) =_{\alpha} (\lambda\ y.M\ \{x \leftarrow y\})$ *where y is a "brand new" variable not appearing in M, and* $M\ \{x \leftarrow y\}$ *is M with all occurrences of x replaced by y.*

The next concept needed in defining the semantics is that of substitutions. A substitution replaces a free variable in a λ-expression with another λ-expression. Formally, substitutions are defined as follows:

Definition 5. *Substitute free variable x in a lambda expression by another lambda expression P:*
$x\ [x = P] = P$
$y\ [x = P] = y$, *if* $x \neq y$
$(M\ N)\ [x = P] = (M[x = P]\ N[x = P])$
$(\lambda\ x.M)\ [x = P] = (\lambda\ x.M)$
$(\lambda\ y.M)\ [x = P] = (\lambda\ y.M[x = P])$, *if* $x \neq y$ *and* $y \notin FV[P]$

$(\lambda\ y.M)\ [x = P] = (\lambda\ y'.(M\ \{y \leftarrow y'\}[x = P]))$, if $x \neq y$ and $y \in FV[P]$ and y' is brand new

Some examples are shown below:
$(\lambda$ x. (x y)) [y = 5] = $(\lambda$ x. (x 5))
$(\lambda$ x. (x y)) [y = (u v)] = $(\lambda$ x. (x (u v)))
Substitution must be done carefully so as not to alter the meaning of the λ-expression, for example,
$(\lambda$ x. (x y)) [y = x] $\neq$ $(\lambda$ x. (x x))
As can be seen, y was a free-variable before, but after the substitution y's value has become bound. Such a case is called a "capture" case, and a way around changing the meaning of the substitutions is first to recognize the fact that we have a "capture" case and then rename the parameter variable in the λ-expression (using an α-equivalence) with a brand new variable and then perform the substitution. So,
$(\lambda$ x.(x y)) [y = x] $=_\alpha$ $(\lambda$ x'.(x' y)) [y = x] = $(\lambda$ x'.(x' x))
The final concept is that of β-reduction, defined as follows:

Definition 6. *$((\lambda\ x.M)\ N) =_\beta M[x = N]$*

As an example, consider the λ-expression, $(\lambda$ x. (* x x)), that denotes the "square" function. To call this function with argument 5, we will construct the "apply" λ-term: ((λ x. (* x x)) 5). β-reduction allows us to "execute or call" a function. We "substitute" the bound variable (parameter), x, of the function abstraction with 5 in the body of the function abstraction.
((λ x. (* x x)) 5) = (* x x) [x = 5] = (* 5 5) = 25
β–reduction can be applied only to a λ-expression of the form ((λ x.M) N). Now, we are ready to define the semantics of a λ-expression. Let β(f) be a single application of β-reduction on f. If there are no "apply" nodes on which β-reductions are possible then β(f) = f. The **semantics/meaning/value** of a λ-expression e is defined as the fixed-point of the function β applied to e at the start, i.e., the value x in the sequence β(e), β(β(e)), β(β(β(e))), ..., for which x = β(x). The order of applying β-reductions is not significant [2]. The end result is the same, especially if the simplification process terminates.

3 Command Line Interface (CLI) Tool

The command line tool, built using Python, allows the users to compute free variables in a lambda-expression, generate an alpha equivalent lambda expression, perform a substitution on a lambda expression, and apply beta reductions on lambda expressions. The command line tool also contains all the necessary functionality that serve as the back-end for the visualization tool described in the next section. The back-end functionality includes the following:

1. the generation of an initial expression tree for a given Lambda expression.
2. the generation of the next expression tree given the previous expression tree and function application node IDs which can be beta-reduced.

3. the generation of the next expression tree given the previous expression tree and "operator" node IDs which can be simplified.

Lambda Expressions, Grammar, Parsing. To generate the initial tree, we use a parser generator library, PLY [8], and code the following grammar rules:

```
expr : NAME
expr : ( LAMBDA NAME expr )
expr : ( expr expr )
```

The above three grammar rules completely define the syntax of the original Lambda Calculus. To make the tool more interesting, we allow arithmetic operations between numbers and thereby include the following two additional types of Lambda expressions:

```
expr : NUMBER
expr : ( OP expr expr )
```

The parser generator validates the syntax of input Lambda expressions and, if valid, produces a tree structure encoded in a Python list.

CLI Tool in Action. The following transcript from the command line illustrates free variable calculation, alpha equivalent expressions, and application of substitutions.

```
$ python3 Lambda.py

LAMBDA> fv[((lambda x x) x)];
Free variables:  {'X'}

LAMBDA> alpha[(lambda x (x x)),u];
(LAMBDA U (U U))

LAMBDA> ((lambda x x) x) [x=(lambda x (x x))];
((LAMBDA X X) (LAMBDA X (X X)))

LAMBDA> exit;
$
```

By default, the command line tool takes as input a lambda expression and produces a final beta reduct expression after repeatedly applying beta reductions until no more reductions are possible. The following is a sample run illustrating the default behavior of the tool.

```
$ python3 Lambda.py

LAMBDA> (((lambda f (lambda x (f x))) (lambda y (* y y))) 12);
```

```
INPUT:  (((LAMBDA F (LAMBDA X (F X))) (LAMBDA Y (* Y Y))) 12.0)
BETA REDUCT:  (* 12.0 12.0)

ANSWER:  144.0
```

In case the user wishes to see the intermediate steps in the beta reductions, they can invoke the tool using the `-d` option as is shown in the following transcript:

```
$ python3 Lambda.py -d
LAMBDA> (((lambda f (lambda x (f x))) (lambda y (* y y))) 12);
INPUT:  (((LAMBDA F (LAMBDA X (F X))) (LAMBDA Y (* Y Y))) 12.0)

BETA:  ((LAMBDA X ((LAMBDA Y (* Y Y)) X)) 12.0)
BETA:  ((LAMBDA Y (* Y Y)) 12.0)
BETA:  (* 12.0 12.0)

BETA REDUCT:  (* 12.0 12.0)

ANSWER:  144.0
```

Another feature of the tool is that the user can provide a startup file named `.startup-lambda` in the current directory containing names for commonly used lambda expressions as shown below.

```
true = (lambda x (lambda y x))
false = (lambda x (lambda y y))

not = (lambda p (lambda a (lambda b ((p b) a))))
and = (lambda p (lambda q ((p q) p)))
or = (lambda p (lambda q ((p p) q)))
```

The tool, when invoked, will read these names and recognize them in lambda expressions. The following is an illustration of the use of names in beta reductions:

```
$ python3 Lambda.py
LAMBDA> ((and true) false);
INPUT:  (((LAMBDA P (LAMBDA Q ((P Q) P))) (LAMBDA X (LAMBDA Y X)))
        (LAMBDA X (LAMBDA Y Y)))

BETA REDUCT:  (LAMBDA X (LAMBDA Y Y))

ANSWER:  (LAMBDA X (LAMBDA Y Y))
```

The example illustrates logical operator "and" on inputs `true` and `false` which returns a value of `false`.

4 Interactive Visualization Tool

The user interface of this interactive tool has been developed using Dash [7], a powerful framework that offers a range of library functions for creating web components with ease, while effectively managing various underlying engineering tasks. By invoking back-end functions *get_initial_tree* and *get_next_tree*, the front-end seamlessly interacts with the back-end. Within the Web interface, four key components play a crucial role.

The first component is a text box, allowing users to input Lambda expressions, accompanied by a submit button. Clicking the "submit" button invokes the back-end's *get_initial_tree*() function. Additionally, it performs necessary adjustments of the resulting tree to ensure compatibility with the front-end, then stores the processed tree within a 'Store' and a 'Canvas' component.

The second component of the front-end is the Canvas. Since the back-end represents Lambda expressions as trees, converting them into the required rooted tree format for display purposes is a straightforward process. To accomplish this, we leverage the "igraph" package [4] and employ the Reingold-Tilford algorithm [10] for tree layout. We also use Python's NetworkX package [6] for intermediate tree representation. To visualize the tree, we utilize the 'Graph' component provided by Dash. To store the current tree, we take advantage of 'Dash's' client-side, in-memory storage solution known as a "Store". However, it is important to note that the contents of the 'Store' will be lost if the browser is refreshed. Whenever another function stores a tree in this in-memory component, an intermediate function is triggered, promptly displaying the updated tree.

The third component allows users to click on and interact with the graph nodes. Within this component, there exist two types of nodes: 'apply' nodes and 'operation' nodes. The back-end incorporates separate functions, namely *get_next_tree*() and *get_next_tree_after_math*(), to handle these distinct node types. These back-end functions perform the necessary computations to generate the appropriate tree, which is subsequently sent to the front-end. As previously discussed, the front-end stores the received tree in the in-memory storage, leveraging the 'Store' component.

The fourth component, the back button, enables users to navigate back and revisit previous trees. To achieve this functionality, we maintain a list of trees that the user has encountered, utilizing the 'Store'component once again. The list of trees is organized as a stack data structure, where the top of the stack represents the current tree. When the user clicks the back button, the top of the stack is popped, triggering the new top of the stack to be sent to the 'Store'. Consequently, the new top of the stack is displayed in the 'Canvas'component, allowing users to view and interact with the previously visited tree.

System in Use. Upon submitting a Lambda expression, the user will be presented with an expression tree with 3 types of interior nodes (Lambda nodes - triangles, apply nodes - green or red circles, and arithmetic operator - squares) and 2 types of leaf nodes (variable and number nodes - rectangles). At any step the user may "click" on a green "apply" node to perform a beta-reduction. The user may also click an arithmetic operator node to "simplify/evaluate" the expression at that node. The system performs the operation and produces a new expression tree. The user can continue with these interactions until the Lambda expression cannot be reduced any further, thereby giving the final value of the expression. At all times the "string" equivalent of the expression tree is shown at the bottom. There is a "back" button that takes the user to the previous tree to possibly try out a different "apply" operation. User "clicks" at all other areas of the expression tree are ignored. Consider the lambda expression: `(((lambda x (lambda y (+ x y))) 10) 5)`. The initial tree produced by our system is shown in part (a) of Fig. 2. A visual interactive expression tree is shown with "green" function application nodes that can be clicked by the user to perform β-reductions. In the initial tree, there is only one "green" node. Arithmetic operator nodes are not yet ready to be simplified. Upon clicking the only green node, a β-reduction is performed and the new tree is shown in part (b) of Fig. 2. Once again, we have an expression tree with just one green node. The user click on this node generates the next tree in the evaluation process and is shown in part (c) of Fig. 2. This tree has an arithmetic operator node that can be simplified. Upon clicking the arithmetic operator node, the final tree in the evaluation is shown in part (d) of Fig. 2.

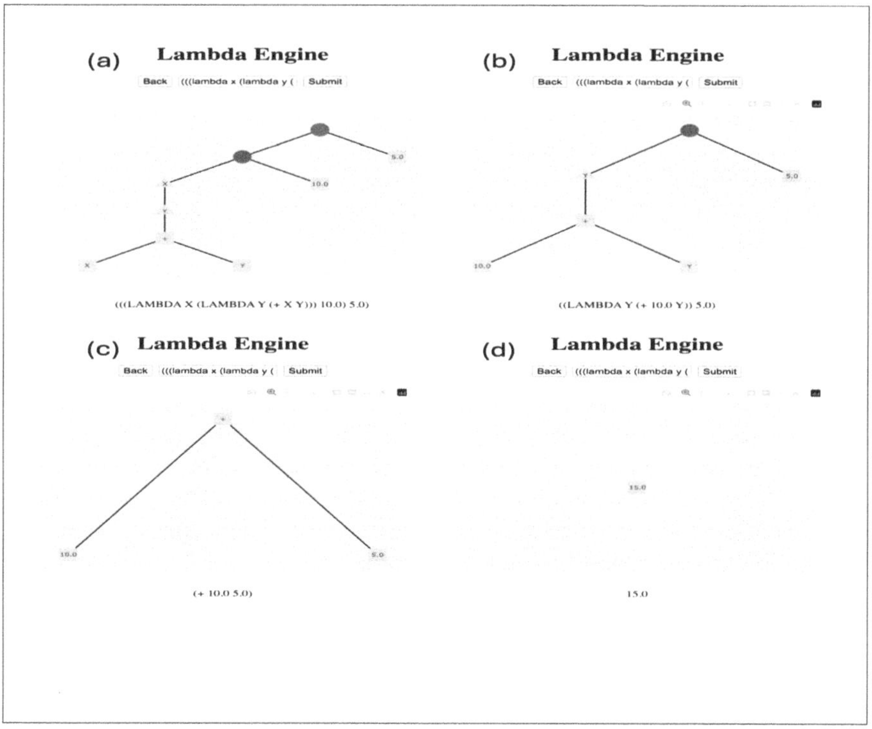

Fig. 2. Expression trees for evaluating `((lambda y (+ 10.0 y))) 5.0)`

5 Evaluation

An evaluation study was conducted in a recent offering of Programming Language Concepts, a junior/senior-level class in the undergraduate (B.S.) Computer Science curriculum. This course covers the syntax and semantics of programming languages and the various programming paradigms such as functional, logic, concurrent, and object-oriented. Lambda Calculus is introduced prior to the module on the Haskell functional programming language. Two versions of the tool were introduced:

1. the command-line version that allows the user to try out various algorithms such as determining free/bound variables, computing alpha-equivalence, applying substitutions, and applying beta-reductions
2. the dynamic interactive visualizer tool that allows the user to interactively apply beta-reductions

At the end of the module, the students were given a problem set to solve by hand and verify their results using the tools. The average grade on the homework was 80%. In addition, a survey was conducted, results of which are shown in Table 1. A total of 31 respondents out of a class of 60 completed the survey. The survey consisted of 5 questions related to the usefulness of the tool, and a free input question asking for comments/feedback on the tools. Overall, the survey indicates that the tools were appreciated by the students, with about half the students finding them "absolutely" useful and another half finding them "somewhat" useful. In the case of the tools for applying beta-reductions, about two thirds of the students found them "absolutely" useful, versus the other third finding them "somewhat" useful. In all cases, only one to three students did not find the tools useful.

In response to the free input question: *Please provide any additional feedback on the tool, including improvements*, most of the written comments were positive, e.g., "awesome tool", "wish we can see more such tools in classes", "I thought the tool overall was great!", "It was a cool tool seeing the tree form", "It was really easy to use and easy to understand!", "Loved using the visualizer especially with how its interactive", "The tools for beta reductions were good". There was one negative comment: "It's not really helpful".

Some suggestions for improvement were given: "I would provide a link to a video explaining the dynamic visual tool that goes into a very in-depth use of it", "I think a better explanation in free/bound variable in the slides would've maybe made the tool a bit better", "some documentation covering the syntax for using the interpreter would be a nice improvement".

Table 1. Survey Results

Question	Not at all	Somewhat	Absolutely
Did the use of the command line Lambda Calculus tool help improve your understanding of the Lambda Calculus concepts?	1	15	15
Did the use of the dynamic Visual Lambda Calculus tool help improve your understanding of the Lambda Calculus concepts?	1	14	16
Please indicate the usefulness of the tools for the concept of Free/Bound variables.	3	15	13
Please indicate the usefulness of the tools for the concept of Substitutions.	1	14	16
Please indicate the usefulness of the tools for the concept of Beta-reductions.	1	11	18

6 Related Work

In this section, we review several Lambda Calculus visualization tools that have been developed in the past. We compare each with our tool and present pros and cons.

Project Ultimatum's Lambda Viewer [9] provides a simple interface wherein users can submit λ-expressions and choose a particular order of evaluation such as normal order, call-by-value, etc., and the system displays a static image containing the expression tree. The system also displays the λ-expression which may be clicked to view the next λ-expression after a single β-reduction. The system seems to have similar capabilities as our tool, however, our tool has a dynamic tree visualization that the user can interact with. In contrast to Lambda Viewer, which is deployed behind a Web server (cgi-bin), our tool can easily be deployed in a Python environment.

Lambda Calculus Calculator [5] is an online tool that enables users to enter λ-expressions and submit for evaluation. The system allows the user to choose the number β-reductions to apply and see the result. The system is linear and does not include a visualization of the expression tree. Users can choose between several strategies of evaluation including innermost and outermost applications. This system is deployed on a Web server and is written in Haskell.

David Ruiz and Mateu Villaret [11] present "TILC: The Interactive Lambda-Calculus Tracer", a user graphical application that helps students learn basic concepts of untyped Lambda Calculus. The user interacts with a tree structure of the Lambda terms and the interactions are reflected in the Lambda terms.

This tool is built as a Desktop application written in Haskell and currently the download is not available at the link provided in the paper.

LambdaLab [3] is another interactive Desktop application that provides the ability to view Lambda Calculus terms graphically and manipulate them via β-reductions. The visualizations are not interactive but employ different coloring schemes to distinguish active parts of the expression tree.

Compared with the above systems, our interactive visualizer for Lambda Calculus has the following advantages:

1. Our system is light-weight and built with Python's universally available packages that can be easily installed in the present and foreseeable future, as long as Python is still a commonplace language.
2. Our system is also highly interactive, with the user under control on which β-reduction to apply, thereby allowing the user to explore different paths to the final reduced form of expressions. This allows the user to try out different evaluation strategies such as inner-most, outer-most, call-by-value, call-by-name, etc.
3. Our system is built using the Plotly graphics package, that uses WebGL or SVG to render the objects. This allows for large λ-expressions to be rendered with zoom in and out possibilities, thereby allowing users to look at different parts of the tree in detail.

7 Conclusion and Future Work

In this paper, we have presented an interactive visualization tool for Lambda Calculus. The tool provides a platform for computer science students to learn about the syntax and semantics of Lambda expressions. A classroom evaluation study was conducted and the results from the study were encouraging and we hope to make the tools available publicly.

As far as future enhancements of the tool, we envision several possibilities including showing the user inner details of β-reductions, exporting a linear trail of reductions starting from the initial expression to it's final value, providing explicit documentation on Lambda Calculus as well as the visualization tool in a Website, and provide other interfaces for the user to try out intermediate steps such as α-reductions, substitutions, and determining free and bound variables in Lambda expressions. The back-end functionalities are already built in for these enhancements and we will need only to build the user interfaces for these enhancements. The source code for this project is available at https://github.com/rajhub28/lambda-animation.

References

1. Church, A.: A set of postulates for the foundation of logic. Ann. Math. **33**(2), 346–366 (1932). http://www.jstor.org/stable/1968337
2. Church, A., Rosser, J.B.: Some properties of conversion. Trans. Am. Math. Soc. **39**(3), 472–482 (1936). https://doi.org/10.2307/1989762

3. Sainati, D., Sampson, A.: LambdaLab: an interactive λ-calculus reducer for learning. https://2018.splashcon.org/track/splash-2018-SPLASH-E?. Accessed 10 Oct 2023
4. igraph: Python-igraph, a Python interface to igraph for manipulating graph data (2023). https://python.igraph.org/en/stable/. Accessed 18 Aug 2023
5. Buchli, L.: Lambda calculus calculator (2023). https://lambdacalc.io/. Accessed 10 Oct 2023
6. NetworkX: Network Analysis in Python (2023). https://networkx.org/. Accessed 18 Aug 2023
7. Plotly: Dash: low-code framework for rapidly building data apps in Python (2023). https://dash.plotly.com/. Accessed 18 Aug 2023
8. PLY: Python Lex-Yacc (2023). https://www.dabeaz.com/ply/. Accessed 18 Aug 2023
9. Project Ultimatum: Lambda Viewer (2023). https://projectultimatum.org/cgi-bin/lambda. Accessed 10 Oct 2023
10. Reingold, E., Tilford, J.: Tidier drawings of trees. IEEE Trans. Softw. Eng. **SE-7**(2), 223–228 (1981). https://doi.org/10.1109/TSE.1981.234519
11. Ruiz, D., Villaret, M.: TILC: the interactive lambda-calculus tracer. Electron. Notes Theor. Comput. Sci. **248**, 173–183 (2009). https://doi.org/10.1016/j.entcs.2009.07.067. https://www.sciencedirect.com/science/article/pii/S1571066109002904. Proceedings of the Eighth Spanish Conference on Programming and Computer Languages (PROLE 2008)
12. Turing, A.M.: On computable numbers, with an application to the Entscheidungsproblem. Proc. Lond. Math. Soc. Second Ser. **42**, 230–265 (1936)
13. Wikipedia: Lambda Calculus (2023). https://en.wikipedia.org/wiki/Lambda_calculus. Accessed 18 Aug 2023

Exploring Recursion Pedagogies: Innovative Strategies and Their Effects on Engineering Students

Pranay Parikh[1], Khush Bajaj[1], Christopher Anand[2], and Jagalingam Pushparaj[1(✉)]

[1] Vellore Institute of Technology, Vellore, Tamil Nadu 632014, India
jagalingam.p@vit.ac.in
[2] McMaster University, Hamilton, ON L8S 4L7, Canada

Abstract. Recursion, a fundamental concept in computer science and engineering, presents both challenges and opportunities for new learners. This paper explores innovative teaching methodologies and empirical insights from a study to enhance freshmen engineering students' understanding of recursion. Additionally, we integrated a prototype study to illustrate the practical application of recursion in real-world scenarios, aiming to deepen student engagement and comprehension. A total of 57 students were divided into four groups (traditional learning - group 1, physical activities - group 2, recursion creator - group 3 and tower of Hanoi problem solving - group 4) consisting of 15,15,14, and 13 students, each taught with a different approach. For each of the groups, a pre-study, and a post-study assessment was taken. Results of this activity were observed and analyzed. It showed that using innovative approaches such as physical activities and the recursion creator improved the understanding of recursion, while the isolated problem solving was not as effective and impactful among the students.

Keywords: Recursion · Education Tools · Computer Science Education · CS Unplugged

1 Introduction

The teaching of recursion has been extensively studied, with a variety of pedagogical strategies to mitigate its inherent complexity. The cognitive challenges associated with recursion often result in student difficulties, such as understanding the concept of function calls and base cases, (Velazquez-Iturbide, 2000) which leads to cognitive overload and confusion. Traditional methods, such as lectures and standard textbook exercises, often fail to foster a deep understanding. Studies have shown that students frequently memorize patterns of recursive solutions rather than comprehending the underlying principles, leading to shallow learning outcomes (Poletiek et al., 2018). Scholtz and Sanders (2010) emphasize the importance of addressing students' mental models of recursion, which are often incomplete or flawed, affecting their ability to understand and apply recursive techniques effectively.

A. Karkare et al. (Eds.): COMPUTE 2024, CCIS 2400, pp. 126–134, 2025.
https://doi.org/10.1007/978-3-031-84391-4_10

To address these challenges, our research aims to develop and test innovative methodologies to improve comprehension of recursion. We have devised several teaching methods including traditional learning (control group 1), physical activities (group 2), recursion creator (group 3) and tower of Hanoi problem-solving approach (group 4).

2 Methodology

These methodologies are accompanied by specially crafted study materials, designed to align with learning objectives and provide comprehensive support throughout the learning process. Conducting a prototype study is considered a crucial aspect of the research process (Malmqvist et al., 2019). Our pilot study involves a small-scale implementation of these methodologies among second-semester computer science engineering students at Vellore Institute of Technology (VIT), Vellore, TN, India. The objective is to evaluate their effectiveness in enhancing students' understanding of recursion. This study serves as a foundation for further research and refinement of these methodologies, contributing to a deeper understanding of effective teaching practices for recursion.

2.1 Participants

The study involved 57 first-year students enrolled in a computer science engineering course at VIT. These students were selected based on their enrollment in the course and their availability to participate in the study. To ensure diversity and mitigate potential biases, participants were divided into four groups, based on a pre-intervention assessment. This was done in order to distribute the highest performers and lowest performers and to achieve the same average performance of each team.

The systematic assignment of students to groups aimed to distribute any inherent differences evenly across groups, thus enhancing the validity of comparisons between teaching methods. Each group consisted of students with varying levels of prior programming experience, ensuring a representative sample of the freshman cohort.

2.2 Study Design

The study was structured into three distinct phases to assess the impact of different teaching methods on students' understanding of recursion:

2.2.1 Pre-Intervention Phase

At the outset of the study, all participants underwent a preliminary assessment comprising 10 questions. These questions were designed to gauge students' baseline knowledge and comprehension of recursion concepts. It also included a few general-programming questions. The assessment results provided a benchmark against which subsequent improvements could be measured.

2.2.2 Intervention Phase

Following the pre-assessment, the intervention phase commenced. Each of the four groups was exposed to a distinct teaching method:

Each group received equal instructional time, assignments, and supplementary materials tailored to their respective teaching methods. This approach ensured consistency and comparability in educational content across groups.

2.2.3 Post-intervention Phase

Following the intervention period, participants completed assignments designed to assess their application of recursion principles. The assignments were structured to evaluate students' problem-solving abilities, algorithmic proficiency, and understanding of recursive strategies. The improvement in assignment scores from the pre-assessment phase served as a primary metric to measure the effectiveness of each teaching method.

2.3 Teaching Methods

All of the teaching materials are included in the GitHub repository linked at the end of the paper. Each teaching method was implemented with specific instructional objectives to enhance students' understanding of recursion:

2.3.1 Traditional Lecture-Based Teaching (Group 1)

This control group utilized structured lectures, code walkthroughs, and theoretical discussions to teach recursive algorithms. Students engaged with textbook examples and exercises, focusing on the efficiency of recursive versus iterative methods and their computational complexity. This approach measured the effectiveness of traditional teaching methods without additional interventions (Rinderknecht, 2014).

2.3.2 Physical Activities (Group 2)

To enhance understanding of recursion, students participated in an interactive real-world binary search simulation, contrasting it with linear search to illustrate time complexity differences. They also explored recursion through reflective surfaces, relating their observations to recursive algorithms. Assignments encouraged critical thinking about base cases and the conditions necessary for recursion to terminate (Kuokkanen et al., 2024).

2.3.3 Educational Tools (Group 3)

The Recursion Creator drawing tool enhances teaching recursion by allowing students to visualize and manipulate recursive function execution. Students can adjust parameters like shape, color, and curvature to see the effects on patterns, such as concentric circles and tree-like structures. To ease learning, the tool's features were adapted to Python, linking recursive concepts to students' prior programming knowledge. Assignments encourage shape recreation using the tool, supported by video lectures and slides to address various learning styles. This multimodal approach fosters a deeper understanding of recursive processes (Stern & Naish, 2002; Wahyuni et al., 2023).

2.3.4 Tower of Hanoi (Problem Based Learning) (Group 4)

The Tower of Hanoi problem is a classic example for learning recursion, highlighting a depth-first approach to problem-solving (Honrales, 2020). Students engaged with recursive concepts through explanations, examples, and video lectures, supported by interactive software. They tackled increasingly complex iterations of the problem, focusing on the rules for moving disks between rods and understanding how recursive calls manage configurations. During the intervention, students practiced solving various problem variations, applying recursive strategies to achieve optimal solutions. This comprehensive approach fostered a deep understanding of recursion's versatility and real-world applicability.

2.4 Post-intervention Evaluation

The evaluation process focused on assessing the effectiveness of each teaching method in enhancing students' comprehension and application of recursion concepts:

2.4.1 Assessment Details

The questions provided assess a range of skills in understanding and applying recursion within the context of computer science. They cover theoretical understanding, practical application, debugging, and critical thinking. Each question challenges students to think deeply about recursion beyond simple mathematical examples, requiring them to recognize and explain its real-life applications (Q1- Question 1), modify and trace recursive functions such as the Fibonacci sequence (Q2 and Q3), identify logical errors in recursive functions (Q4), and propose and justify corrections to faulty recursive algorithms (Q5).

Overall, these questions comprehensively assess students' mastery of recursion, from theoretical foundations to practical implementation and debugging skills.

2.4.2 Comparative Analysis

The comparative analysis focused on evaluating the effectiveness of different teaching methods by analyzing the improvement in assignment scores compared to the pre-intervention assessment. This quantitative approach aimed to provide empirical evidence of how various instructional strategies impacted student learning outcomes. Statistical methods were employed to identify significant differences in performance among the four groups, each exposed to distinct teaching methodologies.

To conduct the analysis, initial assignment scores from pre-intervention assessments served as a baseline measurement. Subsequent scores following the intervention period were compared across groups to assess improvements. These tests allowed us to quantify the degree of improvement attributable to each teaching method, providing insights into which approaches were most effective in enhancing student comprehension and application of recursive concepts.

2.4.3 Experimental Design

In designing our experiment, we meticulously crafted a comprehensive framework that not only assesses the effectiveness of traditional lecture-based approaches but also delves into innovative methodologies aimed at enhancing student comprehension and engagement with the concept of recursion. Recognizing the diverse learning styles and backgrounds of our 57 participants, we curated four distinct experimental groups, each consisting of nearly 15 students, to cater to varied preferences and learning needs.

Before conducting the experiment, we implemented a preliminary assessment on basic programming concepts. This assessment served a dual purpose: firstly, to gauge the students' baseline understanding of programming fundamentals, and secondly, to ensure balanced distribution of participants across the experimental groups. By dividing the students into groups with an equal average score for all, we aimed to minimize potential bias and confounding variables, thus facilitating more accurate and meaningful analysis of the experimental results. Overall, this meticulous pre-experimental step allowed us to establish a level playing field and lay the groundwork for drawing conclusive insights on the efficacy of the different teaching methodologies employed.

By encompassing these diverse experimental groups, we aimed to provide a comprehensive evaluation of various teaching methodologies, ranging from hands-on exploration and physical engagement to in-depth problem-solving activities.

3 Results and Discussions

3.1 Final Assessment Overall Results

Assignment scores were collected from pre-intervention assessments as baseline measurements and compared with scores following a designated intervention period. The interventions varied in approach, emphasizing interactive tools, real-world applications, and traditional lecture-based methods (Table 1).

Table 1. The groupwise improvement of all students

	Total Net Change in Marks (Final - Initial Marks)	No. of Students	Avg Change Per Student	% of students showing improvement
Group 1	99–75 = 24	15	1.60	9/15 = 60%
Group 2	115–74 = 41	15	2.73	13/15 = 86.6%
Group 3	97–69 = 28	14	2.00	12/14 = 85.7%
Group 4	84.5–68 = 16.5	13	1.26	8/13 = 61.5%

Groups 2 and 3 showed the highest improvement rates in assignment scores, with 86.6% and 85.7% of students improving, compared to 60% for Group 1 and 61.5% for Group 4. Specifically, 9, 13, 12, and 8 students improved in Groups 1 through 4, respectively. Graphs in Sect. 3.2 illustrate these changes. The results indicate that teaching methods incorporating physical activities and interactive tools were more effective than traditional lecture-based approaches, as evidenced by higher average score increases and greater percentages of students showing improvement.

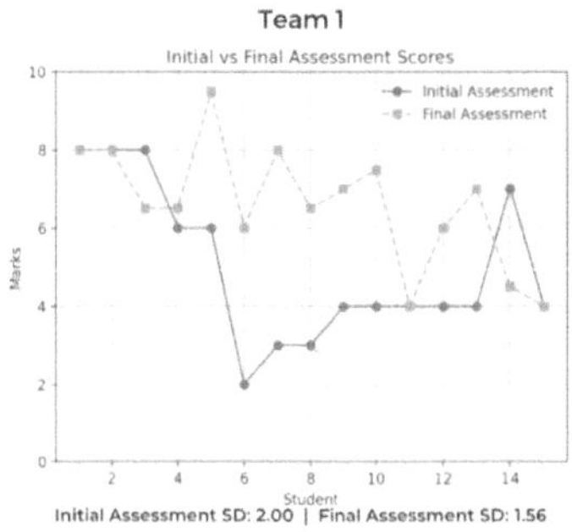

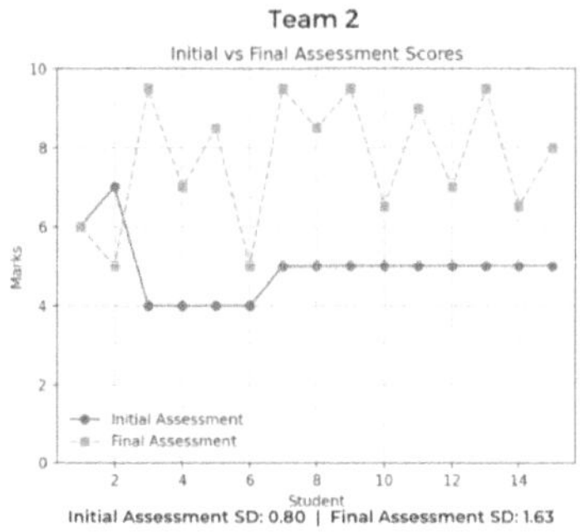

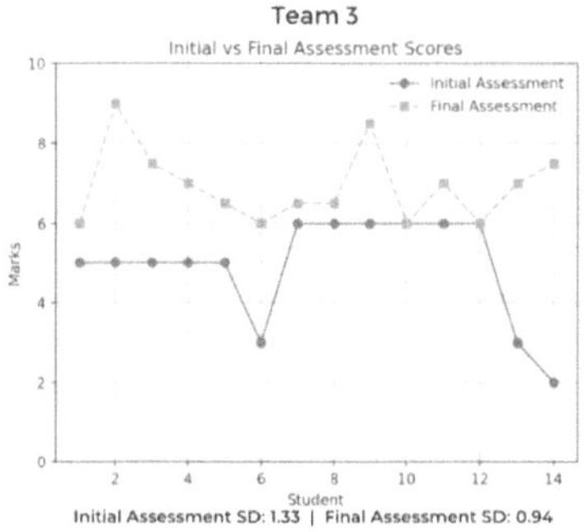

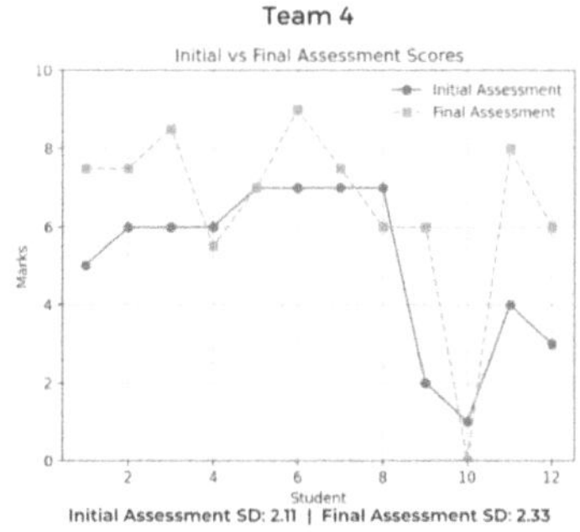

3.2 Group-Wise Performance

Following the intervention phase, students completed post-intervention assignments that assessed their ability to apply recursion principles. The assignments were designed to evaluate various aspects of students' learning outcomes, including:

Correctness: The accuracy of recursive solutions implemented in programming tasks.

Efficiency: The effectiveness and optimization of recursive algorithms in solving computational problems.

Understanding: The depth of comprehension demonstrated in problem-solving approaches and recursive strategy application.

The results of the assignments revealed varying degrees of improvement among the groups, reflecting the relative effectiveness of different teaching methods in enhancing students' understanding and application of recursion (Chakravarty & Keller, 2004).

3.2.1 Group 1

Showed moderate improvement in assignment scores. Students demonstrated proficiency in understanding theoretical concepts and implementing recursive algorithms based on traditional instructional methods (Hughes, 2008).

3.2.2 Group 2

Demonstrated substantial improvement in assignment performance. The hands-on approach of physical activities engaged students actively in recursive processes, facilitating a deeper understanding through kinesthetic learning experiences, and appeared to enhance students' grasp of recursion by reinforcing abstract concepts through tangible experiences.

3.2.3 Group 3

Demonstrated substantial improvement in assignment scores. The interactive and visual learning environment provided by tools like the Recursion Creator facilitated deeper understanding and experimentation with recursive algorithms, leading to enhanced learning outcomes.

3.2.4 Group 4

Showed some improvement in assignment performance, but it was not as much as the other 3 methods. Engaging in problem-solving tasks like the Tower of Hanoi puzzle may have encouraged students to apply recursive strategies effectively in practical scenarios, thereby consolidating their recursive problem-solving skills.

The comparative analysis of the teaching methods used in this study provides valuable insights into their effectiveness in enhancing students' understanding of recursion. Each method—traditional lecture-based teaching, physical activities, educational tools, and problem-based learning—was assessed based on their impact on assessment results and assignment performance.

4 Threats to Validity

While this study provides valuable insights, it is important to acknowledge its limitations and suggest areas for future research:

Sample Size and Generalizability. The study involved a specific cohort of freshman students from a single institution. The high group-SD variability indicates this. Future research should expand the sample size and include participants from different educational backgrounds to enhance the generalizability of the findings.

Long-Term Impact. Assessing the long-term retention of recursion concepts beyond the immediate post-intervention period could provide insights into the sustainability of learning outcomes over time.

Qualitative Insights. In-depth qualitative research should delve deeper into students' perceptions and experiences with different teaching methods to uncover additional factors influencing learning effectiveness.

5 Conclusion

This study provides comprehensive insights into the efficacy of various teaching methodologies in enhancing student understanding of recursion. By carefully designing an experiment with four distinct experimental groups, we evaluated both traditional lecture-based - Group1 and innovative interactive approaches (including Physical Activities - Group 2, Recursion Creator - Group 3, and Tower of Hanoi Problem Solving - Group 4) to teaching recursion. The results, quantified through the total net change in assignment marks and supported by statistical analysis, demonstrate that recursion creator and physical activities significantly improve student performance and engagement compared to conventional methods.

What worked and why?

We observed a clear advantage to Physical Activity and Recursions Creator, in terms of average improvement from the pre- to post-test of 70% and 25% greater than the control group. We hypothesize that these activities created the greatest engagement with the material due to the active learning style. In the future, we propose to use qualitative methods, e.g., interviews and focus groups, to report on differences in students' experiences of these activities. Why do we think the Tower of Hanoi wasn't as effective? We hypothesize that Tower of Hanoi wasn't as effective because the scope for trial and error and open-ended exploration was much less than with the Recursion Creator. In the Recursion Creator, students could adjust floating-point values and immediately visualize the entire recursion, with optional labeling of the generations. In contrast, the Tower of Hanoi simulator provided feedback on one step at a time, making it more of a visualization and demonstration tool rather than an exploration tool like the Recursion Creator.

Importantly, the learning expectation for these first-year students is centered on understanding and creating recursive functions, while the analysis of their complexity is reserved for the second-year data structures course. As part of our current next plan, we are actively working on developing methods to test and identify the most effective approaches for our students, contributing to a collective advancement in engineering education. Institutions are invited to join us in this effort, fostering a shared commitment to enhancing student learning outcomes.

To encourage other educational institutions to adapt, and evaluate these activities, we have made all the slides, videos, questions, and links to the tools that were used by us in the research, available in a publicly accessible GitHub repository (https://github.com/arey-pranay/UnravellingRecursion_StudyMaterials). By sharing our findings and materials, we hope to inspire a collaborative effort to improve the teaching of recursion and other computer science concepts across various educational contexts.

References

Velazquez-Iturbide, J.A.: Recursion in gradual steps (is recursion really that difficult?). In: Proceedings of the Thirty-First SIGCSE Technical Symposium on Computer Science Education, pp. 310–314, March 2000. https://doi.org/10.1145/330908.331876

Poletiek, F.H., Conway, C.M., Ellefson, M.R., Lai, J., Bocanegra, B.R., Christiansen, M.H.: Under what conditions can recursion be learned? Effects of starting small in artificial grammar learning of center-embedded structure. Cogn. Sci. **42**(8), 2855–2889 (2018). https://doi.org/10.1111/cogs.12685

Malmqvist, J., Hellberg, K., Möllås, G., Rose, R., Shevlin, M.: Conducting the pilot study: a neglected part of the research process? Methodological findings supporting the importance of piloting in qualitative research studies. Int. J. Qual. Methods **18** (2019).https://doi.org/10.1177/1609406919878341

Rinderknecht, C.: A survey on teaching and learning recursive programming. Inform. Educ. **13**(1), 87–119 (2014). https://doi.org/10.15388/infedu.2014.06

Kuokkanen, J., Gutierrez, D., Snellman, J.E., Romar, J.E.: Integrating movement and physical education into subject teaching: learning by moving. In: Developing a Didactic Framework Across and Beyond School Subjects, pp. 74–86. Routledge (2024). https://doi.org/10.4324/9781003367260-9

Stern, L., Naish, L.: Visual representations for recursive algorithms. ACM SIGCSE Bull. **34**(1), 196–200 (2002). https://doi.org/10.1145/563340.563414

Honrales, C.C.: Improving solving problem ability with tower of Hanoi puzzle. Solid State Technol. **63**(2s) (2020)

Scholtz, T.L., Sanders, I.: Mental models of recursion: investigating students' understanding of recursion. In: Proceedings of the Fifteenth Annual Conference on Innovation and Technology in Computer Science Education, pp. 103–107, June 2010. https://doi.org/10.1145/1822090.1822120

Acosta Gutiérrez, G.V., Pérez García, A.S., Ildefonso Medina, A.E.: The effects of an educational video game on elementary school students' engagement and motivation in pre Inca cultures learning. In: Rocha, Á., Adeli, H., Dzemyda, G., Moreira, F., Ramalho Correia, A.M. (eds.) WorldCIST 2021. AISC, vol. 1367, pp. 92–102. Springer, Cham (2021). https://doi.org/10.1007/978-3-030-72660-7_10

Bevinakoppa, S., Ray, B., Sabrina, F.: Effectiveness of problem-based learning implementation. Int. J. Qual. Assur. Eng. Technol. Educ. (IJQAETE) **5**(3), 46–58 (2016). https://doi.org/10.4018/IJQAETE.2016070104

Enhancing and Analyzing Log Generation for Collaborative Problem-Solving Activities: Video Analysis and OCR Techniques

Suprabha Jadhav[1(✉)], Parth Jain[2], Harjot Singh Raith[3], Kavi Arya[4], and Sridhar Iyer[1]

[1] Educational Technology, IIT Bombay, Mumbai, India
suprabhaj@iitb.ac.in
[2] Information Technology, Atharva College of Engineering, Malad, India
[3] Artificial Intelligence and Data Science, NMIMS, Navi Mumbai, Kharghar, India
[4] Computer Science and Engineering, IIT Bombay, Mumbai, India

Abstract. This study explores the use of video analysis and Optical Character Recognition (OCR) to generate accurate logs for tracking user search behaviors for external resources during collaborative problem-solving activities on the RoboReady educational platform. The research included 15 teams of engineering students who interacted with a website designed around the PISA 2015 collaborative problem-solving framework. Video recordings of the user's screens were analyzed using image processing and OCR to extract URLs and timestamps of visited web pages. The study compares these logs with those collected through server-side tracking, noting the limitations of the latter in capturing external resource usage. The methodology includes frame extraction, URL isolation, and text recognition using Tesseract OCR and Google Cloud Vision API. Challenges like noisy OCR output and the necessity for manual verification are addressed. The generated logs provide insights into user's navigation and resource usage. However, limitations such as video quality dependency, scalability issues, and the need for manual intervention are also discussed. This research enhances the understanding of user's behavior in online learning environments and offers methodological insights for studying digital learning interactions.

Keywords: Collaborative Problem-Solving · Educational Data Mining · Optical Character Recognition · Video Analysis · User Behavior Tracking

1 Introduction

User behavior logs provide crucial insights into educational platform usage, revealing study habits, content popularity, and engagement patterns. These insights can inform improvements in site structure, content delivery, and student support.

Pattern recognition advancements, particularly in Optical Character Recognition (OCR), have significantly improved document processing efficiency across various industries. With accuracy rates exceeding 99% for printed text, OCR technology has become widely adopted [5].

A. Karkare et al. (Eds.): COMPUTE 2024, CCIS 2400, pp. 135–143, 2025.
https://doi.org/10.1007/978-3-031-84391-4_11

Educational websites have evolved into interactive learning tools, offering personalized and flexible opportunities. Understanding user interactions with videos and content is crucial for predicting performance and improving educational outcomes [1]. Advanced analytics of video and text resources can inform content development, platform optimization, and teaching methods. The growing popularity of free and paid educational platforms provides opportunities to identify best practices for enhancing online learning experiences through comparative analysis [2]. This research aims to understand the role of educational websites in modern education and how data analytics can improve their effectiveness. It continues a previous study [9] that focused on fostering teams' problem-solving skills, with the current study emphasizing collaborative problem-solving skills.

2 Literature Review

In [1], student interactions with video sequences were analyzed from 66 students in a C++ Moodle course, examining 7,423 clicks. K-Nearest Neighbors (KNN) and Multilayer Perceptron (MLP) algorithms were used, achieving 65.07% and 61.13% accuracy, respectively, showing that video interaction patterns can predict student performance. In [2], methods for improving educational video navigation were introduced, including a "Rollercoaster" timeline for visualizing navigation, an enhanced in-video search feature, and a video summarization method highlighting frequently viewed frames.

In [3], web mining techniques were applied to analyze web usage data from www.davkota.org, identifying key metrics like 23,669 hits and 935 unique IP addresses. [4] proposed a privacy-preserving method for mobile screen recordings with on-device event detection, preferred by users over server-based approaches. Meanwhile, [5] highlighted the importance of preprocessing techniques such as noise removal and skew correction in character recognition, improving real-time data extraction.

Methods for extracting visited domains from screen recordings were discussed in [6], utilizing techniques like frame extraction, template matching, and OCR. [7] introduced Web Historian, a Chrome extension for analyzing browsing history with visualization and deletion capabilities. Lastly, [8] explored using perceptual hashes, template matching, and OCR to detect UI events in screen recordings, though OCR accuracy posed challenges during transitions.

3 Methodology

A study was conducted using the 'RoboReady', an educational platform designed to fostered students Collaborative Problem-Solving (CPS) skills. The study had following research questions:

RQ1. How effective is the use of video analysis and OCR techniques in generating accurate log data for tracking undergraduate students' searches for external scaffolds during collaborative problem-solving activities?

RQ2. How can extracted log data be utilized to enhance the understanding of resource utilization during collaborative problem-solving activities?

3.1 Participants

The study involved a total of 15 teams comprising undergraduate students from various departments and years of study. Specifically, participants included students from the Electronics & Computer Engineering department in their second year, Computer and Computer Engineering departments across second and third years, as well as from MBA Tech (B Tech in Computer Engineering + MBA). Additionally, students from Mechanical, Electronics and Telecommunication (EXTC), and Computer Science departments, ranging from first year to third year, also participated. The diversity in departments and years of study provided a broad perspective for the research conducted. Each team comprised of 2–4 students.

3.2 Activity

Participants were required to navigate through a website structured around the PISA 2015 collaborative problem-solving framework [10]. Each stage of this framework included specific activities and quiz questions. To support these tasks, each stage featured a resources page containing various scaffolds, such as conceptual videos, worked examples, and relevant website links, supplemented by additional resources. Teams were tasked with completing activities, including quizzes using the provided scaffolds. With individual student consent, all interactions on the website were logged on the server, and their screens were recorded. This enabled the creation of user log files for analyzing [10] behavioral patterns during the activity.

The video recordings captured both the students' browser windows and live camera feeds. These recordings were analysed using Image Processing tools and Optical Character Recognition (OCR) to extract the URLs of the web pages visited and the corresponding timestamps whenever the screen content changed. This process provided a comprehensive log of teams' behaviour throughout the activity.

3.3 Log Data Collection

Structure of the Log Data. The log data structure, as illustrated in Fig. 1, consists of three main components: user_id, which serves as a unique identifier for each team and acts as the primary key; Page_description, representing the name of the website subsection being accessed; and Timestamp, indicating the date and time of access for a specific page section.

User_id	Page_description	Timestamp
714	Stage 3: Activity	02-03-2024 01:55
723	RoboReady	02-03-2024 02:11
724	RoboReady Website	02-03-2024 02:12
725	Stage 2: Resources	02-03-2024 02:14
727	Stage 4: Activity	02-03-2024 02:14

Fig. 1. Sample server log data

Data Cleaning. To enhance data quality, three main steps were implemented: sorting the data by user_id to facilitate systematic analysis, renaming extracted URLs to their corresponding page titles, and calculating dwell_time by determining the differences between consecutive timestamps.

Limitations. The server-based log collection process has several limitations that affect analysis accuracy: incomplete data collection, as only interactions within the website were captured, the use of external resources, such as Google, YouTube, and AI tools, which were not recorded by the server; and the impact on data accuracy, as the use of external resources introduces significant variance in the calculated engagement time, leading to an underestimation of the actual time spent on activities.

3.4 Generating User Activity Logs from Video Recordings

To overcome server-based log collection constraints, we analyzed video recordings to obtain log data, enabling understanding of external scaffold usage. Figure 2 outlines the workflow: frame extraction, URL extraction, OCR processing, and data cleaning.

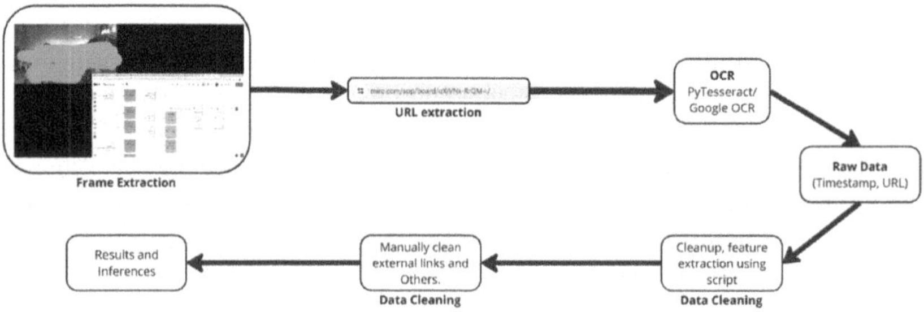

Fig. 2. Log generation process

Data Collection Process. Log file creation from video recordings employed Python libraries, including OpenCV (cv2), NumPy, and Tesseract (Pytesseract), or alternatively, Google Cloud Vision API for OCR. Frames were extracted every second, and those with a mean squared error (MSE) exceeding a threshold of 20 compared to the previous frame underwent further processing, with this threshold determined experimentally. URLs were isolated by identifying the URL bar coordinates using either template matching [6] or manual extraction if the position remained consistent. Preprocessing steps [5], such as grayscale conversion, upscaling, dilation, and sharpening, were applied to enhance OCR accuracy. For text extraction, Tesseract OCR (configured with --psm 6) performed well with high-quality images, while Google Cloud Vision API offered superior accuracy for lower-quality frames, albeit at a higher cost.

Data Cleaning. The procedures generated CSV log files with timestamp and URL columns for each video, though URL accuracy was often compromised due to poor video quality. To address this, we implemented several data cleaning steps. We first discarded redundant data by eliminating consecutive rows with identical URLs and empty URL rows. Next, we matched extracted URLs against a compiled list of known websites and scaffold URLs using the Levenshtein distance metric [11], creating a 'cleaned_url' column. We then categorized known URLs into subtopic lists and matched cleaned URLs against these, creating a 'sub_topic' column with detailed resource information. For external searches, we used the urllib library to parse noisy URLs, extract query parameters, and identify user search inputs. We cleaned these inputs and employed the Llama3-70b LLM to refine and infer likely search terms. Finally, for instances where OCR failed to provide clear URLs, we performed manual verification by reviewing video timestamps and populating remaining fields.

Figure 3 illustrates the keyword extraction process and compares OCR technique accuracy.

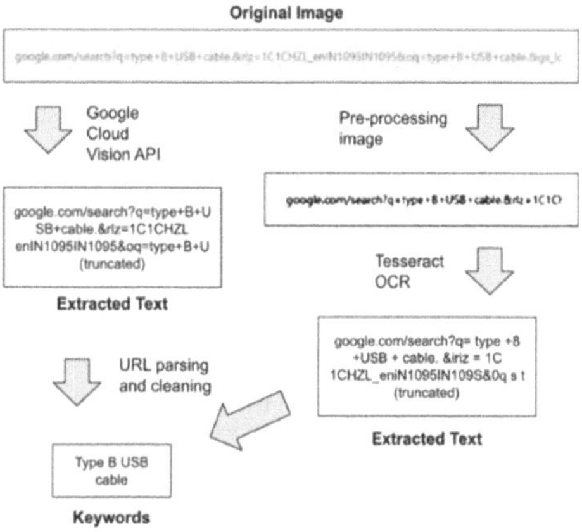

Fig. 3. Example process of keyword extraction

4 Results and Discussions

4.1 Addressing RQ1

The method in this study captured both on-platform activities and external searches, offering deeper insights than server logs alone. By integrating video analysis and OCR, it generated comprehensive logs reflecting a full range of student interactions, including external resources. This provided a more accurate representation of student behavior during collaborative problem-solving on the RoboReady platform.

As shown in Fig. 4, the integration of video analysis and OCR techniques captured detailed records of student activities, including searches for external resources. The log data identifies accessed resources and provides contextual information regarding the timing and nature of these interactions.

Each entry in the log encompasses the key components detailed in Table 1.

user_id	time(in sec)	page	class	cleaned_page	sub_topic	keywords	cleaned_k	page_desc	timestamp	dwell_time
108	4966	robo.personalt	robo	https://robo.personaltutoring.in/resources				Stage 1: Activity	0 days 01:22:46	5
108	4971	docs.google.co	Stage 1: Ac	https://docs.google.com/forms/d/e/1FAIpQLSfBy-hhv	Stage 1: Forms			Stage 1: Activity	0 days 01:22:51	3
108	4974	robo.personalt	robo	https://robo.personaltutoring.in/resources				Stage 1: Activity	0 days 01:22:54	205
108	5179	drive.google.co	Stage 2: Re	https://drive.google.com/file/d/1X0j0vlH6vfGDADcfig	Stage 2: Concept Map			Stage 2: Resources	0 days 01:26:19	170
108	5349	robo.personalt	robo	https://robo.personaltutoring.in/task-stage-2				Stage 2: Resources	0 days 01:29:09	7
108	5356	images.edrawn	Stage 2: Re	https://images.edrawmind.com/templates/cell-conce	Stage 2: Concept Map			Stage 2: Resources	0 days 01:29:16	33
108	5389	robo.personalt	robo	https://robo.personaltutoring.in/task-stage-2				Stage 2: Resources	0 days 01:29:49	4
108	5393	researchgate.n	Stage 2: Re	https://www.researchgate.net/profile/Camila-Cicuto/	Stage 2: Concept Map			Stage 2: Resources	0 days 01:29:53	80

Fig. 4. Sample log data generated from the video recordings

Table 1. Structure of the log data generated using video recordings

Column name	Description
time	Timestamp in seconds
url	Raw URL, extracted using OCR
class	Rough categorization of the data
cleaned_url	Cleaned URL for known webpages
sub_topic	The description for links provided within the website
keywords	Noisy keywords extracted from the URL
cleaned_keywords	Cleaned keywords generated using an LLM
page_desc	Readable title for the known webpages
time_in_minutes	Human readable timestamps
dwell_time	The time spent on the current page

4.2 Addressing RQ2

This comprehensive log data provides valuable insights into student engagement and resource utilization, aiding in the improvement of educational practices and resource design. It supports the creation of detailed process models and dwell time analysis, offering a nuanced understanding of student activity. Process models depict the sequence and flow of actions, while dwell time graphs show the duration spent on specific tasks. Figure 5 presents a sample process model for all teams. In this process model, the numbers on the nodes indicate the frequency of visits to each page, while the numbers on the arcs represent the frequency of transitions between pages. This quantification helps identify popular pages and common navigation patterns among students.

These process models can provide several insights:

- Engagement Pattern Analysis: The models highlight common sequences followed by students, revealing preferred engagement methods. In Fig. 5, the sequential structure suggests students generally accessed pages in the intended order.
- Resource Utilization: As illustrated in Fig. 5, the 'Stage 2: Resources' page was frequently accessed alongside 'Stage 2: Activity,' with longer dwell times indicating that students found these resources relevant. However, further analysis is needed to assess their effectiveness in supporting learning outcomes.

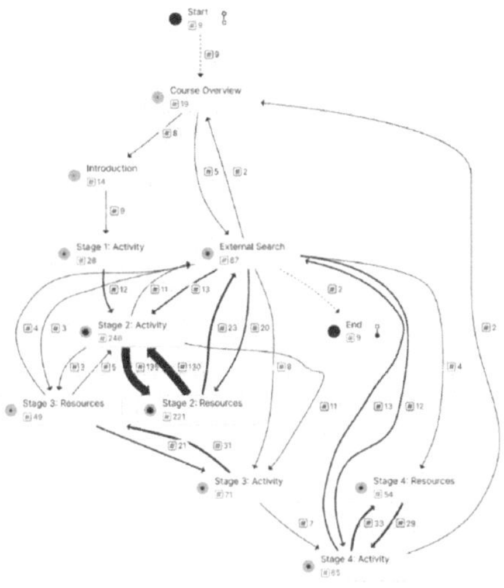

Fig. 5. Combined process model of all the teams

- External Resource Integration: Tracking external searches offers insights into additional information students seek, which can inform improvements to existing resources or the integration of commonly searched external content into the platform.

4.3 Educational Implications

The integration of video analysis and OCR for log generation has significant implications for computing education, particularly in enhancing learning analytics and supporting more effective problem-solving approaches. For example, analyzing search behaviors and resource use during debugging or algorithm design tasks can provide valuable insights into students' learning processes and strategies.

In collaborative learning environments, such as team-based coding or software development projects, this approach can offer deeper understanding of group dynamics and how students engage with external resources like coding forums or documentation repositories. Educators can identify patterns that suggest over-reliance on external tools, signalling potential gaps in foundational knowledge that may need to be addressed through curriculum adjustments or targeted interventions.

Moreover, the data generated through this method can be integrated into automated feedback systems, enabling real-time guidance for students as they engage with computational tasks. Additionally, such data can inform predictive algorithms that flag students who may be at risk of underperforming, allowing for timely interventions in both in-person and online learning environments.

5 Limitations

While our method provides rich interaction data, frequency of access alone doesn't necessarily indicate engagement quality or learning outcomes. Future research could combine this log data with qualitative assessments for a more comprehensive understanding of the learning process in computing education.

Scalability is a limitation, as this data collection method is feasible only for smaller sample sizes. For larger-scale implementations, browser extensions like Web Historian could be used, though they can't provide information about behavior within webpages.

Video quality significantly affects OCR accuracy, with lower quality compromising log data. While Google Cloud Vision API improved performance, it's a paid service. Open-source alternatives like Tesseract could be considered for cost-effectiveness.

6 Conclusion and Future Work

In conclusion, the use of Optical Character Recognition (OCR) combined with process models and data analysis techniques provides a powerful approach to understanding and enhancing educational systems. Our approach provides a more nuanced understanding of resource utilization and learning patterns than traditional server logs alone.

Future research will focus on enhancing data collection methods, interaction techniques, and analysis for improved understanding and usability of digital platforms. Expanding our current project, which uses OCR methods to extract log data from video recordings, we aim to support multiple browsers and mobile devices through new extensions and applications. Ethical data collection practices will be prioritized by allowing participants to review and selectively delete sensitive data before submission, while advanced filtering algorithms will enhance data accuracy. Web usage mining techniques will be applied to analyze metrics like hits, page views, and visitor patterns, providing insights for improving website usability and design. By integrating these advanced techniques, our research will contribute to a comprehensive and ethical understanding of user behavior, promoting the development of user-centric digital platforms.

Acknowledgments. The authors express their gratitude to the participants who took part in the study and provided us with valuable feedback. This study was conducted in the e-Yantra Lab, a project funded by the Ministry of Education (MoE).

Disclosure of Interests. The authors have no competing interests to declare that are relevant to the content of this article.

References

1. El Aouifi, H., El Hajji, M., Es-Saady, Y., Douzi, H.: Predicting learner's performance through video sequences viewing behavior analysis using educational data-mining. Educ. Inf. Technol. (2021)

2. Kim, J., Guo, P.J., Cai, C.J., Li, S.W., Gajos, K.Z., Miller, R.C.: Data-driven interaction techniques for improving navigation of educational videos. In: Proceedings of the 27th Annual ACM Symposium on User Interface Software and Technology, pp. 563–572 (2014)
3. Sharma, A.K., Gupta, P.C., Kota, R.I.: Identifying the number of visitors to improve website usability from educational institution web log data. Int. J. Comput. Appl. Technol. Res. **2**(1), 22–26 (2012)
4. Krieter, P.: Can I record your screen? Mobile screen recordings as a long-term data source for user studies. In: Proceedings of the 18th International Conference on Mobile and Ubiquitous Multimedia, pp. 1–10 (2019)
5. Alginahi, Y.: Preprocessing techniques in character recognition. Character Recognit. **1**, 1–19 (2010)
6. Heidarysafa, M., Reed, J., Kowsari, K., Leviton, A.C.R., Warren, J.I., Brown, D.E.: From videos to urls: a multi-browser guide to extract user's behavior with optical character recognition. In: Advances in Computer Vision: Proceedings of the 2019 Computer Vision Conference (CVC), vol. 1, no. 1, pp. 503–514. Springer International Publishing (2020)
7. Menchen-Trevino, E.: Web historian: enabling multi-method and independent research with real-world web browsing history data. In: IConference 2016 Proceedings (2016)
8. Krieter, P., Breiter, A.: Analyzing mobile application usage: generating log files from mobile screen recordings. In: Proceedings of the 20th International Conference on Human-Computer Interaction with Mobile Devices and Services, pp. 1–10 (2018)
9. Jadhav, S., Iyer, S., Arya, K.: Enhancing problem-solving in robotics education: analysis of scaffolds and interactions. In: 2024 IEEE International Conference on Advanced Learning Technologies (ICALT), pp. 121–123. Nicosia, North Cyprus, Cyprus, 2024 (2024)
10. OECD: PISA 2015 collaborative problem-solving framework, in PISA 2015 Assessment and Analytical Framework: Science, Reading, Mathematic, Financial Literacy and Collaborative Problem Solving, OECD Publishing, Paris (2017)
11. Po, D.K.: Similarity based information retrieval using Levenshtein distance algorithm. Int. J. Adv. Sci. Res. Eng. **6**(04), 06–10 (2020)

Beyond CS1: Computing Education Research in Upper Level Courses

Identifying the Root Cause of a Cyber Attack Through Log Data Analysis: An Overview of the Challenges Faced by Novice Learners

Priya V. Nagvekar, Syaamantak Das(✉), and Sridhar Iyer

Centre for Educational Technology, Indian Institute of Technology Bombay, Mumbai, India
{priyalotlikar,syaamantak.das,sri}@iitb.ac.in

Abstract. Cyber security has become a critical concern in today's digital age, and log data analysis plays a pivotal role in investigating the root causes of cyber attacks. However, the teaching and learning of the log data analysis process is intricate, especially in root cause analysis (RCA), necessitating diverse domains of expertise and background knowledge. This study addresses a significant research gap in the existing literature by a comparative analysis of cyber attack RCA performed by novices and experts through log data analysis. The study design process initially involved novices with limited cyber security experience (senior undergraduate Computer Science students) performing a log data analysis of a cyber attack, followed by industry professionals (subject matter experts) performing the same log data analysis. In the research, the participants identified the root causes of a cyber attack through log data analysis, culminating in generating an attack tree as an outcome. The objective was to assess novices' ability to identify and deduce the root causes of cyber attacks from log data and generate a comprehensive attack tree through causal reasoning. The follow-up observation and reflections were supplemented by artefact analysis and simulated recall interviews. The study's findings shed light on the disparities in log data analysis skills between novices and subject matter experts. It reveals novices' key challenges compared to experts and the nature of novices' difficulties. The results of this research also offer valuable insights into the industry practices of log data analysis by experts and their advice contributing to developing more effective teaching-learning methodologies for cyber security education.

Keywords: cyber security · log data analysis · novice vs expert · root cause analysis

1 Introduction

Cyber security has become a critical concern in today's digital age, as cyber-attacks pose severe threats to individuals, businesses, and national security.

A. Karkare et al. (Eds.): COMPUTE 2024, CCIS 2400, pp. 147–160, 2025.
https://doi.org/10.1007/978-3-031-84391-4_12

Effective incident response and root cause analysis (RCA) of cyber-attacks are crucial for mitigating their impact and preventing future occurrences. RCA involves investigating the underlying causes of a security breach and identifying vulnerabilities that enabled the attack. However, performing RCA is a complex task that requires diverse domains of expertise and background knowledge, making it challenging for novice learners in cyber security. This study addresses a significant research gap by analyzing the differences between novice learners and industry professionals (subject matter experts) in performing RCA of cyber attacks using log data analysis. The primary objective is to assess novices' ability to identify and deduce the root causes of cyber attacks from log data and generate comprehensive attack trees through causal reasoning.

While there is a substantial body of literature on RCA methods and techniques, there is a lack of comparative evidence on the processes followed by experts and the specific challenges faced by novices in this domain. Understanding these differences is crucial for developing effective teaching-learning methodologies and bridging the gap between novice and expert performance in cybersecurity education. The study focuses on the following research question:

What are the various challenges and difficulties encountered by novice learners when undertaking the task of performing RCA?

To address these research questions, the study employs a mixed-methods approach. Novice participants (senior undergraduate Computer Science students) and industry professionals analyze simulated cyber attack log data using RCA methods such as the 5 Whys, fault tree analysis, fishbone diagrams, and attack tree creation. Observations, reflections, artefact analysis, and simulated recall interviews are used to collect both quantitative and qualitative data, providing insights into the decision-making processes and challenges faced by novices and experts. By identifying the root causes of the difficulties faced by novice learners and contrasting their approaches with those of experts, this study contributes to the ongoing efforts to enhance cybersecurity education and practice.

This paper is organized as follows: Sect. 2 briefly describes the existing literature and how the work connects to the skills of RCA. Section 3 details the design of the study, participants, resources used and experimental phases. Our findings are presented and discussed in Sects. 4 and 5 while highlighting various challenges faced by novices and industry experts' opinions, including the limitations involved with the study in subsections. The paper is concluded in Sect. 6.

1.1 Problem Background: Log Data Analysis Techniques for RCA

Performing vulnerability assessment through RCA is a crucial step in incident response after a cyber attack. RCA involves systematically investigating the underlying causes of a security breach to identify vulnerabilities and develop mitigation strategies [18]. In a rapidly evolving cybersecurity environment, a multifaceted approach to analyzing cyberattacks is critical to understanding their nature, origin, and potential impact. This study uses a comprehensive set of analytical tools to analyze and interpret cyber attack data, including reading log files, the 5 Whys technique, fault tree analysis, fishbone diagrams, and attack trees. The following methods show how log data can be used for RCA.

- **Log file reading (Identifying tags):** It involves examining detailed records of system events focusing on key elements such as UserID, URLs, requests, responses, timestamps and duration. This method helps in identifying patterns and anomalies associated with cyber attacks [24].
- **5 Whys Technique:** It is a root cause analysis technique that involves repeatedly asking "why" questions to dig deeper into the root cause of a problem. In cyber security, this helps uncover the underlying reasons for an attack and go beyond the surface-level symptoms to identify key vulnerabilities [25].
- **Fault Tree:** Constructing a fault tree for a scenario is a deductive failure analysis method. It helps to visualize the logical combinations of different factors that could result in a successful attack [26].
- **Fishbone Diagram:** Also known as the Ishikawa diagram, is a cause-effect diagram that helps in identifying potential causes for a problem. In cyber security, it can be used to categorize and analyze various factors that contribute to security breaches, such as environmental factors, people, technology and processes [27].
- **Attack Tree:** It is a conceptual diagram that shows how an asset can be attacked through various routes. Starting with the target as the root node, the tree branches out to show different ways as attacker can reach the target, which helps in threat modeling and risk assessment [28].

Various frameworks, such as NIST SP 800-61, the SANS Incident Handling Process, and ISO/IEC 27035 [35], provide guidelines for conducting RCA and analyzing log data to determine the appropriate response.

2 Literature Review

While the importance of RCA in cyber security is well-established, the existing literature primarily focuses on the technical aspects and methodologies involved. However, there is a lack of research exploring the challenges faced by novice learners in acquiring and applying these skills effectively. Most studies in this domain concentrate on expert practitioners' perspectives and industry best practices [14,23,36], overlooking the unique difficulties encountered by novices during their learning journey.

Several studies have investigated the differences between novice and expert performance in cybersecurity-related tasks. For instance, Silva et al. [34] examined expert and novice performance within computer security incident response teams, while Koutcheme et al. [21] explored how students solve open-ended assignments in SQL injection. However, these studies do not specifically address the challenges faced by novices in performing RCA using log data analysis, which is a critical component of incident response and vulnerability assessment.

While the literature acknowledges that log analysis is an essential part of RCA [35], there is a lack of research investigating the specific difficulties novice learners encounter when analyzing log data to identify root causes. A study was done by Scheponik et al. [36] where they interviewed 26 learners on cyber security concepts. Related similar cyber security studies were the work of Silva et.al [34] which focused on Expert-Novice performance in cyber security incidence response and the study by Koutcheme et al. [21] which explored how students solve open-ended assignments in SQL injection. Most existing studies focus on technical aspects, such as log analysis tools [1,23] or machine learning techniques [4], rather than the cognitive and pedagogical challenges faced by novices in this domain. Additionally, the literature lacks a comparative analysis of the approaches and strategies employed by experts and novices when performing RCA using non-technical methods, such as the 5 Whys, fishbone diagrams, fault tree analysis, and attack tree creation. While these methods are often recommended for novice learners [12,14,22], there is limited empirical evidence on the specific challenges encountered by novices in applying these techniques and the differences in approaches compared to experts.

Addressing this research gap is crucial for developing effective teaching-learning methodologies and interventions to bridge the gap between novice and expert performance in cybersecurity education. By identifying the root causes of the difficulties faced by novice learners and contrasting their approaches with those of experts, this study aims to provide valuable insights for enhancing introductory-level cyber security education, particularly in the context of log data analysis and RCA.

3 Study Design

In order to address the research questions, it was suggested to utilize a mixed-methods approach [6]. The study process involves several stages: Stage 1 includes providing log data of cyber attacks to both novice students and industry experts. Stage 2 consists of an orientation session, detailing the specific instructions for student participants (novices) and industry experts, respectively. Following the orientation, Stage 3 involves analyzing log data using the 5 why method, identifying and creating the fault tree, also focusing on constructing a fishbone model by identifying all potential causes, and developing an attack tree to identify the root cause of the attack. The process was followed by stage 4 - observations and reflections by the participants which were supplemented by artefact analysis [34] and a simulated recall survey [7]. Figure 1 shows the entire study design process.

For this study, the quantitative data is collected through the log data analysis and the fishbone and attack tree models, while the qualitative data is collected through observations, reflections, artefact analysis, and simulated recall interviews. The 5 Why method and fault tree analysis are quantitative techniques that help to identify the root cause of the attack. The fishbone model and attack tree are visual tools that help to organize and analyze the data. The observations and reflections of the participants provide qualitative insights into the decision-making process and the effectiveness of the techniques used. The artefact analysis and simulated recall interviews validate the findings and provide additional insights into the participants' experiences and perspectives.

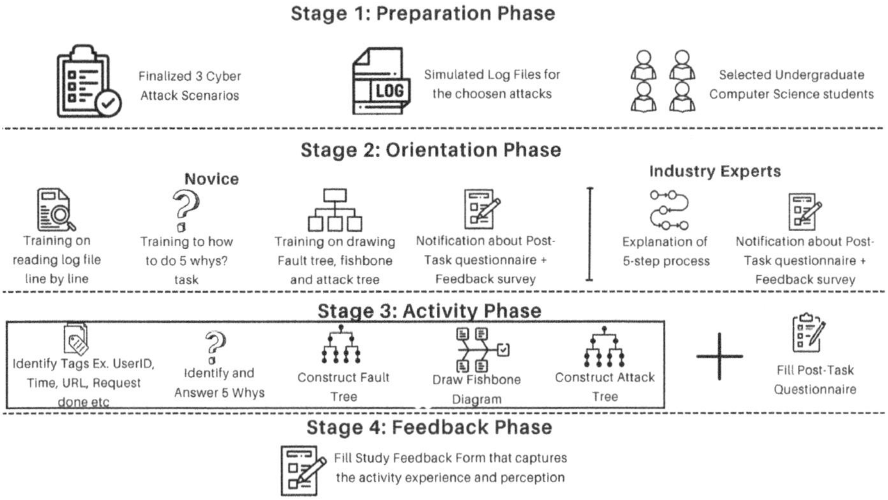

Fig. 1. Study design process

3.1 Datasets and Resource Material

To ensure a fair assessment of expertise, participants were required to have completed standard undergraduate-level Computer Science Network courses (semester subjects) as a prerequisite. This baseline knowledge was deemed essential for all participants. The study included a diverse group of Indian students, categorized as follows in Table 1. This breakdown of participants allows for a comparison between novice and expert approaches to cyber attack log analysis.

Table 1. Participant Profile.

Participant Type	Gender	Age Range	No.
Novice	Male	21–24	17
Novice	Female	21–24	7
Expert	Male	35–40	3

3.2 Sample Log Data

Below is a sample log file of a simulated DoS attack:

```
Timestamp: 2023-11-05T13:03:12-08:00
IP Address: 192.168.1.100
User Agent: "Mozilla/5.0(X11; Linux x86\_64)AppleWebKit/537.36
(KHTML, like Gecko) Chrome/107.0.0.0 Safari/537.36"
Request: GET /index.php HTTP/1.1
Response: 200 OK
```

This log file records a single HTTP request for the page index.php from the IP address 192.168.1.100. The response code is 200 OK, indicating a successful request.

Root Cause: The root cause of the DoS attack is the attacker flooding the server with numerous requests for the same page. This overloads the server, rendering it inaccessible to other users.

The following logfile parameters help determine the root cause of the DoS attack:

- **Timestamp:** Shows when the request was received.
- **IP Address:** Identifies the attacker's location.
- **User Agent:** Reveals the browser and operating system the attacker is using i.e. tools being used.
- **Request:** Indicates the specific page the attacker is targeting, aiding in pinpointing the vulnerability being exploited.
- **Response:** The HTTP response code 200 OK suggests that the attacker successfully exploited the vulnerability.

Analysis of web server log files can reveal patterns indicative of Denial of Service (DoS) attacks, distinguishing them from regular web traffic. In this study, we examined log data from an experimental setup designed to demonstrate DoS attack patterns to students. The logs exhibited several key characteristics consistent with a DoS attack: high-frequency requests from a single IP address, with multiple identical GET requests targeting the same URL and using the same user agent, all occurring within seconds. Notably, these requests consistently resulted in 499 status codes, suggesting the server's inability to process the high volume or potentially invalid nature of the requests. The uniformity of these requests—identical IP, URL, and user agent—maintained over an extended period, as evidenced by the broader dataset, serves as a significant indicator of malicious activity. While log files do not inherently differentiate between regular access and DoS attacks, the presence of these patterns provides strong evidence for distinguishing between benign traffic and potential security threats.

3.3 Experiment Phase

Phase 1: Pilot Study Phase. This study was conducted as a proof of concept, to get better clarity on various aspects of complexity that a student might face while doing the activity. It was an open resource study, where participants were allowed to access the internet to seek help on certain concept explanations. However, they had to mention in their answer sheets wherever they used the internet for help mentioning the details. Approximately 120 min were given to a student to perform the entire activity.

- **Participants:** - 7 novices and 1 expert
- **Purpose:** - Face validity testing

- **Task:** - Participants were given log files of three distinct cyber attacks(SQL Injection, XSS, DoS) to identify the tentative root cause of an attack using the 5 Why method. They were also tasked with generating a Fault tree, preparing a fishbone model, and creating an Attack tree. This was followed by a post-task questionnaire to gather their observations and reflections. The questionnaire consisted of 9 open-ended questions based on the five methods performed and the challenges the participant faced while working with the 5 Why methods. For instance, *"What are the five whys you identified, and why did you choose those?"*, *"What Challenges did you encounter when using the 5 whys method and why?"*. Participants were needed to answer the questionnaire after every attack analysis, thus having 3 responses for all three attacks. Once the analysis task was completed, all the participants had to answer the feedback survey, which was designed to gather the various challenges faced while doing the activity using all 5 methods and their perspective on the entire RCA activity. The feedback form comprised of 16 choice-based and 1 open-ended questions.

Phase 2: Extensive Study Phase

- **Participants:** - 24 novices and 3 experts
- **Task:** - Similar to Phase 1, participants were asked to identify the root cause of an attack using the 5 Why method, generate a Fault tree, prepare a fishbone model, and create an Attack tree. However, this phase included structured questions for each method. There were two sets of questions: Question Set 1 focused on the procedural aspects of the task, for e.g. *"What were the 5 Whys you identified, and why did you choose those?"*; while Question Set 2 addressed the challenges and obstacles faced by the participants during task execution, regardless of the outcome. For e.g. *"What challenges did you encounter when using the 5 Whys method, and why?"*.

4 Data Analysis and Result

4.1 Methodology

The research methodology employed a mixed-methods approach, combining quantitative and qualitative analysis to investigate challenges faced by novice students in the cybersecurity domain. The data sources used for analysis included student and industry expert answer sheets, post-task questionnaire responses and post-study feedback responses from both student and industry experts. Initially, 4 teacher interviews were conducted to identify student challenges in cyber security problem analysis, which followed the approach suggested by Seidman [29]. These insights, along with a comprehensive literature review [30–32], informed the development of a set of categories and themes as shown in Table 2 capturing various challenges faced by students and teachers. This framework was then used as the basis for a deductive coding process on student and Industry experts' post-task questionnaires and feedback responses as outlined by Saldana

[33]. The deductive coding process aimed at identifying common categories and themes of challenges that students could encounter during the RCA process and also identifying the gap between novice and industry expert approaches for RCA. To identify challenges faced by novices while doing RCA, the following meta-analysis approaches were employed on the student answer sheets: 1) Structural Analysis: i) Examining the completeness of each diagram. ii) Evaluating the coherence and logical flow of the 5 whys responses. 2) Content analysis: i) Analyze the accuracy and relevance of identified causes and effects. ii) Evaluate the use of cyber security terminology and concepts. 3) Pattern identification: i) identify common mistakes or misunderstandings across artefacts. ii) Identifying gaps in knowledge. iii) Identify patterns of misinterpreted log data. 4) Time-based analysis: analyzing time spent on each method. 5) Thematic analysis: Identify recurring predefined themes and categories.

Table 2. An Overview of Challenges faced by Novices - Themes and Categories

Themes	Categories
Teaching Methods	Traditional Teaching methods, Practical Teaching
Learning Challenges	Knowledge Gap, Curriculum constraints, Teaching challenges
Pre-requisite Knowledge	Programming skills, OS understanding, CS foundations
Motivation	Interest and importance, Emerging career options, Passion for cyber security

4.2 Result

Time Duration Analysis for Each Attack. The distribution of time for experts was more consistent, as evidenced by the lower standard deviation (17.85) compared to novices (32.60). Both groups had a similar minimum time (15 min), indicating that the fastest individuals in each group solved problems at a comparable speed. Table 3 shows a comparison of the time taken for problem analysis between Novice and Experts.

Table 3. Comparison of Time taken for problem analysis between Novice and Experts

Metrics	Group	
	Novice	Experts
Mean(mins)	57.05	41.67
Standard Deviation(mins)	32.60	17.85
Min(mins)	15	15
Max(mins)	141	60
25th Percentile(mins)	35	25
50th Percentile (Median - mins)	45	45
75th Percentile(mins)	85	60

However, the maximum time for novices (141 min) was much higher than for experts (60 min), suggesting that some novices took considerably longer to solve problems. The median time for both groups was 45 min, indicating that half of all participants, regardless of their expertise, solved the problems within this time frame.

The first problem (SQL injection) proved to be the most time-consuming, with each student spending over an hour on it. However, the time required for subsequent attacks (XSS and DoS) showed a significant reduction, indicating a learning curve as participants became more familiar with the analytical methods.

5 Discussion

5.1 Challenges Faced by Novices

To seek answers to the given Research Question and get deeper insights into the challenges faced by novices while doing RCA using log files, the study analyzed the post-task questionnaire. The key findings of the meta-analysis on challenges faced by novice learners are as follows:

1. Difficulty in identifying the attack activities i.e. difficulty in understanding the meaning, which required additional effort to comprehend each line of the log file and the mode of attack.
2. Superficial Analysis: Stopping the analysis too early and not addressing deeper root causes. Not digging deep enough to uncover the root cause.
3. Assumption and Bias: Influence of preconceived notions or biases on the analysis.
4. Single-Cause Bias: Oversimplification of complex problems by attributing them to a single cause.
5. Lack of Cross-Functional Input: Narrow analysis due to not involving various other computer science concepts.
6. Not familiar with XSS-based malware attack. Almost 71% of students found this as a major challenge.
7. Complexity of the System: Difficult to capture all potential failure modes accurately in complex systems with numerous dependencies and interactions.
8. Assumption of Linear Causality: Oversimplification by assuming linear cause-and-effect relationships, potentially overlooking interconnected factors. This also shows a lack of critical thinking ability.
9. Inadequate Expertise: Lack of necessary expertise to conduct a thorough analysis.
10. Insufficient Information: Incomplete or ambiguous data due to limited access to information, complex systems, or lack of comprehensive documentation.

At the end of the study, the student also had to answer a feedback survey which was designed to gather their experience and perception about the RCA activity using log files. Based on the analysis of student responses, four main themes were identified: teaching challenges, knowledge gaps, curriculum constraints, and resource limitations. The findings reveal that teaching challenges were the most prominent issue, accounting for 43.9% of the responses. This was closely followed by knowledge gaps, which represented 39.0% of the feedback. Curriculum constraints were cited in 14.6% of the responses, indicating a less significant but still notable concern. Resource limitations appeared to be the least prevalent issue, mentioned in only 2.4% of the responses. Figure 2 demonstrates the graphical representation of the analysis. These results suggest that improvements in teaching methods and addressing students' knowledge deficits should be prioritized to enhance the effectiveness of log analysis activities also emphasizing the need for more orientation sessions on how to read and interpret log files, while curriculum adjustments and resource allocation may require attention but to a lesser extent.

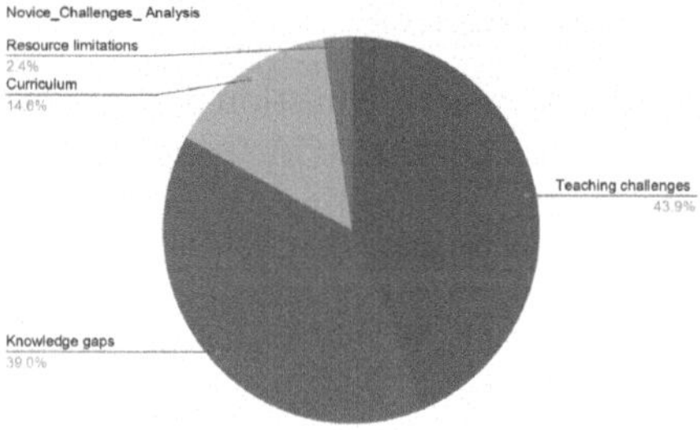

Fig. 2. Challenges faced by Novice learners

5.2 Analysis of Industry Experts Study

Based on the expert analysis, the methods for RCA of cyber attack i.e. 5 whys, fault tree, fishbone and attack tree, using log files each have their strengths and limitations. Common challenges across these 5 methods as mentioned by the experts in their responses include incomplete data resources, time constraints, and the need for deep technical knowledge. The analysis suggests that these methods can be subjective, potentially leading to biased interpretations. They also struggle to capture the full complexity of modern cyber attacks, which often involve multiple layers of technology and diverse techniques. The experts noted that creating comprehensive analyses is challenging without complete information, and that staying updated with emerging attack techniques is crucial. Based on the analysis of industry experts' responses to the post-activity feedback survey, several key themes emerged. The most significant issue identified was the lack of expertise, accounting for 15.6% of the responses. This was followed by three equally prominent themes: lack of foundational knowledge, log data analysis tools, and simulation demos, each representing 9.4% of the feedback. Several themes tied at 6.3% of responses, including cyber security upskilling, continuous learning, emerging challenges, introductory SIEM education, and real-world examples. Less frequently mentioned but still notable were themes such as infrastructure upgradation, curriculum enhancement, student growth and success, passion for cyber security, interest and importance, operating systems understanding, networking expertise, and cyber security foundations, each accounting for 3.1% of the responses. Figure 3 summarizes the analysis graphically. These findings suggest that while addressing the lack of expertise is crucial, a multi-faceted approach encompassing foundational knowledge, practical tools, and hands-on experience is necessary to improve log analysis education and training in the cyber security field.

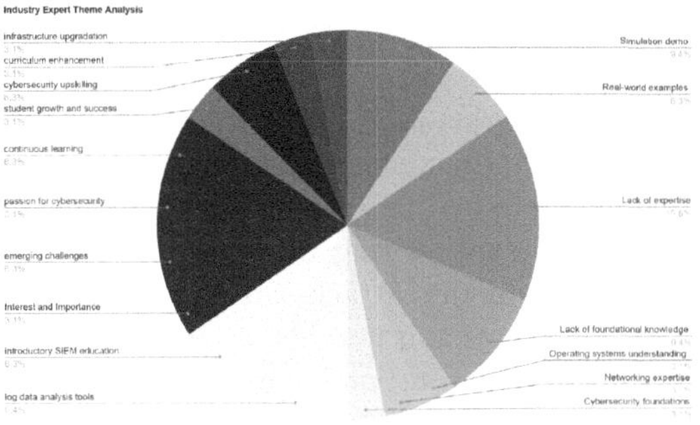

Fig. 3. Themes from industry expert analysis

Suggestions by Industry Experts. In response to the open-ended question in the feedback form *"What additional resources or support would help a novice better understand and apply these analysis methods to cyber attacks?"*, the following themes emerged:

1. Use of tools in classroom - experts recommend teaching tools like machine learning techniques [37], and SIEM tools [1,23] to analyze log data.
2. Inclusion of log analysis in the curriculum - experts proposed revising the digital forensics curriculum to include data analysis.
3. Experts also suggest More practices and case studies with log data.

5.3 Takeaway for the Computer Science Education Community: Pedagogy Perspective

Novice learners face distinct challenges in cyber security problem solving compared to experts. The analysis reveals the following pedagogical factors:

1. Lack of Foundational Knowledge: The pieces of evidence indicate a significant gap in basic cyber security knowledge among novice learners, which hinders their ability to tackle complex problems effectively. The frequent mention of "*lack of theoretical knowledge*" in student responses, coupled with the industry perspective emphasizing the need for concept understanding in Networks and Data Communication, underscores the critical need for a stronger theoretical base in cyber security education.

2. Technical Complexity and Comprehension: Novice participants struggle with interpreting technical data, in particular the log files. This difficulty is evident from both students ("*Wasn't able to understand the URL so I used Chatgpt*")and industry ("*Difficulty in interpreting data*") responses. The fact that some students adopted tools like ChatGPT for understanding URLs suggests a need for more training sessions on how to read and interpret log files, as comprehending and analysing log data is fundamental in cyber security.
3. Methodology Implementation: The evidence shows that novices struggle with formulating appropriate "Why" questions and constructing logical flow charts ("*finding the proper questions starting from why was challenging.*", "*To link the questions that sequence wise explains the attack.*"). This indicates that while the students are taught about these methodologies, they need more practice and guidance in applying these methods to real-world scenarios.
4. Analytical Thoroughness: The analysis reveals that novices face difficulties in connecting events and synthesizing information into a coherent analysis. Given that cyber security issues/attacks are often interconnected, the challenge of synthesizing information is notable. As reported by the student, "*Cannot synthesize the attack information*", mandates the need for developing a more holistic view of cyber security scenarios.
5. Information Synthesis and Interpretation: Developing a comprehensive analytical model from sparse information is a skill that novices find challenging. The evidence of students being "*unable to create final output*" points out to a gap in their ability to make informed inferences and construct meaningful analyses from limited data resources. In real-world cyber security attack scenarios, this skill is crucial where complete information is rarely available.

5.4 Limitations of the Study

The study has limitations due to the small size of the expert group, the use of simulated data, and insufficient training sessions for students. However, it provides valuable insights for cyber security education and suggests the need for further research to address challenges faced by novice learners. Future research could involve expanding the scope of participants from Indian undergraduate students to computer science students worldwide.

6 Conclusion

This research contributes in the quest to enhance cyber security education and practice through an in-depth analysis of novice challenges and industry expert insights. The study identifies the areas where novices face the most difficulties and highlights essential elements for effective log analysis.

The findings emphasize on the identification of key parameters for analyzing cyber attack log data. By addressing the cognitive biases and technical obstacles that novices encounter, this research also offers valuable guidance for educators and curriculum developers to enhance cybersecurity training programs.

References

1. Abbott, R.G., McClain, J., Anderson, B., Nauer, K., Silva, A., Forsythe, C.: Log analysis of cyber security training exercises. Procedia Manufacturing **3**(2015), 5088–5094 (2015)
2. Ahmad, A., Desouza, K.C., Maynard, S.B., Naseer, H., Baskerville, R.L.: How integration of cyber security management and incident response enables organizational learning. J. Assoc. Inf. Sci. Technol. **71**(8), 939–953 (2020)
3. Aldawood, H., Skinner, G.: Educating and raising awareness on cyber security social engineering: a literature review. In: 2018 IEEE International Conference on Teaching, Assessment, and Learning for Engineering (TALE), pp. 62–68. IEEE (2018)
4. Švábensky, V., Vykopal, J., Čeleda, P., Tkáčik, K., Popovič, D.: Student assessment in cybersecurity training automated by pattern mining and clustering. Educ. Inf. Technol. **27**(7), 9231–9262 (2022)
5. Angelini, M., Blasilli, G., Catarci, T., Lenti, S., Santucci, G.: Vulnus: visual vulnerability analysis for network security. IEEE Trans. Vis. Comput. Graph. **25**(1) , 183–192 (2018)
6. Buchanan, L., D'Amico, A., Kirkpatrick, D.: Mixed method approach to identify analytic questions to be visualized for military cyber incident handlers. In: 2016 IEEE Symposium on Visualization for Cyber Security (VizSec), pp. 1–8. IEEE (2016)
7. Burden, S., Topping, A., O'Halloran, C.: The value of artefacts in stimulated-recall interviews. Nurse Researcher **23**, 1 (2015)
8. Chockalingam, S., Pieters, W., Teixeira, A., Khakzad, N., van Gelder, P.: Combining Bayesian networks and fishbone diagrams to distinguish between intentional attacks and accidental technical failures. In: Cybenko, G., Pym, D., Fila, B. (eds.) GraMSec 2018. LNCS, vol. 11086, pp. 31–50. Springer, Cham (2019). https://doi.org/10.1007/978-3-030-15465-3_3
9. Conti, M., Dragoni, N., Lesyk, V.: A survey of man in the middle attacks. IEEE Commun. Surv. Tutor. **18**(3), 2027–2051 (2016)
10. Anderson Bergamini de Neira, Burak Kantarci, and Michele Nogueira. 2023. Distributed denial of service attack prediction: Challenges, open issues and opportunities. Computer Networks 222 (2023), 109553
11. Dong, S., Abbas, K., Jain, R.: A survey on distributed denial of service (DDoS) attacks in SDN and cloud computing environments. IEEE Access **7**(2019), 80813–80828 (2019)
12. Fantin, I.: Applied Problem Solving: Method, Applications, Root Causes, Countermeasures, Poka-Yoke and A3 (2014). Ivan Fantin
13. Flores, R., Namin, A.S., Tavakoli, N., Siami-Namini, S., Jones, K.S.: Using experiential learning to teach and learn digital forensics: educator and student perspectives. Comput. Educ. Open **2**(2021), 100045 (2021)
14. Furnell, S.: The cybersecurity workforce and skills. Comput. Secur. **100**(2021), 102080 (2021)
15. Goel, S.: National cyber security strategy and the emergence of strong digital borders. Connections **19**(1), 73–86 (2020)
16. Grammatikakis, K.P., Koufos, I., Kolokotronis, N., Vassilakis, C., Shiaeles, S.: Understanding and mitigating banking trojans: from zeus to emotet. In: 2021 IEEE International Conference on Cyber Security and Resilience (CSR), pp. 121–128. IEEE (2021)

17. Hatfield, J.M.: Social engineering in cybersecurity: the evolution of a concept. Comput. Secur. **73**(2018), 102–113 (2018)
18. Hellesen, N., Torres, H., Wangen, G.: Empirical case studies of the root-cause analysis method in information security. Int. J. Adv. Secur. **11** (2018)
19. Kanta, A., Coisel, I., Scanlon, M.: A survey exploring open source Intelligence for smarter password cracking. Forensic Sci. Int. Digit. Investig. **35**(2020), 301075 (2020)
20. Khan, F., Kim, J.H., Mathiassen, L., Moore, R.: Data breach management: an integrated risk model. Inf. Manag. **58**(1), 103392 (2021)
21. Koutcheme, C., Tilantera, A., Peltonen, A., Hellas, A., Haaranen, L.: Exploring how students solve open-ended assignments: a study of SQL injection attempts in a cybersecurity course. In: Proceedings of the 27th ACM Conference on on Innovation and Technology in Computer Science Education, vol. 1, pp. 75–81 (2022)
22. Lallie, H.S., Debattista, K., Bal, J.: A review of attack graph and attack tree visual syntax in cyber security. Comput. Sci. Rev. **35**(2020), 100219 (2020)
23. Landauer, M., Skopik, F., Wurzenberger, M., Rauber, A.: System log clustering approaches for cyber security applications: a survey. Comput. Secur. **92**(2020), 101739 (2020)
24. Kent, K., Souppaya, M.: Guide to Computer Security Log Management. NIST Special Publication 800-92 (2006)
25. Serrat, O.: The five whys technique. In: Knowledge Solutions, pp. 307–310. Springer, Singapore (2017)
26. Ericson, C.A.: Fault tree analysis – a history. In: Proceedings of the 17th International System Safety Conference (1999)
27. Ishikawa, K., Loftus, J.H.: Introduction to quality control, vol. 98, p. 31. Tokyo: 3A Corporation (1990). https://www.scirp.org/reference/referencespapers?referenceid=1272669, June 2024
28. Schneier, B.: Attack trees. Dr. Dobb's J. **24**(12), 21–29 (1999)
29. Seidman, I.: Interviewing as qualitative research: a guide for researchers in education and the social sciences. Teachers college press, 2006
30. Triplett, W.J.: Addressing cybersecurity challenges in education. Int. J. STEM Educ. Sustain. **3**(1), 47–67 (2023)
31. Cybersecurity in Higher Education: Problem and Solutions | Toptal®, May 2024. https://www.toptal.com/insights/innovation/cybersecurity-in-higher-education
32. Top Challenges in Faced by Students in Cybersecurity Education. https://3university.io/challenges-faced-by-students-in-cybersecurity/. Accessed May 2024
33. Saldaña, J.: The coding manual for qualitative researchers, pp. 1–440 (2021)
34. Silva, A., Emmanuel, G., McClain, J.T., Matzen, L., Forsythe, C.: Measuring expert and novice performance within computer security incident response teams. In: Foundations of Augmented Cognition: 9th International Conference, AC 2015, Held as Part of HCI International 2015, Los Angeles, CA, USA, 2–7 August 2015, Proceedings 9, pp. 144–152. Springer (2015)
35. Svacina, J., et al.: On vulnerability and security log analysis: a systematic literature review on recent trends. In: Proceedings of the International Conference on Research in Adaptive and Convergent Systems, pp. 175–180 (2020)
36. Scheponik, T., et al.: How students reason about cybersecurity concepts. In: 2016 IEEE Frontiers in Education Conference (FIE), pp. 1–5. IEEE (2016)
37. Yin, C., Minatoya, D., Zhao, F.: Factor analysis for performance prediction using e-book learning logs. In: 2023 International Conference on Artificial Intelligence and Education (ICAIE), pp. 42–43 (2023). https://doi.org/10.1109/ICAIE56796.2023.00021

Teaching NLP in the Age of Large Language Models: Challenges and Strategies for Indian Universities

Manu Madhavan[1(✉)] and Jeena Kleenankandy[2]

[1] Department of Computer Science and Engineering, Indian Institute of Information Technology Kottayam, Kottayam, India
manum@iiitkottayam.ac.in

[2] Department of Computer Science, Cochin University of Science and Technology, Kochi, India
jeenakk@cusat.ac.in

Abstract. This paper examines the challenges and opportunities in teaching Natural Language Processing (NLP) at the undergraduate level, particularly in the era of Large Language Models (LLMs). It discusses the diverse backgrounds of students, including those from computer science and non-computer science disciplines, and the need to incorporate Indian languages into the curriculum. The study identifies key challenges, such as integrating classical NLP methods with contemporary deep learning techniques, and outlines practical issues in syllabus design. By focusing on the unique context of Indian universities, this paper offers actionable recommendations for educators to enhance NLP education. The insights and strategies proposed aim to address the evolving landscape of NLP and prepare students for the demands of the field.

Keywords: Teaching NLP · Large Language Models · Curriculum

1 Introduction

Natural Language Processing (NLP) technology is a dynamic and evolving area that touches every corner of the world nowadays. The evolution of deep learning and Large Language Models (LLM) is creating an unprecedented impact on the AI landscape. Innovations in terms of models and use cases are happening every day. This has also fascinated industry and academic researchers to explore the area, irrespective of the domain, including but not limited to humanities, business studies and finance. This has resulted in a growing demand for NLP courses, not only in engineering streams but also among non-engineering streams. In earlier days, such courses were mostly confined to computer science and linguistics students.

Though the significance of NLP is widely acknowledged in the academic community, there is concern that the most part of the NLP curriculum is outdated

A. Karkare et al. (Eds.): COMPUTE 2024, CCIS 2400, pp. 161–169, 2025.
https://doi.org/10.1007/978-3-031-84391-4_13

and needs a thorough reform to equip students with the skills necessary for today's language technologies. On the other hand, updated syllabi are a mix of classical NLP algorithms and deep learning models, including LLMs. The vast nature of such syllabi pose another big challenge to the educators handling NLP courses as they struggle to cover the topics to imbibe the skills for the state-of-the-art (SOTA) advancements. Education 4.0 [22] aims to make students competent with technological advancements and make them industry-ready. At this juncture, educators face a dilemma: while the classical methods are important for understanding the challenges of NLP, advanced models must also be effectively discussed. The challenge doubles when the course is offered to all students, irrespective of their Computer Science and Engineering (CSE) background. Additionally, in a multilingual country like India, the course should be taught in a way that enables students to understand the linguistic challenges related to their native languages and contribute to the development of language technologies for Indian languages.

Highlighting the gap between the NLP curriculum and state-of-the-art NLP technologies, this paper discusses the challenges faced in teaching NLP courses to engineering students, specifically in the Indian context. Our discussion primarily focuses on the challenges in teaching NLP within university and affiliated systems of education, which cover the majority of students in India. Many of the challenges discussed are global, though. The analysis is based on a comparison of syllabi of NLP courses offered at various Indian universities and the authors' experiences in teaching NLP courses at undergraduate and postgraduate levels. Compiling various challenges and opportunities, this paper emphasises the need for active research in teaching NLP to develop a comprehensive curriculum for Indian needs. The main contributions of the paper are:

1. Presenting a comparative analysis of syllabi of various Indian universities and identify major challenges in teaching NLP
2. A discussion on the pressing need for NLP curriculum reform and the opportunities from the Indian context.

The rest of the paper is organised as follows: Sect. 2 briefly discusses the research in teaching NLP. Section 3 gives an overview of the various syllabi followed for NLP courses in India. Section 4 presents the practical challenges faced by educators in teaching NLP. Section 5 provides opportunities and suggestions for future research, followed by the conclusion.

2 Research in Teaching NLP

Research in NLP is highly active, but research on teaching NLP rarely receives attention from educators. The diversity in the curricula, level of students, motivation of the course, and the background may be the reason for limiting the education research in NLP. The workshop on Teaching NLP [1] in association with ACL is one of the prominent venues discussing the challenges and innovative ideas of teaching NLP. Many of the recent works in teaching NLP discussed the use of innovative and interactive tools such as NLTK [7] and GATE [11] to illustrate the NLP concepts. These tools help students to understand the concepts easily without the difficulty of coding. Some past works [3,13] have discussed challenges in handling NLP courses, such as a lack of coding knowledge among students and identifying good reference materials. The points raised in these papers remain relevant today, and current educators continue to experience a plethora of additional challenges. The necessity of including ethics in the NLP course is highlighted in [8,12]. Many teachers reported their experiences and insights from offering NLP courses to non-CSE students like Humanities, social sciences [14] and massive online programs for the general audience [7]. Few of the papers presented the experiences and challenges in offering NLP for schools [17]. A recent paper by Joshi et al., [15] presents an analysis of model curricula for NLP which balances both classical and deep learning based NLP. The discussion in the paper is quite interesting and gives strong arguments for classical methods in the NLP curriculum, the analysis is limited to tier-1, research oriented institutes. Literature discussing the challenges in teaching conventional education such as Universities and affiliated colleges, especially in the Indian context is not present.

3 Current NLP Curriculum (in India)

In most of the Indian universities the NLP is typically offered as a seventh semester elective course within Computer Science and Engineering (CSE) programmes. These courses are designed from a theoretical perspective starting from the morphological parsing, finite state transducers, and various parsing techniques, followed by statistical methods, word embedding, machine learning and deep learning methods. Many popular NLP use cases such as machine translation, text classification, Part-of-Speech Tagging, Named Entity Recognition (NER), and Word Sense Disambiguation(WSD) are also included in the syllabus. Few of the recently updated syllabus[1],[2] includes Transformers [21] and LLMs in addition to the traditional NLP topics. The course is offered in the final year and at many places without any lab or project component. Most syllabi follow well-known textbooks such as "Statistical NLP" by Manning [18] and "Speech and Language Processing" (SLP) by Jurafsky [16], with some also referencing James Allen's "Natural Language Understanding" (NLU) [5]. The lab follows NLTK and the related book by Bird et al., [10]. Many courses, especially those that offer only a single NLP course, do not cover Large Language Models (LLMs) in detail. They may only briefly discuss recent trends in this area. Some premier research institutes[3] offer NLP in two courses- *Introduction to NLP* for fundamentals and *Advanced NLP* for more complex architectures such as Transformers and LLMs. NPTEL offers 3 MOOC courses[4] for NLP out of which two

[1] https://www.cse.iitk.ac.in/pages/CS698O.html.
[2] https://www.cse.iitd.ac.in/mausam/courses/col772/spring2024/.
[3] Example IIIT Hyderabad.
[4] https://nptel.ac.in/courses/106105158, 106101007, 106106211.

follow traditional computational linguistics approaches while "Applied NLP"[5] course focuses on the more practical side of the area, excluding some of the topics from traditional linguistics. There are few universities[6] that offer specific courses in Statistical NLP, Deep Learning for NLP, and recently Introduction to LLM [7].

4 Challenges in Teaching NLP

4.1 Vast Nature of Syllabus

One of the predominant challenges in offering NLP courses is covering the vast syllabus in a single semester. The syllabi are filled with topics from linguistics, statistics, machine learning, deep learning, complemented with a long list of NLP tasks. Students, especially from Engineering background may be unfamiliar with linguistics concepts, due to which instructors are compelled to spend more time on each of these topics. This approach eats away majority of the semester and they struggle to cover the syllabus. This also alleviates students' opportunity to learn practical skill and in depth knowledge in the subjects. Coverage of syllabus is important in an affiliated college system, where the students are appearing for a common examination across the university.

4.2 Multi-disciplinary Nature

The vastness of NLP curriculum results from the inherent complexity of the field. NLP lies at the intersection of multiple disciplines, including linguistics, computer science, mathematics, and statistics. A very broad curriculum covering all relevant areas may not allow for deep exploration of any single topic. Focusing deeply on one area (e.g., Deep learning for NLP) might result in students missing out on important foundational knowledge in linguistics or classical NLP techniques. Integrating concepts from linguistics (syntax, semantics, pragmatics) with technical aspects from computer science (algorithms, data structures, machine learning) in a cohesive manner is challenging. The curricullum has to ensure that students understand how these disciplines interact and complement each other.

4.3 Prerequisites for the Course

From an engineering perspective, probability, statistics, machine learning and deep learning are some of the prerequisites for deep understanding of modern NLP algorithms. Students are expected to have a sound programming competence to develop NLP applications. Since NLP is a buzzword in the current AI landscape, the course will be opted by a large number of students. Though the

[5] https://nptel.ac.in/courses/106106211.
[6] Example: VIT Vellore, CUSAT.
[7] https://www.amrita.edu/course/introduction-to-nlp-transformers-llm/.

prerequisites are already covered in the undergraduate curriculum, it is observed that students are not able to connect the background concepts to NLP topics. In many cases, instructors need to devote time to cover the essence of prerequisite concepts such as probability, Python programming etc. This also affects the course delivery and is unable to capture the essence of NLP concepts.

4.4 Balancing the Importance Between Classic Methods and Deep Learning Methods

Transformers and LLMs are the state-of-the-art NLP algorithms, and many of the problems approached by classical methods are solved to a near perfection by LLMs. Most of the current NLP curriculum (except for some premier research institutes) is dominated by classic methods and vaguely describe recent trends to discuss transformers and LLMs. The paper by Joshi et al., [15] demonstrates a curriculum that balances both the classical and deep learning NLP techniques. They also argue that classical methods are required in the NLP curriculum for developing an intuitive understanding of the domain. However, in-depth discussion and proper balancing of classical methods and LLM techniques is still challenging for an NLP educator.

4.5 Resource Constraints References Materials, Compute and Data

The major bottlenecks faced when delivering NLP courses is lack of teaching materials. The classics books commonly followed in the majority of the curriculum are excellent in the content, but depth and breadth are not suitable for covering NLP for the contemporary needs. Thousands of online short courses on social media are popping up daily and students mostly rely on these contents. The quality of these contents needs thorough scrutiny. In the view of experimentation with LLMs, constraints on compute resources will be more prevalent nowadays. Many of the prominent models are proprietary closed models and even open source alternatives are also resource hungry. In either case, most students except those from premium institutes, do not have access to High Performance Computing (HPC) facilities required for adequate laboratory work. This makes them highly dependent on APIs to gain these expertise. Unavailability of massive quality data demanded by current neural NLP models is another major bottleneck to both teachers and students working on Indian Language Computing.

4.6 Rapid Advancement in NLP

The technological advancements in NLP has been too rapid lately. This poses a challenge not just in keeping the curriculum up-to-date, but also in equipping the educators with the required expertise to deliver these contents effectively. For instance, the rise of transformer-based language models like BERT and GPT has happened in just 6 years and has been evolving ever since. Lack of expertise in the field may be one of the reasons for the lag in integrating them in the NLP curriculum.

4.7 Offering NLP as Open Elective for Non-CSE Students

Till the recent years, NLP or Computational Linguistics courses were offered either to CSE students or PG Linguistics students. Considering the impact of NLP research in all domains, we can observe a mass interest in NLP techniques in all branches including Engineering and non-Engineering students. Clinical NLP, NLP for Digital Humanities are few of the examples. The main challenges in offering NLP courses for non-CSE students are the diversity of the students and unfamiliarity with the technical jargons. Hippala et al., discussed their experience in offering an online course on language technology for Humanities students [14]. There are many inherent challenges of teaching computational methods like algorithmic thinking and programming to non-CSE students, especially from humanities and medical streams [20]. One could argue that the humanities students (or non-CSE students) can learn applied NLP in their domain. But these applied NLP courses focus more on tools than algorithms and don't prepare humanities students to make actual contributions in Digital Humanities.

4.8 Delivering Course for Non-English Language Background

This challenge is not intended to discuss the scope of native language as a medium of instruction. The point we would like to highlight is discussing the NLP tasks specific to the Indian Language. Most of the NLP curriculum follows the foreign references and uses the textbook examples to illustrate the NLP tasks. This pedagogical approach fails to appreciate the cultural and linguistic challenges of Indian languages for NLP tasks. The diversity of language families, with distinct structures and scripts, makes it harder to develop teaching methodologies that cater to students from different linguistic backgrounds. Though the gap can be addressed by choosing Indian language related tasks for projects/practicals, major challenges may be left untouched in the curriculum. The experience in offering Russian [6] and Italian [19] specific NLP courses are really positive. Identifying/preparing good reference material will be the main task to address this challenge. "NLP: A Paninian Perspective" [9] is an attempt towards this goal, and we require more advanced materials to achieve this task.

4.9 Satisfaction of Students with the Course Outcome

The term NLP is too misleading in the era of LLM and GenAI. Most of the students want to explore the LLMs and explore the trending topics. Though the students may not have sufficient in-depth knowledge to appreciate the LLMs, the discussions on classic methods and detailing often diminishes their enthusiasm. Attempts to convey the importance of thoroughly understanding classical methods are usually futile in most cases. Meeting the student's expectations from the course point of view becomes more challenging.

4.10 Teaching Ethics in NLP

The understanding of responsible use of NLP is the predominant concern in the research community. The conventional curriculum however is not able to discuss these issues effectively. Ender et al., highlights dual use of NLP, bias in the model and privacy issues are the key ethical concerns as far as NLP is concerned [8]. The incorporation of ethics and responsible computing concepts make the curriculum more comprehensive.

5 Suggestions and Future Directions

The challenges posed in the previous section clearly necessitate the need for an urgent reformation of the NLP curriculum. The first challenge will be choosing the topics to make the curriculum that helps the students to get an in-depth understanding of classical and advanced NLP algorithms. In an educational set up of affiliated universities, offering specialised NLP courses in two levels (introductory and advanced) may not be practicable. The most feasible thing is to shift the focus towards deep learning and statistical techniques, since the SOTA NLP techniques are based on these related concepts. Aligning to the National Education Policy 2020 [4], introducing a course on Linguistics to CSE students at the early years of their UG curriculum will help to understand the linguistic background for NLP. This also helps to understand the NLP challenges from an Indian language perspective. Introducing deep learning and machine learning concepts in the context of NLP within their respective courses will help students grasp NLP use cases while allowing more time for detailed discussions on NLP algorithms. However, this approach may require redesigning other courses, which could be challenging.

Challenges related to computing resources pose significant obstacles to implementing effective practicals in the course. To overcome these challenges, labs and projects should encourage students to work with Indian languages and motivate them to contribute to ongoing efforts in this area. There are notable initiatives by state and central governments, non-profit organizations like TinkerHub, and tech giants such as Google Colab, Amazon Cloud, HuggingFace, and Kaggle, which provide free computing resources to the public and students. Unfortunately, these resources are often underutilised due to a lack of awareness among educators and limited access to high-speed internet.

Given the importance of NLP, it is crucial to design a curriculum tailored to the Indian context. The syllabus should include foundational topics in classic NLP while placing greater emphasis on statistical methods and deep learning algorithms. Introducing students to the concept of Large Language Models (LLMs) is essential, along with incorporating assignments and projects that allow them to explore recent advancements in the field. Adapting the ACM CSE Curriculum recommendations from 2023 [2] for an Indian-specific NLP course can serve as a valuable starting point.

6 Conclusion

The paper discussed the challenges in designing and teaching a NLP course for undergraduate students of Universities and affiliated colleges. The multiple challenges including the vastness of the syllabus, relevance of classical algorithms in the time of deep learning and LLMs, lack of expertise, relevant reference materials and the conflict between student expectation and course outcomes were discussed. Importantly, the need for revamping the NLP course specific to Indian languages and context is also presented. The importance of incorporating a curriculum that adequately covers foundational concepts alongside advanced topics is emphasised, as these are crucial for understanding and analysing the reasoning and errors of LLMs. In conclusion, this paper calls on educators and institutions to re-evaluate and update their NLP curricula, ensuring it is robust, inclusive, and reflective of both classical and cutting-edge technologies.

Disclosure of Interests. The authors have no competing interests to declare that are relevant to the content of this article.

References

1. ACL: Workshop on Teaching Natural Language Processing - ACL Anthology — aclanthology.org. https://aclanthology.org/venues/teachingnlp/. Accessed 23 July 2024
2. ACM: Curricula Recommendations. https://www.acm.org/education/curricula-recommendations. Accessed 30 July 2024
3. Agarwal, A.: Teaching the basics of NLP and ml in an introductory course to information science. In: Proceedings of the Fourth Workshop on Teaching NLP and CL, pp. 77–84 (2013)
4. Aithal, P., Aithal, S.: Analysis of the indian national education policy 2020 towards achieving its objectives. Int. J. Manage., Technol., Soc. Sci. (IJMTS) **5**(2), 19–41 (2020)
5. Allen, J.: Natural Language Understanding. Benjamin-Cummings Publishing Co., Inc. (1988)
6. Artemova, E., Apishev, M., Sarkisyan, V., Aksenov, S., Kirjanov, D., Serikov, O.: Teaching a massive open online course on natural language processing. arXiv preprint: arXiv:2104.12846 (2021)
7. Baglini, R., Hjorth, A.: Natural language processing 4 all (NLP4All): a new online platform for teaching and learning NLP concepts. arXiv preprint: arXiv:2105.13704 (2021)
8. Bender, E.M., Hovy, D., Schofield, A.: Integrating ethics into the NLP curriculum. In: Proceedings of the 58th Annual Meeting of the Association for Computational Linguistics: Tutorial Abstracts, pp. 6–9 (2020)
9. Bharati, A., Chaitanya, V., Sangal, R., Ramakrishnamacharyulu, K.: Natural Language Processing: A Paninian Perspective. PHI Learning (1995)
10. Bird, S., Klein, E., Loper, E.: Natural Language Processing with Python: Analyzing Text With the Natural Language Toolkit. O'Reilly Media, Inc. (2009)
11. Bontcheva, K., Cunningham, H., Tablan, V., Maynard, D., Hamza, O.: Using gate as an environment for teaching NLP. In: Proceedings of the ACL-02 Workshop on Effective Tools and Methodologies for Teaching Natural Language Processing and Computational Linguistics, pp. 54–62 (2002)

12. Friedrich, A., Zesch, T.: A crash course on ethics for natural language processing. In: Jurgens, D., Kolhatkar, V., Li, L., Mieskes, M., Pedersen, T. (eds.) Proceedings of the Fifth Workshop on Teaching NLP. pp. 49–51. Association for Computational Linguistics, Online (2021). https://doi.org/10.18653/v1/2021.teachingnlp-1.6
13. Hearst, M.A.: Teaching applied natural language processing: triumphs and tribulations. In: Proceedings of the Second ACL Workshop on Effective Tools and Methodologies for Teaching NLP and CL, pp. 1–8 (2005)
14. Hiippala, T.: Applied language technology: NLP for the humanities. arXiv preprint: arXiv:2105.01052 (2021)
15. Joshi, A., Renzella, J., Bhattacharyya, P., Jha, S., Zhang, X.: Striking a balance between classical and deep learning approaches in natural language processing pedagogy (2024). https://arxiv.org/abs/2405.09854
16. Jurafsky, D.: Speech & Language Processing. Pearson Education India (2000)
17. Katuka, G.A., et al.: Integrating natural language processing in middle school science classrooms: an experience report. In: Proceedings of the 55th ACM Technical Symposium on Computer Science Education V.1, pp. 639–645 (2024)
18. Manning, C., Schutze, H.: Foundations of Statistical Natural Language Processing. MIT press (1999)
19. Messina, L., et al.: A dissemination workshop for introducing young Italian students to NLP. arXiv preprint: arXiv:2104.12405 (2021)
20. Öhman, E.: Teaching computational methods to humanities students. In: DHN, pp. 479–494 (2019)
21. Vaswani, A., et al.: Attention is all you need. In: Advances in Neural Information Processing Systems, vol. 30 (2017)
22. Vyas, P.S., Bhattacharya, S., Mahmud, M.: Co-designing education 4.0 in the Indian context. In: Proceedings of the 16th Annual ACM India Compute Conference, pp. 94–99 (2023)

Bridging Ethics and Code: A PBL Framework for Digital Citizenship in CS

Pratik Rana(✉)

Plaksha University, Mohali, Punjab, India
pratik.rana@plaksha.edu.in

Abstract. As technology increasingly permeates society, integrating digital citizenship concepts into computer science (CS) education has become crucial. This paper presents a novel framework that seamlessly merges digital citizenship principles with project-based learning (PBL) in CS curricula. The framework emphasizes competencies such as digital literacy, ethical decision-making, and online safety, fostering the development of responsible innovators capable of addressing the societal implications of their work. By aligning digital citizenship themes with relevant CS topics, the framework encourages critical thinking and collaborative problem-solving while providing hands-on learning experiences. The paper outlines specific integration strategies for various CS subjects and proposes comprehensive assessment methods to evaluate both ethical reasoning and technical proficiency. Case studies demonstrate the framework's practical application, showcasing its effectiveness in cultivating a holistic understanding of technical skills and ethical considerations. This approach aims to empower the next generation of computer scientists to engage in responsible innovation, ensuring ethical practices are at the forefront of technological advancement. The paper concludes by discussing potential evaluation methods for future research and exploring the broader implications of this integrated approach for CS education and the technology industry.

Keywords: Digital citizenship · Project-based learning · Computer science education · Ethical computing · Curriculum integration · STEM ethics · Technology literacy · Responsible innovation

1 Introduction

In today's digital age, the importance of digital citizenship in computer science (CS) education cannot be overstated. As technology becomes increasingly integrated into every aspect of society, it is crucial that CS students not only develop technical skills but also understand the ethical, social, and cultural implications of their work. Digital citizenship encompasses a wide range of competencies, including online safety, digital literacy, ethical behavior, and responsible use of technology [1].

A. Karkare et al. (Eds.): COMPUTE 2024, CCIS 2400, pp. 170–180, 2025.
https://doi.org/10.1007/978-3-031-84391-4_14

Project-based learning (PBL) has emerged as an effective pedagogical approach in CS education, offering students hands-on experience in applying theoretical concepts to real-world problems [3]. PBL encourages critical thinking, collaboration, and creativity, skills that are essential in the rapidly evolving field of technology [2].

This paper proposes a framework for integrating digital citizenship concepts into CS project-based learning. By combining these two educational approaches, we aim to create a holistic learning experience that prepares students to become not just skilled programmers, but also responsible digital citizens capable of navigating the complex ethical landscape of modern technology. Several researchers have highlighted the importance of integrating ethics into CS education [5,6]. Our framework builds on these works by providing a structured approach to embedding digital citizenship concepts within project-based learning.

The remainder of this paper is structured as follows: Sect. 2 provides background on digital citizenship and current approaches to teaching it, as well as an overview of project-based learning in CS. Section 3 presents our proposed framework, including its core components and integration strategies. Section 4 offers implementation guidelines, followed by case studies in Sect. 5. Section 6 discusses potential evaluation methods for future research, and Sect. 7 concludes with a discussion of the implications and future directions of this work.

2 Background

2.1 Defining Digital Citizenship

Digital citizenship refers to the responsible and ethical use of technology. It encompasses various aspects, including:

- Digital literacy: Understanding how digital technologies work and how to use them effectively.
- Digital ethics: Making ethical decisions in digital environments.
- Online safety and security: Protecting oneself and others in online spaces.
- Digital rights and responsibilities: Understanding one's rights and obligations in the digital world.
- Digital health and wellness: Managing the physical and mental health aspects of technology use.

These components align with the ISTE Standards for Students [4], which emphasize the importance of digital citizenship in education.

2.2 Current Approaches to Teaching Digital Citizenship

Current approaches to teaching digital citizenship often involve standalone courses or modules that are separate from the core CS curriculum [7].

While these approaches have merit, they may not provide students with opportunities to apply digital citizenship concepts in practical, technology-focused contexts. This separation can lead to a disconnect between ethical considerations and technical implementation, potentially limiting students' ability to integrate these crucial skills in their future careers [8].

2.3 Project-Based Learning in CS: Benefits and Challenges

Project-based learning in CS offers numerous benefits, including:

- Practical application of theoretical concepts
- Development of problem-solving skills
- Encouragement of creativity and innovation
- Enhancement of collaboration and communication skills

These benefits have been well-documented in CS education research [9]. However, challenges in implementing PBL in CS include:

- Time constraints in covering all required material
- Ensuring projects align with learning objectives
- Assessing individual contributions in group projects
- Balancing technical content with broader educational goals

Our framework aims to address these challenges while leveraging the benefits of PBL to foster digital citizenship skills.

3 Proposed Framework

Our proposed framework aims to seamlessly integrate digital citizenship concepts into CS project-based learning, addressing the challenges mentioned above while leveraging the benefits of both approaches. The framework is designed to be flexible and adaptable to various CS courses and institutional contexts.

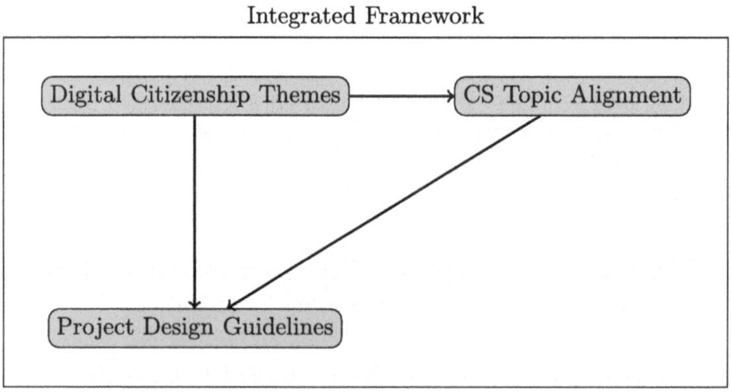

Fig. 1. Core Components of the Integrated Framework

Figure 1 illustrates the core components of our framework and their interrelationships.

3.1 Core Components of the Framework

The framework consists of three core components:

1. Digital Citizenship Themes: Key aspects of digital citizenship that will be integrated into projects, such as ethical decision-making, privacy, societal impact, online safety, and accessibility.
2. CS Topic Alignment: Mapping of digital citizenship themes to relevant CS topics, ensuring a natural integration that enhances rather than detracts from technical learning.
3. Project Design Guidelines: Principles for designing projects that incorporate both CS skills and digital citizenship concepts, including assessment strategies and implementation tips.

3.2 Integration Strategies for Different CS Topics

The framework provides strategies for integrating digital citizenship themes into various CS topics. The mapping of digital citizenship themes to CS topics is based on a careful analysis of the natural alignment between ethical concerns and technical concepts. This alignment ensures that students can see the direct relevance of ethical considerations to their technical work. Table 1 provides an overview of these integration strategies.

The rationale behind each pairing is rooted in the potential ethical implications of each CS topic. For example, data structures and algorithms are paired with ethical decision-making because the design choices in these areas can significantly impact fairness and bias in computational systems [10]. Similarly, database topics are linked to privacy concerns due to the critical role of data management in protecting personal information [11].

3.3 Assessment Considerations

Quantifying digital citizenship skills presents a unique challenge due to the often subjective nature of ethical reasoning. To address this, we propose a multi-faceted assessment approach:

1. Knowledge Tests: Pre- and post-project quizzes on digital ethics concepts (20% of total score)
2. Ethical Analysis Rubric: Evaluation of students' ability to identify and address ethical issues in their projects (30% of total score)
3. Peer Evaluation: Assessment of ethical considerations in group work (15% of total score)
4. Reflective Essays: Analysis of students' depth of ethical reasoning (25% of total score)
5. Behavioral Metrics: Tracking of students' engagement with ethical resources and discussions (10% of total score)

Table 1. Integration Strategies for CS Topics

CS Topic	Citizenship Theme	Integration Strategy	Rationale
Data-Structures & Algorithms	Ethical Decision Making	Discuss algorithmic bias and fairness	Algorithms can perpetuate or amplify biases, making ethical considerations crucial in their design and implementation
Databases	Privacy	Focus on responsible data management	Databases often contain sensitive personal information, necessitating strong privacy protections
Artificial-Intelligence	Societal Impact	Emphasize ethical AI-development	AI systems can have far-reaching societal effects, requiring careful consideration of their impacts
Networking	Online Safety	Address cybersecurity concerns	Network vulnerabilities can compromise user safety, making security a key ethical concern
Software-Engineering	Accessibility	Integrate inclusive design principles	Software should be usable by all, including those with disabilities, promoting equal access to technology

These measures are combined into a composite 'Digital Citizenship Score' ranging from 0–100, allowing for quantitative comparison between students and over time. This approach addresses the challenge of objectively evaluating ethical reasoning while providing a comprehensive view of students' digital citizenship competencies [12].

In summary, our proposed framework provides a comprehensive approach to integrating digital citizenship into CS project-based learning. By aligning ethical themes with CS topics, providing clear integration strategies, and offering a multi-faceted assessment approach, we aim to create a learning environment that fosters both technical proficiency and ethical awareness.

4 Implementation Guidelines

To aid educators in applying the framework, we provide detailed guidelines for project design and implementation:

1. **Theme Selection**: Choose a digital citizenship theme that aligns with the CS topic being taught. For example, when teaching databases, focus on data privacy and ethical data management.
2. **Project Scoping**: Design projects that require students to engage with both technical CS concepts and digital citizenship issues. For instance, in a web development course, students could create a social media platform with a focus on user privacy controls.
3. **Ethical Considerations**: Incorporate explicit discussions and assignments related to ethical considerations. For example, in an AI course, require students to write a reflection on the potential biases in their machine learning models.

4. **Stakeholder Analysis**: Encourage students to consider various stakeholders affected by their projects. In a software engineering course, students could conduct a stakeholder analysis for their application, considering issues of accessibility and inclusivity.
5. **Peer Review**: Implement peer review processes that include evaluation of both technical implementation and ethical considerations.
6. **External Engagement**: Where possible, engage with external stakeholders or experts in digital ethics to provide real-world context and feedback on student projects.

5 Case Studies

To illustrate the application of the framework, we present three case studies across different CS courses:

5.1 Data Structures and Algorithms: Fair Sorting Algorithm

Course: Advanced Data Structures and Algorithms
Digital Citizenship Theme: Ethical Decision Making
Project Description: Students are tasked with developing a sorting algorithm for a job application screening system. They must consider how different sorting criteria might impact various demographic groups and implement measures to ensure fairness.

Learning Outcomes:

- Technical: Proficiency in algorithm design, complexity analysis, and implementation
- Ethical: Understanding of algorithmic bias, fairness in machine learning, and the societal implications of automated decision-making systems

Project Deliverables:

1. Implementation of the sorting algorithm
2. Technical report on algorithm efficiency and fairness measures
3. Ethical analysis of potential biases and mitigation strategies
4. Presentation on the societal implications of algorithmic decision-making in hiring processes

Assessment:

- Technical skills (50%): Algorithm correctness, efficiency, and code quality
- Ethical analysis (30%): Depth of consideration of ethical issues, quality of proposed mitigation strategies
- Presentation (20%): Clarity of communication, demonstration of understanding of both technical and ethical aspects

5.2 Databases: Privacy-Preserving Health Data System

Course: Database Management Systems
Digital Citizenship Theme: Privacy
Project Description: Students design and implement a database system for a healthcare provider, focusing on protecting patient privacy while allowing necessary data access for medical research.

Learning Outcomes:

- Technical: Proficiency in database design, SQL, and data encryption techniques
- Ethical: Understanding of data privacy regulations, ethical considerations in health data management, and balancing research needs with individual privacy

Project Deliverables:

1. Database schema and implementation
2. Data access control system
3. Privacy impact assessment report
4. Presentation on ethical considerations in health data management

Assessment:

- Technical implementation (40%): Database design, query efficiency, security measures
- Privacy protection (30%): Effectiveness of privacy-preserving techniques
- Ethical analysis (20%): Depth of consideration of ethical issues in health data management
- Presentation (10%): Clarity of communication, demonstration of understanding of both technical and ethical aspects

5.3 Artificial Intelligence: Ethical Chatbot Development

Course: Introduction to Artificial Intelligence
Digital Citizenship Theme: Societal Impact
Project Description: Students develop a chatbot for a mental health support service, focusing on creating an AI system that is both effective and ethically responsible.

Learning Outcomes:

- Technical: Proficiency in natural language processing, machine learning, and chatbot development
- Ethical: Understanding of AI ethics, responsible AI development, and the societal implications of AI in healthcare

Project Deliverables:

1. Functional chatbot implementation
2. Technical report on the AI model and its performance
3. Ethical impact assessment of the chatbot
4. Presentation on responsible AI development in healthcare contexts

Assessment:

- Technical implementation (40%): Chatbot functionality, AI model performance
- Ethical considerations (30%): Depth of ethical analysis, implementation of ethical safeguards
- User experience (20%): Appropriateness of chatbot responses, user safety considerations
- Presentation (10%): Clarity of communication, demonstration of understanding of both technical and ethical aspects

These case studies demonstrate how the framework can be applied across different CS domains, integrating digital citizenship themes with technical content in a meaningful way.

6 Potential Evaluation Methods for Future Research

While we have not conducted a full-scale empirical study, we propose the following methods for evaluating the effectiveness of this framework in future research:

1. **Comparative Studies**: Longitudinal studies comparing learning outcomes between students in traditional CS programs and those in programs implementing our framework. These studies could measure both technical proficiency and ethical reasoning skills over time [13].
2. **Skill Transfer Assessment**: Evaluate how well students apply ethical reasoning skills in real-world scenarios or internships after completing courses using this framework. This could involve case studies or simulations of ethical dilemmas in professional settings [14].
3. **Industry Feedback**: Gather input from employers on the ethical decision-making capabilities of graduates from programs using this framework compared to traditional programs. This could be done through surveys or interviews with hiring managers and team leaders [15].
4. **Ethical Dilemma Simulations**: Develop and administer standardized ethical dilemma scenarios to assess students' ability to apply digital citizenship concepts in complex situations. These simulations could be based on real-world ethical challenges in technology [16].
5. **Portfolio Analysis**: Evaluate student portfolios over time to assess the integration of ethical considerations in their technical projects. This could provide insights into how students' approach to ethical issues evolves throughout their education [17].

These methods would provide robust empirical support for the framework's effectiveness and guide further refinements. Future research could also explore the long-term impact of this integrated approach on students' career trajectories and their contributions to ethical technology development.

7 Discussion and Future Directions

The proposed framework for integrating digital citizenship into CS project-based learning represents a significant step towards developing ethically-minded technologists. By combining technical skill development with a strong foundation in digital citizenship, we can better prepare students for the complex ethical landscape of modern technology.

One of the primary strengths of this approach is its flexibility and adaptability to various CS topics and educational contexts. The framework provides a structure for integrating ethical considerations across the CS curriculum, rather than treating ethics as a separate, isolated topic. This integrated approach may help students see the relevance of ethical considerations to their technical work and develop a habit of ethical reasoning that carries into their professional lives [18].

However, implementing this framework is not without challenges. Educators may need additional training and resources to effectively integrate digital citizenship concepts into their courses. There may also be resistance from students or faculty who view ethics as secondary to technical skills. Addressing these challenges will require institutional support, ongoing professional development, and clear communication about the importance of ethical reasoning in technology development [19].

Future research directions could include:

- Exploring the framework's applicability across different types of institutions (e.g., large research universities, liberal arts colleges, community colleges) and student populations.
- Investigating the long-term impact of this integrated approach on students' career trajectories and ethical decision-making in professional settings.
- Developing more sophisticated assessment tools for measuring digital citizenship skills and their integration with technical proficiency.
- Examining how this framework might align with or influence CS education standards and accreditation criteria.
- Investigating the potential for technology-enhanced learning tools, such as ethical reasoning simulations or AI-assisted feedback systems, to support the implementation of this framework.

As we move forward, it is crucial that the CS education community continues to innovate in this space, refining and expanding upon this framework to ensure that our educational approaches keep pace with the rapidly evolving technological and ethical landscape. By doing so, we can help create a generation of technologists who are not only skilled in their craft but also deeply committed to the responsible and ethical use of technology.

8 Conclusion

The integration of digital citizenship into CS education through project-based learning offers a promising approach to preparing students for the ethical challenges they will face in their careers. Our framework provides a structured yet flexible way to incorporate these crucial concepts across the CS curriculum.

The case studies and implementation guidelines offered in this paper demonstrate the practical applicability of the framework across various CS topics. While empirical validation is still needed, the potential benefits of this approach are significant, including enhanced relevance of CS education to real-world ethical issues, improved student engagement, and the development of well-rounded technologists with strong ethical foundations.

As technology continues to shape our society in profound ways, the need for ethically-minded technologists has never been greater. By adopting and refining approaches like the one presented in this paper, we can ensure that the next generation of computer scientists is equipped not only with technical excellence but also with the ethical reasoning skills necessary to navigate the complex landscape of modern technology development.

Future work should focus on empirical evaluation of the framework's effectiveness, refinement of assessment methods, and exploration of how this approach can be scaled and adapted across diverse educational contexts. Through continued research and collaboration, we can work towards a future where ethical considerations are seamlessly integrated into every aspect of computer science education and practice.

The impact of this work extends beyond the classroom, potentially influencing how technology is developed and deployed in society. By fostering a generation of ethically-minded computer scientists, we can contribute to the creation of more responsible, inclusive, and beneficial technological innovations.

References

1. Ribble, M.: Digital Citizenship in Schools: Nine Elements All Students Should Know. International Society for Technology in Education (2015)
2. Grover, S., Pea, R.: Computational thinking in k-12: a review of the state of the field. Educ. Res. **42**(1), 38–43 (2013)
3. Boss, S., Larmer, J.: Project Based Teaching: How to Create Rigorous and Engaging Learning Experiences. ASCD, Alexandria (2018)
4. International Society for Technology in Education (ISTE) Standards for Students. https://www.iste.org/standards/for-students. Accessed 12 July 2023
5. Zhang, B.G., Li, Y.L.: Integrating ethical and societal implications of computing in CS education. In: Proceedings of the 52nd ACM Technical Symposium on Computer Science Education, pp. 1209–1215 (2021)
6. Saltz, J., et al.: Integrating ethics within machine learning courses. ACM Trans. Comput. Educ. **19**(4), 1–26 (2019)
7. Skirpan, M., et al.: Ethics education in context: a case study of novel ethics activities for the CS classroom. In: Proceedings of the 49th ACM Technical Symposium on Computer Science Education, pp. 940–945 (2018)

8. Mittelstadt, B.: Principles alone cannot guarantee ethical AI. Nat. Mach. Intell. **1**(11), 501–507 (2019)
9. Ko, A.J., et al.: Teaching explicit programming strategies to adolescents. In: Proceedings of the 51st ACM Technical Symposium on Computer Science Education, pp. 469–475 (2020)
10. Barocas, S., Selbst, A.D.: Big data's disparate impact. Calif. Law Rev. **104**, 671 (2016)
11. Tene, O., Polonetsky, J.: Privacy in the age of big data: a time for big decisions. Stanford Law Rev. Online **64**, 63 (2011)
12. Shilton, K.: Values and ethics in human-computer interaction. Found. Trends Hum.-Comput. Inter. **12**(2), 107–171 (2018)
13. Fincher, S., Petre, M.: Computer Science Education Research. CRC Press (2004)
14. Herkert, J.R.: Engineering ethics education in the USA: content, pedagogy and curriculum. Eur. J. Eng. Educ. **25**(4), 303–313 (2000)
15. Colby, A., Sullivan, W.M.: Rethinking Undergraduate Business Education: Liberal Learning for the Profession. John Wiley & Sons (2011)
16. Fleddermann, C.B.: Engineering Ethics. Prentice Hall, Hoboken (2011)
17. Brey, P.: The strategic role of technology in a good society. Technol. Soc. **52**, 39–45 (2018)
18. Grosz, B.J., et al.: Embedded EthiCS: integrating ethics across CS education. Commun. ACM **62**(8), 54–61 (2019)
19. Reich, J., et al.: Remote learning guidance from state education agencies during the COVID-19 pandemic: a first look. AERA Open **7**, 2332858420983574 (2021)

Mapping Challenges in Teaching-Learning Software Testing: Limitations and Unaddressed Issues in Contemporary Research

Setu Maheshwari(✉), Ramkumar Rajendran, and Sridhar Iyer

Educational Technology, Indian Institute of Technology, Bombay, India
214380006@iitb.ac.in

Abstract. Software testing systematically evaluates and verifies that a software application meets specified requirements and functions correctly. Consequently, proficiency in software testing is a key skill demanded by graduates in the software development industry. Despite its importance, software testing has not received sufficient attention in curricula and teaching practices in undergraduate computer science courses. Teaching-learning software testing brings various challenges for students and instructors, e.g., generating an exhaustive list of test cases, dividing code into testable chunks, fixing the size of projects, etc. Contemporary research reveals that researchers have used TDD to teach software testing and integrated it with programming/SE courses. TDD suggests writing tests before writing code. Gamification and Project-based/ Problem-based learning are also widely used pedagogies for teaching testing. This paper is a meta-review that maps challenges with existing teaching methods/tools to understand current research's limitations for addressing and unexplored challenges. Analysis of this paper is based on three latest systematic reviews, an additional 28 empirical studies on teaching testing, and three papers discussing challenges in detail.

Keywords: Software Testing · Teaching · Industry Expectations · CS education

1 Introduction

Software testing systematically evaluates and verifies whether a software application or system meets specified requirements and functions correctly. Consequently, proficiency in software testing is a crucial skill demanded by the software industry from computer science graduates. According to (Hamid & Ikram, 2023), 98.86% (out of 160) job advertisements demanded testing skills. Studies by (Kassab et al., 2021) and (Florea & Stray, 2019) also mentioned the high demand for test case design and test automation in the industry. Given software testing's critical role in the industry, rigorously evaluating its effective teaching is essential for developing skilled professionals.

While reviewing the literature, we found that researchers argue that software testing is not adequately taught in computer science education (e.g., Blanco et al., 2023) recently argued that it is frequently neglected in computer science education despite the importance of software testing. To further evaluate the current standards in teaching-learning

A. Karkare et al. (Eds.): COMPUTE 2024, CCIS 2400, pp. 181–191, 2025.
https://doi.org/10.1007/978-3-031-84391-4_15

software testing, we have done a comparative analysis of the ACM 2023 curricula[1] and curricula adopted by five universities in India chosen with convenience sampling. The outcome is ACM recommends teaching preliminary testing concepts, such as the need for testing, types of testing, and basic introduction to testing tools, etc., in introductory programming courses. In contrast, professional tools and practices for performing testing are recommended for teaching software engineering or equivalent courses. However, curricula followed by universities typically fail to include ACM recommendations for teaching software testing and are often limited to theoretical instruction without incorporating the practical use of tools. Here, the ACM curriculum is used just as a reference point. Still, the focus is to establish despite the importance of testing in CS education, it is often overlooked or insufficiently covered in academic programs.

Given the evidence that software testing is inadequately taught in undergraduate computer science programs, it is likely that there are significant challenges involved in teaching learning software testing (Garousi et al., 2020). Section 3 presents a detailed analysis of these challenges. To understand to what extent these challenges are addressed, we examine contemporary research for teaching-learning software testing. In this direction, we analyzed three recent review papers (Garousi et al., 2020; Scatalon et al., 2019; Scatalon et al., 2020) to gain a broad understanding of teaching and learning software testing in CS education. Findings from these review papers are presented in Sect. 2.3.

Additionally, to gain a deeper understanding, we have analyzed 28 empirical studies and documented their important details, such as pedagogical approaches, study designs, etc. By manually counting, we found that gamification and problem/project-based learning (specifically using (F)OSS projects) are the widely used pedagogies for teaching software testing. Section 2.3 details how these pedagogies are used for teaching software testing.

This paper provides a mapping of challenges in teaching-learning software testing (identified from the literature) to contemporary empirical studies, aiming to evaluate which challenges are well-addressed and which still need to be explored (Sect. 3). To our knowledge, this targeted mapping has not been previously undertaken. The section-wise distribution of this paper is as follows. Section 2 is the Background and Related Work, Sect. 3 provides challenges for students and instructors in teaching learning software testing and mapping them, Sect. 4 is the Discussion, and Sect. 5 is the conclusion.

2 Background and Related Work

2.1 Importance of Software Testing

Generally, at least half of the development budget for software projects is spent on quality assurance activities to ensure software quality (Deng et al., 2020). Companies like Facebook, Google, and Microsoft take testing seriously and require their engineers to master such techniques (Aniche et al., 2019). According to (Hamid & Ikram, 2023), 98.86% (out of 160) job advertisements have demanded testing skills. According to (Kassab et al., 2021), test case generation and automation in testing kept the most in-demand skills as per industry expectations. The most significant industrial demand is

[1] https://dl.acm.org/doi/10.1145/3626253.3633405.

placed on high-level testing, with acceptance testing and system testing occupying the first two positions in ranking skills for test levels (Florea & Stray, 2019). Therefore, students need to learn Software Testing properly.

2.2 Lack of Focus on Teaching Testing in Undergraduate Computer Science Courses

The ACM releases a detailed CS education curriculum every decade, with the latest on December 1, 2023. A comparative analysis of the ACM 2023 curriculum and the curricula of selected universities (five universities in India, including three public and two private, chosen through convenience sampling) highlights two key areas where the teaching-learning of software testing is insufficient: 1)The ACM recommends incorporating fundamental concepts e.g. unit testing and its types, basic introduction of testing tools within IPCs however, universities' curricula often fail to do this 2)The ACM's Software Engineering (SE) knowledge area stresses on teaching software testing using professional tools and practices but universities' curricula predominantly focus on theoretical instructions only. Besides this comparison, various researchers have also noted the limited inclusion of software testing in undergraduate CS programs. e.g., according to (Wei, 2023), Educators should teach testing through a test-driven development approach, but it is often taught theoretically, so students rarely apply it in their projects. Computer science education prioritizes software development languages, tools, and design principles over testing (Smith et al., 2017).

2.3 Existing Research to Integrate Testing with Programming Courses

According to (Garousi et al., 2020), testing is integrated into either programming or software engineering courses, with fewer incorporating it across multiple courses, and the majority of integrations were with programming courses. According to (Scatalon et al., 2019), modifying assignments is the most commonly used method, and modification in the curriculum is the least adopted method for integrating testing in programming courses. According to (Scatalon et al., 2020), about 90% of empirical studies used TDD or its variations, like TBC or test-first programming, as a teaching technique for software testing. According to (Baldassarre et al., 2021), TDD (Test-driven development) is a cyclic development approach where each development cycle starts with the writing of unit tests for an unimplemented piece of functionality, and the cycle ends when unit tests pass as well as the existing regression test suite.

The following paragraphs overview various pedagogical approaches used in teaching software testing. Gamification has been used frequently by researchers to teach software testing. A study by (Blanco et al., 2023) taught software testing and linked the effectiveness of test suites with rewards to achieve immortality, this has increased students' engagement. A melee game named Code Defender was developed by (Fraser et al., 2019) and received positive feedback from students for learning software testing. A game-based learning approach (GAMUT) was introduced by (Gomes and Lelli., 2021) for teaching unit testing, the approach successfully engaged students. The puzzle game *Testing Maze* created by (Severo & Lelli, 2023) was employed to teach functional testing.

Project-Based/Problem-Based Learning using FOSS (Free and Open Source Software) is also a widely used pedagogical approach for teaching software testing. This approach emphasizes immersing students in professional testing tools, real-world projects, and industry practices. Using this pedagogy (Deng et al., 2020) taught software testing through five activities and tools like GitHub, JUnit, and Travis-CI. The study of (Chow et al., 2021) employed PBL to provide professional experience to students while teaching software testing using tools like JUnit 5, Cypress, etc. Apart from PBL, another approach is TILE (Test Informed Learning with Examples) used by (Doorn et al., 2023). This approach integrated testing while teaching OOP concepts without overwhelming students cognitively. The proposal of (Heckman et al., 2020) suggested integrating software testing in multiple courses; however, its adequate implementation is still a future work.

2.4 Challenges in Integrating Software Testing

According to (Gopal 2022), dividing and prioritizing code into testable chunks, integrating testing holistically, etc., are major challenges. (Aniche et al., 2019) highlight the difficulty of generating exhaustive test cases and managing testing activities in programming assignments. (Scatalon et. al., 2017) identify setting appropriate project sizes, student reluctance, and timely, accurate assessment as key challenges. Sections 3 and 4 present a detailed analysis and discussion of these challenges.

3 Comprehensive Analysis of Challenges and Related Research

3.1 Challenges for Students and Their Underlying Reasons

Table 1 presents students' challenges in learning software testing and their underlying three reasons: 1) Increased cognitive load, 2) Increased workload, and 3) Adoption of wrong practices. In Table 1, "Y" indicates the reason contributes to the corresponding challenge, while "N" signifies it does not. These underlying causes are interrelated to each other, this interrelation between causes is explained in Sect. 4. Challenges 1 through 7 listed in Table 1 are attributed to increased cognitive or workload or both. The other challenges listed in Table 1 are due to wrong practices.

Table 1. List of challenges for students and their underlying causes

S.no	Challenge	The reason behind the challenge		
		Cognitive Load	Workload	Wrong practices
1	Test case creation is time-consuming and complex	Y	Y	N

(continued)

Table 1. (*continued*)

S.no	Challenge	The reason behind the challenge		
		Cognitive Load	Workload	Wrong practices
2	Prioritizing Requirements	Y	Y	Y
3	When and where to start testing?	N	N	Y
4	Establishing clear and fine-grained exit criteria for testing an application	N	N	Y
5	Developing an exhaustive list of tests	Y	Y	N
6	Accurate Test Coverage	Y	Y	N
7	Students' reluctance - students tend not to do it until it is not made compulsory	N	N	Y
8	Lackofmotivationtofind issues/bugs in their own code	N	N	Y
9	Students are often surprised to receive poor grades	N	N	Y
10	Aligning tests with modifying code	Y	Y	Y
11	How to divide and prioritize their code into testable chunks	N	Y	Y
12	Converting application requirements into test cases at the unit testing level	Y	Y	Y
13	Unawareness of potential difficulties in using professional testing tools	N	N	Y

3.2 Challenges for Instructors and Their Underlying Reasons

Table 2 presents the list of challenges for instructors along with three underlying reasons: 1) Increased Workload, 2) Improper Guidelines, and 3) Wrong practices. In Table 2, "Y" and "N" hold the same meaning as in Table 1. These underlying causes are also interrelated. Section 4 discusses this interrelation in detail. Challenge no. 3 in Table 2 addresses the holistic integration of testing, which refers to a gradual increase in complexity level to avoid making it feel like an explicit part of the course.

Table 2. List of Challenges for instructors and their underlying causes.

S.n o	Challenge	Thereasonbehindthe challenge		
		Work Load	Improper Guidelines	Wrong Practices
1	Choosing Project size in introductory courses	N	Y	N

(*continued*)

Table 2. (*continued*)

S.n o	Challenge	Thereasonbehindthe challenge		
		Work Load	Improper Guidelines	Wrong Practices
2	Holistic Integration of Testing	Y	Y	N
3	Preparing test cases for students is time-consuming	Y	N	Y
4	Quick assessment and timely feedback on students' assignments	Y	N	Y
5	How to conduct testing activity	N	Y	Y
6	Programming courses are too full to include testing due to time constraints	N	Y	Y

3.3 How Existing Research Addresses Challenges Given in Table 1 and Table 2

Researchers have utilized both teaching methods and tools to address these challenges (listed in Table 1 and Table 2). Among teaching methods, Gamification (used by Blanco et al., 2023; Gomes & Lelli, 2021; Severo & Lelli, 2023, etc.) is useful in increasing students' engagement which helps to reduce student's reluctance towards performing testing (Challenge no. 7 in Table 1). Use of project/problem-based learning (used by Deng et al., 2020, Chow et al., 2021, etc.) using (F)OSS projects is useful to provide industry-relevant development and testing experience to students, which in turn helps to address students' unawareness of potential difficulties in learning the required technological tools (challenge no. 13 from Table 1). The TILE (Test Informed Learning with Examples) pedagogy by (Doorn et al., 2023) helps in developing the right practices to start testing without cognitively overwhelming students. It helps to reduce Students' reluctance (Challenge No. 7 in Table 1) and Challenge No. 9 in Table 1, i.e., students are often surprised to receive poor grades.

Besides the above-mentioned teaching methods, the following tools are also used for teaching-learning software testing. Auto-grading tools like FEAT (Smith et al., 2017) are useful in assessing assignments and providing accurate and timely feedback to students (challenge no. 4 in Table 2). Tools used for automatic test case generation are useful in addressing challenges related to test case generation (challenges no. 1, 6 in Table 1 and challenge no. 3 in Table 2). Another challenge (Challenge no. 8 in Table 1) i.e., students' lack of motivation to find bugs in their own code, is addressed by (Missiroli et al., 2017) through peer evaluation. Table 3 maps the challenges given in Table 1 and Table 2 to their corresponding solutions in existing research.

Table 3. Mapping of Existing Solutions with Existing Challenges

Solution Approach	Challenge Addressed	How challenge has been addressed
Automatic test-case generation	1,5,6 from Table 1and 3 from Table 2	Reduces cognitive load and workload
Gamification	7 from Table 1	Increase engagement
Peers tested projects	8 from Table 1	Students were highly motivated to find bugs in peer's projects/codes
Auto grading	4 from Table 2	It provides immediate feedback

3.4 Limitations of Existing Empirical Research on Addressing Challenges

This section outlines the limitations of current empirical research regarding challenges and highlights unaddressed challenges. Existing auto-grading tools effectively provide immediate feedback but are limited in scope, as they are designed for specific assignment types and lack generalizability across different tasks. The TILE approach fosters early testing habits in programming courses, but its simplicity limits students' grasp of real-world testing complexities. Gamification boosts student engagement and reduces students' reluctance towards testing, but leaderboard scores only rise with successful test case design, while creating exhaustive test cases is complex; hence, current testing games are useful only for small-scale applications. (Heckman et al., 2020) suggest integrating testing into multiple courses (challenge no. 2 in Table 2, i.e., Holistic Integration), but this concept is still under exploration. Evaluating its effects requires multiple longitudinal studies, with controlling various variables being a key challenge for researchers. As previously noted, this section also identifies challenges that have been overlooked by existing research, Table 4 presents an examination of these unexplored challenges, explaining the difficulties involved in these challenges for researchers.

Table 4. Unexplored Challenges and Their Research Difficulties

Challenge	Difficulty involved in it for researchers
It is difficult for students to select values for test cases, using testing techniques and criteria	There is no established rule for teaching how to select values for test cases which is applicable for all types of projects
Students struggle to prioritize test cases i.e. linking business requirements, previous test cycle experiences and the current performance	In industry, specialized teams with distinct skills operate with a structured hierarchy but in academic settings, it may not be achievable
Fixing project size, specifically in introductory programming courses	To create a balance among students' prior knowledge, industry expectations, and course time constraints is challenging

It is important to note that certain software testing concepts, such as Black Box techniques like Equivalence Class Partitioning and Boundary Value Analysis, offer test case selection guidelines. However, their exclusion from introductory programming courses due to inadequate curriculum, heavy workload, and time constraints hinders practical discussion of these topics.

4 Discussion

For teaching-learning testing in CS education, researchers majorly have given three important recommendations: 1) Testing should be introduced early (in IPCs), 2) Teach testing using the latest professional tools and industry-relevant practices, and 3) Testing should not overwhelm students cognitively in programming courses. However, it is important to understand that there is a trade-off between these three guidelines. Introducing testing in IPCs and learning through professional tools increases cognitive load, on the other hand introducing testing early but using some easy testing exercises will not let students learn industry-relevant testing techniques, lastly delaying testing until later semesters when students are more mature fosters reluctance, reducing their likelihood of adopting testing practices.

While current empirical research effectively applies these recommendations individually, it significantly overlooks this trade-off. For example, Project-based learning with FOSS projects introduces industry-relevant tools but significantly increases cognitive load. The TILE approach fosters essential testing habits without overwhelming students but doesn't meet industry requirements for software testing. Gamification boosts engagement in small-scale applications but is unsuitable for industry-standard projects. Integrating testing across various programming courses is not been implemented yet.

Apart from the above trade-off, the interrelation among underlying causes given in Sect. 3 also needs to be discussed. The underlying causes in Table 1 are interrelated with each other. For example, adopting wrong practices hampers learning testing adequately, this reduces student engagement and increases cognitive load and workload. Similarly, sometimes a task becomes time-consuming because it is complex. For instance, in software testing tasks such as converting requirements to unit tests and aligning them with constantly changing code are cognitively complex, hence it takes a lot of time and increases students' workload. The reverse is also true; developing exhaustive test cases for large projects is time-consuming, leading to cognitive exhaustion while aiming for accurate test coverage. Similar relation can be seen in causes mentioned for instructors also (Table 2) e.g. lack of proper guidelines (e.g. not using tools for auto-grading or automatic test case generation) leads to wrong practices and increases instructors' workload, exercises like planning a testing activity in programming courses or fixing project size requires exhaustive work to be done which also involve sincere cognitive effort.

5 Conclusion

This meta-review identifies challenges in teaching software testing, evaluates current methods and tools, highlights unresolved issues, and provides a comprehensive mapping of unexplored challenges as a key novelty. This paper offers a clear objective for researchers aiming to create novel methods and tools for teaching software testing. One limitation of this research is its major reliance on three papers for identifying challenges. Our future implication is to explore how the latest tools and technologies can be leveraged to address the trade-off and remaining challenges in teaching learning software testing.

References

Aniche, M., Hermans, F., van Deursen, A.: Pragmatic software testing education. In: Proceedings of the 50th ACM Technical Symposium on Computer Science Education, pp. 414–420 (2019). https://doi.org/10.1145/3287324.3287461

Avellar, G.M.N., Silva, R.F. da, Scatalon, L.P., Andrade, S.A., Delamaro, M.E., Barbosa, E.F.: Integration of software testing to programming assignments: an experimental study. In: 2019 IEEE Frontiers in Education Conference (FIE), pp. 1–9 (2019). https://doi.org/10.1109/FIE43999.2019.9028519

Blanco, R., Trinidad, M., Suárez-Cabal, M.J., Calderón, A., Ruiz, M., Tuya, J.: Can gamification help in software testing education? Findings from an empirical study. J. Syst. Softw. **200**, 111647 (2023)

Chow, S.P., Komarlu, T., Conrad, P.T.: Teaching testing with modern technology stacks in undergraduate software engineering courses. In: Proceedings of the 26th ACM Conference on Innovation and Technology in ComputerScience Education, vol. 1, pp. 241–247 (2021). https://doi.org/10.1145/3430665.3456352

Deng, L., Dehlinger, J., Chakraborty, S.: Teaching software testing with free and open source software. In: 2020 IEEE International Conference on Software Testing, Verification and Validation Workshops (ICSTW), pp. 412–418 (2020). https://ieeexplore.ieee.org/abstract/document/9155837/

Doorn, N., Vos, T., Marín, B., Barendsen, E.: Set the right example when teaching programming: Test Informed Learning with Examples (TILE). In: 2023 IEEE Conference on Software Testing, Verification and Validation(ICST), pp. 269–280 (2023). https://ieeexplore.ieee.org/abstract/document/10132188/

Gopal, B.: Teaching software testing and devops in undergraduate software engineering: a comparison of peer instruction and POGIL [PhD Thesis, The University of Nebraska-Lincoln]. https://www.proquest.com/openview/6ebfc4c430db47f10808bb6ebf8557ea/1?pq-origsite=gscholar&cbl=18750&diss=y

Lemos, O.A.L., Silveira, F.F., Ferrari, F.C., Garcia, A.: The impact of software testing education on code reliability: an empirical assessment. J. Syst. Softw. **137**, 497–511 (2018)

Ramasamy, V., Alomari, H.W., Kiper, J.D., Potvin, G.: A minimally disruptive approach of integrating testing into computer programming courses. In: Proceedings of the 2nd International Workshop on Software Engineering Education for Millennials, pp. 1–7 (2018). https://doi.org/10.1145/3194779.3194790

Smith, R., Tang, T., Warren, J., Rixner, S.: An Automated system for interactively learning software testing. In: Proceedings of the 2017 ACM Conference on Innovation and Technology in Computer Science Education, pp. 98–103 (2017). https://doi.org/10.1145/3059009.3059022

Wei, B.: Teaching test-driven development and object-oriented design by example. In: 2023 IEEE International Conference on Software Testing, Verification and Validation Workshops (ICSTW), pp. 413–421 (2023a). https://ieeexplore.ieee.org/abstract/document/10132265/

Baldassarre, M.T., et al.: Studying test-driven development and its retainment over a six-month time span. J. Syst. Softw. **176**, 110937 (2021)

Garousi, V., Rainer, A., Lauvås, P., Jr., Arcuri, A.: Software-testing education: a systematic literature mapping. J. Syst. Softw. **165**, 110570 (2020)
Perspectives on the gap between the software industry and the software engineering education. IEEE J. Mag. I IEEE Xplore. (n.d.). https://ieeexplore.ieee.org/abstract/document/8808915. Accessed 24 Feb 2024
Scatalon, L.P., Barbosa, E.F., Garcia, R.E.: Challenges to integrate software testing into introductory programming courses. In: 2017 IEEE Frontiers in Education Conference (FIE), pp. 1–9 (2017). https://doi.org/10.1109/FIE.2017.8190557
Scatalon, L.P., Carver, J.C., Garcia, R.E., Barbosa, E.F.: Software testing in introductory programming courses: a systematic mapping study. In: Proceedings of the 50th ACM Technical Symposium on Computer Science Education, pp. 421–427 (2019). https://doi.org/10.1145/3287324.3287384
Scatalon, L.P., Garcia, R.E., Barbosa, E.F.: Teaching practices of software testing in programming education. In: 2020 IEEE Frontiers in Education Conference (FIE), pp. 1–9 (2020). https://doi.org/10.1109/FIE44824.2020.9274256
Zivkovic, T., Zivkovic, M.: Survey of learning environments for software testing education. In: 7th Conference on the Engineering of Computer Based Systems, pp. 1–9 (2021). https://doi.org/10.1145/3459960.3459971
Clarke, P.J., Davis, D.L., Chang-Lau, R., King, T.M.: Impact of using tools in an undergraduate software testing course supported by WReSTT. ACM Trans. Comput. Educ. **17**(4), 1–28 (2017). https://doi.org/10.1145/3068324
Fraser, G., Gambi, A., Kreis, M., Rojas, J.M.: Gamifying a software testing course with code defenders. In: Proceedings of the 50th ACM Technical Symposium on Computer Science Education, pp. 571–577 (2019). https://doi.org/10.1145/3287324.3287471
Gomes, R.F., Lelli, V.: GAMUT: GAMe-based learning approach for teaching Unit Testing. XX Braz. Symp. Softw. Qual., 1–11 (2021). https://doi.org/10.1145/3493244.349326
Gren, L.: A flipped classroom approach to teaching empirical software engineering. IEEE Trans. Educ. **63**(3), 155–163 (2020)
Heckman, S., Schmidt, J.Y., King, J.: Integrating testing throughout the CS curriculum. In: 2020 IEEE International Conference on Software Testing, Verification and Validation Workshops (ICSTW), pp. 441–444 (2020). https://ieeexplore.ieee.org/abstract/document/9155661/
Jin, H., Zeng, F.: Research on the definition and model of software testing quality. In: The Proceedings of 2011 9th International Conference on Reliability, Maintainability and Safety, pp. 639–644 (2011). https://doi.org/10.1109/ICRMS.2011.5979352
Missiroli, M., Russo, D., Ciancarini, P.: Learning agile software development in high school: an investigation. In: Proceedings of the 38th International Conference on Software Engineering Companion, pp. 293–302 (2016). https://doi.org/10.1145/2889160.2889180
Missiroli, M., Russo, D., Ciancarini, P.: Teaching test-first programming: assessment and solutions. In: 2017 IEEE 41st Annual Computer Software and Applications Conference (COMPSAC), vol. 1, pp. 420–425 (2017). https://ieeexplore.ieee.org/abstract/document/8029637/
Severo, J., Lelli, V.: Testing maze: an educational game for teaching functional testing. In: Proceedings of the XXXVII Brazilian Symposium onSoftware Engineering, pp. 407–415 (2023a). https://doi.org/10.1145/3613372.3614191
Aasheim, C., Shropshire, J., Li, L., Kadlec, C.: Knowledge and skill requirements for entry-level IT workers: a longitudinal study, vol. 23 (n.d.)
Exter, M., Caskurlu, S., Fernandez, T.: Comparing computing professionals' perceptions of importance of skills and knowledge on the job and coverage in undergraduate experiences. ACM Trans. Comput. Educ. **18**(4), 1–29 (2018). https://doi.org/10.1145/3218430
Florea, R., Stray, V.: A qualitative study of the background, skill acquisition, and learning preferences of software testers. In: Proceedings of the Evaluation and Assessment in Software Engineering, pp. 299–305 (2020). https://doi.org/10.1145/3383219.3383252

Florea, R., Stray, V., Sjøberg, D.I.: On the roles of software testers: an exploratory study. J. Syst. Softw., 111742 (2023)

Hamid, B., Ikram, N.: Industry perceptions of the competencies needed by novice software tester. Educ. Inf. Technol., 1–32 (2023)

Hung, B.K.H., To, C.C.N., Fung, R.K.H., Chan, C.C.S.: Addressing proficiency gaps in future skills between employers and learners through data visualization. SN Comput. Sci. **4**(3), 308 (2023). https://doi.org/10.1007/s42979-023-01722-3

Kassab, M., Laplante, P., Defranco, J., Neto, V.V.G., Destefanis, G.: Exploring the profiles of software testing jobs in the United States. IEEE Access **9**, 68905–68916 (2021)

Pham, R., Kiesling, S., Singer, L., Schneider, K.: Onboarding inexperienced developers: struggles and perceptions regarding automated testing. Software Qual. J. **25**(4), 1239–1268 (2017). https://doi.org/10.1007/s11219-016-9333-7

Qadir, J., Yau, K.-L.A., Imran, M.A., Al-Fuqaha, A.: Engineering education, moving into 2020s: Essential competencies for effective 21st century electrical & computer engineers. In: 2020 IEEE Frontiers in Education Conference (FIE), pp. 1–9 (2020). https://ieeexplore.ieee.org/abstract/document/9274067/

Radermacher, A., Walia, G., Knudson, D.: Investigating the skill gap between graduating students and industry expectations. In: Companion Proceedings of the 36th International Conference on Software Engineering, pp. 291–300 (2014). https://doi.org/10.1145/2591062.2591159

Scaffidi, C.: Employers' needs for computer science, information technology and software engineering skills among new graduates. Int. J. Comput. Sci., Eng. Inf. Technol. **8**(1), 1–12 (2018)

Valstar, S., Krause-Levy, S., Macedo, A., Griswold, W.G., Porter, L.: Faculty views on the goals of an undergraduate CS education and the academia-industry gap. In: Proceedings of the 51st ACM Technical Symposium on Computer Science Education, pp. 577–583 (2020). https://doi.org/10.1145/3328778.3366834

Author Index

A. Karkare et al. (Eds.): COMPUTE 2024, CCIS 2400, p. 193, 2025.
https://doi.org/10.1007/978-3-031-84391-4

The manufacturer's authorised representative in the EU is Springer Nature Customer Service Centre GmbH, Europaplatz 3, 69115 Heidelberg, Germany. If you have any concerns regarding our products, please contact ProductSafety@springernature.com

Printed and bound by CPI Group (UK) Ltd, Croydon, CR0 4YY
30/09/2026
02225597-0012